60 SHORT HIKES IN THE SANDIA FOOTHILLS

■ ■ ■

60 SHORT HIKES IN THE SANDIA FOOTHILLS

Tamara Massong

■ ■ ■

UNIVERSITY OF NEW MEXICO PRESS, ALBUQUERQUE

Cover illustration: <comment>[! Designer: Add
cover illustration credit/caption info. !]
COVER DESIGNED BY LILA SANCHEZ
TEXT DESIGNED BY TERESA W. WINGFIELD
Composed in Scala Pro and Scala Sans Pro

LIBRARY OF CONGRESS
CATALOGING-IN-PUBLICATION DATA

Names: Massong, Tamara, 1969– author.
Title: 60 Short Hikes in the Sandia Foothills /
Tamara Massong.
Other titles: Sixty Short Hikes in the Sandia
Foothills
Description: Albuquerque : University of
New Mexico Press, 2018. | Includes bibli-
ographical references and index. | Description
based on print version record and CIP data
provided by publisher; resource not viewed.
Identifiers: LCCN 2017005530 (print) | LCCN
2017011576 (ebook) | ISBN 9780826358868
(E-book) | ISBN 9780826358851 (pbk. : alk.
paper)
Subjects: LCSH: Hiking—New Mexico—
Sandia Mountains—Guidebooks. | Trails—
New Mexico—Sandia Mountains—
Guidebooks. | Sandia Mountains
(N.M.)—Guidebooks.
Classification: LCC GV199.42.N62 (ebook) |
LCC GV199.42.N62 S265 2017 (print) |
DDC 796.5109789—dc23
LC record available at https://lccn.loc.gov/2017
005530

CONTENTS

▦ PART TWO. CENTRAL TRAILS

▉ PART THREE. SOUTH CENTRAL TRAILS

ACKNOWLEDGMENTS

A big thank-you to all my hiking friends who explored trails, gave advice, shared information, tested data, helped with contacts, and were willing to just talk with me about my ideas: Susan, Julie, Sarah, Will, Arianne, Sandra, Kerry, Champ, Erik. Special thanks to the Press and their reviewers, John, Sonia, Matt, and Bob, whose suggestions improved the content of this work. I am particularly grateful to my family, Neill, Emily, Conor, Mom, and Cookie, for being my partners on many hikes that didn't make the book, for putting up with my repetitive need to verify trails and maps, for the numerous photographs, and, of course, for all the support to make this possible.

INTRODUCTION

An early-morning walk is a blessing
for the whole day.

—HENRY DAVID THOREAU

ONE OF THE MAJOR ATTRACTIONS OF
life in Albuquerque is the variety of public
lands within the city, which yield access to
the Rio Grande, petroglyphs, volcanoes,
and the Sandia Mountains. With our busy
lifestyles we have precious little time to do
the homework about these places. When
we are able to free up a couple of hours
on a sunny afternoon, we flock to places
like the foothills and swarm the popular
trails, joining a steady stream of hikers
enjoying the splendid views and the joy
of outdoor exercise. Rarely do these hikes
result in a true visit with nature and all
that this normally quiet world has to offer.
With the Sandia Mountains right there
at the edge of the city, blocking the early
morning sun and beckoning for us to
visit, it seems ridiculous that hikers congregate along a few trails. There are nooks
and crannies everywhere. A hiker with a
couple of free hours and a little desire can
visit breathtaking falls, hidden springs
and canyons, ruins, forests, and mountain
benches frequented by deer or simply get
off the beaten track on a quiet trail.

This guide is for everyone who not
only likes the big, popular trails, but also
would like to explore a few of those nooks
and crannies. These short excursions
through the foothills, into canyons, and
onto the lower mountains create a perfect
introduction for less-experienced hikers,
for people who are new to high-desert
hiking, and for hard-core hikers who
haven't yet taken the time to look around.
Some routes, although short, are harder
than others, creating a number of choices
for every skill and endurance level. Introductory information about the geography,
plant community, and wildlife you are
likely to encounter is included to broaden
your general awareness while enriching
the hiking experience as you explore the
variety of environments and ecosystems
that exist throughout the western Sandia
Mountains and its foothills.

Hiking safely should always be a prior-
ity. A variety of safety considerations are
discussed, with specific information given
for each hike, including details about
nearby private lands. With neighborhoods
bounding the foothills areas, being aware
of public versus private property is a must
for every hiker. In a couple of locations,
private lands have actually been made
available for public use. This wonderful
sharing needs to be respected so that
the owners keep those lands open to the
public.

The short hikes described here are typically two to four miles in length and will usually take less than two hours. They range from easy to hard and explore the greater foothills area and the lower (western) Sandia Mountains. They encompass many different landscapes and ecosystems, including the large outwash plain of the foothills, tight canyons, outwash fans, waterfalls, springs, and the steep lower mountains and their grassy benches. Some routes make use of old roads or small trails leading to cabin ruins, while others are serious treks straight up the mountains. Some of the trails are exceptionally busy; others have more rabbits than people.

These routes are full of fantastic views and beautiful scenery. They are also teeming with wildlife of all kinds. Birds flock to these open areas. The abundant population of local, year-round inhabitants includes roadrunners and robins, along with a noticeable influx of migratory birds, such as the ever-curious and all-time favorite hummingbirds, which show up in the late spring and stay until early fall. The land animals most encountered are deer, coyotes, and rabbits, all of which will run and hide from hikers. But don't be surprised to see a snake sunning itself, or to hear about the occasional black bear visit.

NATURAL HISTORY OF THE LAND

Geologic Background

The oldest rocks in the Sandia Mountains are the Precambrian Sandia granite and mica schist of the Rincon Ridge metamorphics, both more than 1.5 billion years old. The Sandia granite is the most abundant rock and is along nearly every trail in this guide. Its color and composition varies, but is generally characterized by large pink or white crystals surrounded by smaller crystals. Mica schist is found only in the far north of the Sandia Mountains, in the hills at the Jaral Watershed, and along the full length of Juan Tabo Canyon Watershed, including the Rincon Ridge on the Piedra Lisa Trail. This metamorphic rock has relatively thick bands of light-colored mica and quartz crystals intertwined with less-distinct darker layers.

About three hundred million years ago, during the Pennsylvanian geologic period—after the granite and schist basement rocks formed but long before the Sandia Mountains came to be—this area of New Mexico was a shallow sea. An abundance of shelled creatures lived and died in these warm ocean waters, creating a thick layer of calcium carbonate at its bottom. As the sea drained, the sediments hardened, becoming limestone, which is found in two forms today at the Sandia Crest: the dark-gray Sandia and the lighter-gray Madera. The Madera limestone is the more exposed of the two, extending from the top of the crest nearly to New Mexico State Route 14 in the East Mountains. Chunks of limestone are scattered throughout the western mountains, especially in drainages and their valleys within the foothills.

The Sandia Mountains began forming ten to fifteen million years ago, as the Rio Grande Rift–Albuquerque Basin pulled apart this section of the continent. As the land stretched, deep north–south trending faults split the terrain, creating a large valley (also known as a graben). On the edges of the rift/fault zone, the Sandia Mountains rose up as the valley continued to sink. The stretching of the land occurred slowly, with many faulting

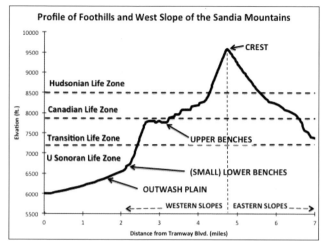

Profile of Foothills and West Slope of the Sandia Mountains

this plain is obviously tilted but looks smooth. Closer inspection reveals a series of valleys running from the top of the plain near the mountains to its bottom at the Rio Grande. These features, known locally as arroyos (a Spanish word for "ephemeral channels") continuously change the surface of the outwash plain as they move sand and rocks downhill in flash floods; in a single season, a pulse of sediment can fill in an entire arroyo valley, causing the channel to jump (avulse) to a new location. This dynamic system, with continued uplift of the mountains along with ongoing erosion of the rock, has created a varied landscape that remains active today.

episodes. Eventually the top limestone layers, along with the Sandia granite, began to tilt toward the east and form the steep and rugged western face of the mountains. The Sandia Crest has continued moving to the east as fault blocks slide down the edge of the mountains to fill in the bottom of the rift. Many of these blocks lie deep in the valley depression and are covered with river sediment and rock debris from the mountains. Others, not yet buried, form the lower mountains. Many of these blocks have relatively flat tops, creating a series of benches near the outwash plain.

Erosion, meanwhile, has been slowly and continually chipping away at the uplifted bedrock, chemically altering it and gradually crushing it into small pieces that break free and are transported downhill. Over the same millions of years of mountain formation, enough sand, gravel, and boulders have been carried downstream through the canyons and deposited at the base of the mountains to completely cover the lower fault blocks and form a broad outwash plain, also known as the foothills. From a distance,

Life Zones

In 1889 naturalist C. Hart Merriam described all terrains in North America as belonging to one of seven elevation-driven life zones, each with its own characteristic plant and animal life. Although somewhat outdated in its field, this simple classification is still a good and easy-to-use system for describing the plant communities in the Sandia Mountains, where four of the seven life zones are present: the Upper Sonoran, Transition, Canadian, and Hudsonian. Most of the routes described in this guide start and are fully contained in the Upper Sonoran life zone, although a few climb higher up, reaching the Transition zone. However,

Merriam's simplistic model isn't perfect, as specific site conditions overrule these general trends. Finding and recognizing these unusual and unexpected communities can be a lot of fun, and long-time avid hikers in this area usually have their favorites.

In the Sandia Mountains, gaining altitude results in drastic changes not only in the plant community but also to hiking conditions. The highest elevations have a solid winter period, accompanied by snowpack, ice, and a colder year-round climate. Hiking in higher elevations is beyond the scope of this book; thus, hikes through the Canadian and Hudsonian life zones are not covered here.

The Upper Sonoran Zone, the most common life zone in this guide's hikes, extends up to about 7,200 ft. (~2,200 m) above sea level. This zone is officially characterized by juniper, piñon, and oak trees, chamisa, Apache plume, yuccas, cacti, bear grass, many species of native grasses including the popular grama grasses, and a variety of other forbs and flowering plants. Observant hikers will note that within this life zone, the vegetation can be notably different depending on elevation as well as specific geography: the steepness of the hillside, ridgeline, or valley bottom and, of course, slope aspect. In this high desert, many north-facing slopes are full of significantly thicker patches of juniper, piñon, Apache plume, and bear grass, while the small, almost indistinct ridgelines along the main foothills area are dominated by grama and other grasses. There are many differences between the lower and higher elevations within the Upper Sonoran life zone: for example, at the Elena Gallegos Picnic Area, the piñon-juniper forest is relatively thick

and expansive, but this gradually thins to the south as the foothills' elevation decreases, such that there are almost no trees present at U-Mound.

The Transition life zone, characterized by ponderosa pine forests, extends from about 7,200 to 7,800 ft. (2,200 to 2,400 m). Some plant species common in the Upper Sonoran life zone also thrive here, among them piñon, oak, banana yucca, and a variety of cacti. Oaks actually change character between the Upper Sonoran and Transition zones: a deciduous variety thrives in the former, but changes to an evergreen variety in the higher elevations and colder winters of the Transition zone.

NATIVE AMERICAN CONNECTION TO THE SANDIA MOUNTAINS

Local Native American pueblos and tribes have lived in this area, hunted game, harvested trees and other vegetation, and simply gathered resources from the Sandia Mountains for thousands of years. The resources are used for everyday life as well as for culturally important activities, such as ceremonies and dances. The trees, the animals, and simply the mountains are sacred in many tribal cultures, a reverence that transcends time.

With such a long history in the area, ruins of Native American camps and villages, along with artifacts such as potsherds or corn-grinding stones (metates and manos) can be found throughout the mountains. It is unlawful to dig in, pillage, damage, or take artifacts from these sites. If you are lucky enough to stumble upon an old camp, please be respectful, as these places are and always will be sacred to our Native American friends.

HISTORY OF LANDOWNERSHIP
IN THE FOOTHILLS

With the return of Spanish settlers after
the Pueblo Revolt of the late 1600s, the
government of Spain divided the majority
of the foothills into two sections: the Villa
de Alburquerque land grant in the south
and what later became known as the
Elena Gallegos Land Grant in the north.
The Villa de Alburquerque slowly trans-
formed into what we know today as the
City of Albuquerque. The Elena Gallegos
property extended from near the Rio in
today's northern section of Albuquerque
to the crest of the Sandia Mountains.
These two large land grants contained
most of the foothills, and both used the
foothills and lower mountains as open
space for things such as timber harvest
and cattle grazing. In both cases, descen-
dants of the grantees subdivided the lands
and eventually sold them to outsiders.

Meanwhile, in the late nineteenth and
early twentieth centuries, the US government became concerned about overuse
of public land resources, in particular the
hunting of game species and tree harvest.
In a national effort, it began setting aside
public land and limiting the resource use
on those lands. This led to the formation
of National Forests, which were and are
managed by the federal government. In
1906, the United States Forest Service
(USFS) formed the Manzano National
Reserve, which included a collection
of unowned foothills and mountain
properties in the Manzano and Sandia
Mountains.

In the 1930s, the Manzano National
Reserve was joined with several other
nearby federal lands as the Cibola
National Forest and National Grasslands,
and the Sandia Ranger District was

created to manage the Sandia Mountains.
In 1978, 30,981 acres of Sandia Ranger
District land was designated as wilderness and strict land-use restrictions were
implemented for land managers and
recreationists alike. The major constraints
included no bicycle or motorized vehicle
use within the Wilderness Area.

Although the USFS public lands in the
Sandia Mountains were quite extensive,
for a long time they didn't include the
northern foothills or northwestern mountain areas. These lands are part of the former Elena Gallegos Land Grant and took
a different path to public ownership, as
the grant heirs kept the lands "in the family" until the 1930s. After returning from
Washington, DC, where he had been a
Congressional representative for New
Mexico, Albert G. Simms and his wife,
Ruth Hanna McCormick Simms, began
purchasing parcels of the former Elena
Gallegos Land Grant. On his death in
1964, Mr. Simms bequeathed a large portion of these properties to the Albuquerque Academy, a day school for students of
middle- and high-school age.

In the late 1970s, the Academy decided
to sell a portion of the bequeathed lands,
which eventually led to a complicated
land purchase and exchange among the
school, the City of Albuquerque, and the
USFS in 1982. This brought approximately eight thousand acres of the northwestern Sandia Mountains into public
land status. Some of it became USFS
land; another portion became part of the
city's Open Space Division and is maintained by Albuquerque as a public park
and recreation area.

Appendix B of this volume gives a
detailed timeline of post–Pueblo Revolt
landownership and management of the
foothills.

CURRENT LAND MANAGEMENT AGENCIES

United States Forest Service

The USFS, an agency of the US Department of Agriculture, describes itself as "a multi-faceted agency that manages and protects 154 national forests and 20 grasslands in 44 states and Puerto Rico" and states that its mission is "to sustain the health, diversity, and productivity of the nation's forests and grasslands to meet the needs of present and future generations." Among the properties it oversees is the Cibola National Forest and National Grasslands, which covers more than 1.6 million acres in New Mexico and extends into Texas and Oklahoma. The terrain there rises from 2,700 to 11,300 feet above sea level. The Cibola National Forest includes four wilderness areas, among them the one that is the focus of this guide: the 37,200 acres that was designated as the Sandia Mountain Wilderness Area in 1978.

USFS Sandia Ranger District

Contact Information:
Address: 11776 Highway 337, Tijeras, NM 87059
Phone: (505) 281-3304
E-mail: r3_cibola_sandia_information@ fs.fed.us
Website: http://www.fs.usda.gov/main /cibola/home

City of Albuquerque Open Space Division

In 1988 the City of Albuquerque revised its comprehensive plan to identify and designate more than twenty-nine thousand plots of land in and around the metropolis as "major public Open Space." Its Open Space Division works to acquire and protect these lands' natural character in order to, in their words,

- Conserve natural and archaeological resources
- Provide opportunities for outdoor education
- Provide a place for low impact recreation
- Define the edges of the urban environment.

Contact Information:
Address: Open Space Division, Parks and Recreation, P.O Box 1293, Albuquerque, NM 87103
Phone: (505) 452-5200 or 311 (Citizen Contact Center)
Website: https://www.cabq.gov/parksand recreation/open-space/open-space

PRIVATE LANDS

The private landowners who live along the edges of these public areas will ultimately evaluate the success of recreation in the foothills. And, appropriately, they will grade the users on their behavior on and respect for private property as well as public land. Stay off posted private land (that is, with "No Trespassing" or similar signs along its perimeter). Also be certain that when you park your vehicle, you do not block owners' access to their properties. When walking along the edge of private lands with houses, keep your voices down and don't peer into windows or backyards; these people have a right to privacy. If you desire to cross private property, ask the landowner for permission before you do so. Many residents are concerned about loose dogs and messes on their property, so please keep your pets on leash near private lands and clean up after them, whether this entails dislodged landscape rocks or poop.

SAFETY CONSIDERATIONS

Although this area doesn't seem all that dangerous—after all, it is at the edge of the city—there are many safety concerns for hikers to consider and plan for. The most common injury stories seem to revolve around the vegetation, especially stepping on, brushing up against, or sitting on cacti. Many hikers are concerned about wildlife, but luckily most creatures are very wary of humans and tend to keep their distance. Being prepared for trail and obvious weather-related conditions is the easiest and most important plan for every hiker. Here are some tips for staying safe.

Picking a Good Hike Based on Your Skills and Preparedness

Although it is rare for hikers to get in trouble in the Sandia Mountains, it does happen, typically because a trail or route turns out to be too difficult for the hiker's skill/athletic level, or the trail conditions are unexpected (e.g., deep snow). These types of problems can be avoided easily by being honest with yourself and learning in advance about the trails. If the trail is too hard, turn around before you have a problem. The hikes in this book have information about difficulty and skill level recommendations. Know your abilities and be honest with yourself, and you'll stay safe.

Predicting trail conditions can be tough, as this status can change from season to season and year to year. In this guide, trail maintenance, trail size (large vs. small) and seasonal safety concerns are noted for each hike. Most of the small trails described are unmaintained pathways, while the large trails are well-maintained. Small-trail conditions range greatly, but generally small foothill trails are in better condition than those that

climb up the mountain slopes. Mountain trails may fade out or become filled with loose rocks, requiring more navigation and athletic skills than their flat counterparts below.

Even with the best planning, unexpected conditions may exist on these trails. Two important examples of this are summer weather and lingering snowpack. Thunderstorms in the Sandia Mountains usually last for less than half an hour, but they can turn a nice afternoon hike into a dangerously slippery adventure. Although snow conditions may seem easy to research, many hikers have discovered that lingering deep snowpacks in the late spring (especially on the La Luz Trail) are crazy scary when the trail turns into a long, bumpy slab of ice. If in doubt about the current trail conditions, call the USFS Sandia Ranger District at (505) 281-3304 or search for information on their web page.

Altitude

Altitude sickness is unlikely on the routes in this book, which range in elevation from 5,000 to 8,000 feet. However, hikers will definitely notice how difficult exercise is at a mile-high elevation due to the thin and dry air. For Albuquerque residents who are acclimatized to the elevation, the high altitude should not be a concern. Visitors who live at lower elevations should not find altitude sickness a problem either, but if you are concerned, wait a few days before hiking in the foothills to partially acclimate to the altitude. Take it slow on the hike and bring along extra water to help keep your body hydrated.

Summer: Sun, Water, and Heat Exhaustion/Hyperthermia

Summer begins early in New Mexico, and often lasts longer than in the rest of the country: April to October. Every trail in this guide starts in the high-desert environment, and most hikes do not have abundant shade. Hikers should take extra precautions for the sun and the hot, dry, thin air. Simply stated, the high-desert sun is intense, and it can be daunting in the summer months as it endlessly shines down. Protecting your skin is paramount. Sunburns on your head, face, and shoulders can happen quite quickly. A light hat is advised, not only to keep the sun off your head but also to provide a little shade for your shoulders. Sunscreen is highly recommended even if you are wearing a hat, as the sun's rays are continually reflected off the desert sand. In fact, the winter sun also causes sunburns, so sunscreen is recommended year-round. The higher the sun protection factor (SPF) number, the better, preferably 30 or higher. If you are sweating, reapply it often.

Drinking water is advisable on every hike, regardless of the route's length. Carry at least one quart/liter of water per person for every hour of hiking expected. More may be needed in the summer, and keeping an extra supply in the car for after the hike is highly recommended.

Overexertion leading to heat exhaustion or, even worse, heat stroke is a primary concern in the hot summer months. The best way to avoid this issue is to hike in the early morning, when the temperatures are lower and the sun is less daunting. Dress in light clothing, wear a hat, and drink lots of water before, during, and after the hike. Even if you take these precautions, you can still suffer from heat exhaustion, which is caused by a lack in the body of either hydration or essential salts. The symptoms for heat exhaustion, as described by the Mayo Clinic, are cool, moist skin with goose bumps while in the heat, heavy sweating, faintness, dizziness, fatigue, weak and rapid pulse, lightheadedness, muscle cramps, confusion, nausea, and headache. The treatment is to stop all activity, rest in a cool spot out of the sun, and drink water or a sports drink. If untreated, heat exhaustion can lead to heat stroke, which has many of the same symptoms but also involves a rapid rise in body temperature (104°F or more). If heat exhaustion symptoms worsen or don't improve within the hour, or you think you may have heat stroke, seek medical assistance immediately.

Thunderstorms and Lightning

It is hard to overemphasize the importance of being aware of the high-desert weather and how quickly it can change. As most Albuquerqueans know, when it rains, it usually pours. Thunderstorms are possible year-round but are most common in July and August when the monsoon season is in full swing. If you happen to find yourself hiking in one, you will likely get soaking wet and very cold. You also face a notable risk of being struck by lightning. After the storm has passed, you'll have two other major concerns to face: slipping and falling on wet rocks or muddy trails, and being stranded in the foothills by flooded arroyo channels that block your exit route. However, the largest storms generally travel across New Mexico from southwest to northeast, so hikers in the foothills can easily see them coming. Additionally, the National Weather Service and all the local news stations track thunderstorms and send out weather alerts. Given the wide-open views of the western horizon and the copious amounts of real-time data available, hikers can easily avoid being caught out in bad weather.

STORM SAFETY

Thunder equals lightning. If you see lightning, you can estimate how close it is by counting the seconds between the flash and the thunder: every five seconds equals about one mile. Here is a summary of the current recommendations provided by the National Park Service for lightning within five miles of your position:

• Lightning often strikes the tallest object in the area. Avoid seeking shelter under tall, isolated, or solitary trees. Avoid locations with water, metal, and power lines.
• Find an open, low space on solid ground. If in the forest with no clearing, position yourself under the shortest trees you can find.
• Leave ridgelines and other high points such as mounds or hills. If on a ridgeline trail, hike off the ridge and wait out the storm.
• Remove metal objects and electrical devices from your body.
• Space yourself at least fifteen feet from your hiking companions.
• As a last resort, make yourself a small target by crouching on your toes, hands covering your ears, head between your knees. Crouch down on a sleeping pad, pack, or other nonmetal material to insulate yourself from ground currents. The ground conducts electricity, so touch the ground with as little of your body as possible.
• Do not lie flat.
• Stay alert and remain in a safe position until thirty minutes after the last thunder.

POST-STORM FLOOD SAFETY

Flood safety is a real concern when hiking in a canyon or when your route crosses any valley or arroyo. Canyons should be avoided during inclement weather as they are prone to dangerous flash floods during and after rainstorms. Most of the canyons in this guidebook have steep valley walls and can quickly become death traps. They also commonly contain smooth bedrock steps that become slippery when wet, creating an extremely dangerous situation for falling.

General arroyo safety applies to just about every hike in this book. Don't cross an arroyo that contains floodwaters. As little as one foot of fast-flowing water can knock hikers off their feet and sweep them away. Pay particular attention to storms brewing over the mountains, and be smart and avoid hikes that cross arroyos or valleys if rain is on the way.

Winter Snow and Ice

The most common hiking mistake in the winter is being unprepared for snow and ice, which generally leads to an uncomfortable hike, an injury, or worse. Snow regularly blankets Albuquerque and the Sandia Mountains from late November to late March. Even though the foothills get more snow than the city, there is rarely enough there for cross-county skiing or snowshoe hiking. Although it generally melts quickly, large sections of bumpy, slippery ice often form on the foothill trails in the winter months. With only a little foot traffic, these patches form quickly, most commonly on north-facing hills and in deep valleys. The primary concern for hiking on snow and ice is slipping; even if you don't fall, this can jar your back and cause an injury.

At a minimum, winter conditions require good hiking shoes with a "grippy" tread and extra clothing. It's possible to avoid most of the snow and ice on the lower-elevation foothill trails by waiting for a few days after a snowstorm to go out, but still be mentally and physically prepared for icy sections. Regardless of your athletic level, refrain from any hike that climbs into the mountains unless you are prepared for winter mountain conditions and have some sort of shoe cleats (crampons) with you.

Mine Safety

Mining in the Sandia Mountains ended in the 1970s. Many mines were simply abandoned without any regard for safety, and none of them are marked with warning signs. Although several trails in this area pass right next to a mine shaft or test pit, hikers may not notice it, as trees or the tailings may obscure the actual hole. Unfortunately, many of these features are simply holes in the ground, with shafts that may drop straight down or lead into the hillside. The walls of the vertical shafts often fall in under their own weight and aren't necessarily scalable. Shafts that enter the hillsides at an angle or are horizontal are often stabilized with wood structures or concrete; however, the wood is likely old and rotten and may collapse without warning. Best practice is to stay out of these features, while treading lightly and very carefully around them.

Animals and Wildlife Safety

There is a surprising amount of wildlife within the foothills and lower Sandia Mountains. A general list of species to be aware of includes black bears, cougars, bobcats, deer, coyotes, snakes, lizards, rabbits, squirrels, prairie dogs, mice, scorpions, tarantulas, roadrunners, quail, ducks, hawks, ravens, and a wide variety of migratory and other birds. All wildlife can be dangerous and should be viewed from a distance. Given a chance, every wild animal wants to flee from a hiker, but just in case they don't, never try to

touch them, even if they approach you. Do not feed or leave food for the wildlife along the trails. Doing so makes the animals associate human contact with easy food. This leads them to seek humans out for food and often results in the destruction of the animal.

Here are some specific tips for the more worrisome creatures.

BLACK BEARS AND COUGARS

The two largest predator species in the foothills are black bears and cougars (also called pumas or mountain lions). Although it is *extremely* rare to have an encounter with either of these animals, hikers should know what to do if they do meet one. Although brown bears (grizzlies) resided in the Sandia Mountains at one time, black bears are the only bear species there today; luckily, these are the least aggressive of the bears in North America. In some years, especially when it is extra dry in the mountains, bears will venture down into the lower foothills looking for food and water. Cougars are found throughout the North American mountains but are very private animals that actively avoid humans.

The most dangerous encounters with either of these animals occur when you surprise them, somehow threaten

them, or seem to pose a danger to their offspring. The best way to avoid this is to be a noisy hiker so these animals will hear you and retreat. Being noisy does not mean that you need to shout: just talk with the other hikers in your group and scuff your feet as you walk or—if you are alone—sing to yourself.

If you do meet a bear or cougar, the general recommendations from the USFS and the National Park Service are to

- stop, stay calm, and talk calmly to the animal; do not shout or act aggressively;
- stand firm: do not turn your back or run away; let them know you are not prey;
- try to look bigger by waving your arms and standing tall;
- group together and pick up small children to help them stay calm;
- hold your dog's collar; and
- wait for the animal to leave, as they usually do quickly once they see you. If the animal doesn't leave right away, hold your ground and be patient.

Additional information on what to do when encountering bears and cougars is often posted at major trailheads and is also readily available on both the USFS and the National Park Service websites.

RATTLESNAKES AND OTHER SNAKES
The Sandia Foothills, with its granite rocks and sandy terrain, has the perfect habitat for a variety of venomous and nonvenomous snakes. Although snake encounters can be common for frequent users of this area, the most important thing to know about snakes is that they do not want to bite humans. Usually, a snake will hide or leave an area if it realizes you are nearby, so making obvious movements and walking heavily on the trail is a good precaution. Because

humans are not prey for snakes, their biting is strictly a defensive action and is always their last resort. The most likely encounter for hikers is when the snake is sunning itself on a warm, sandy trail. They also live in piles of boulders or brush, so it is ill-advised to stick your hands into rock crevices and holes where you can't see what's inside.

Although all snakes will coil, act defensive, and potentially strike out if they feel threatened, it is the rattlesnake that most folks fear. Luckily, rattlesnakes do not like to be around humans, so encounters are rare. As with all snakes, a rattlesnake does not want to strike at hikers or their dogs; however, it will if threatened.

The best course of action if you encounter any snake is to stop and back up if you are too close, stand still for a moment, and assess it. Is it rattling or acting defensive? If not, take a picture, then turn around and leave. Do not touch the snake or try to pick it up, even if it is nonvenomous. If the snake is cold, it may just lie there, so you will need to hike around it. Give all snakes a wide berth, as they can reach beyond their body length with multiple strike attempts. If the snake is not leaving on its own, be smart and safe: turn around and leave the area. If you *must* pass a rattlesnake, back off to a safe distance, stomp on the ground, and wait for the snake to leave. Have patience: it may take a while.

Although snakebites are rare and usually nonfatal, all bites (including those from nonvenomous species) should be seen immediately by a medical professional to decrease the risk of infection. The venom from rattlesnakes is of particular concern for many hikers and their dogs. If you are bitten, the Food and Drug Administration and New Mexico Department of Game and Fish recommend that

Many-Legged Desert Dwellers

Maybe it's because of all those scary insect movies from our childhood, but three small animals seem to elicit an unjustified amount of fear in our society: tarantulas, scorpions, and centipedes. Luckily for us, none of them in this part of New Mexico have lethal venom. As predators, they primarily use their venom to hunt insects and small animals such as lizards. They often wander into garages or outbuildings along the open space, but because these creepy crawlers hide during the day, hikers will likely never see one.

Tarantulas (also known as "big hairy spiders") live in holes in the ground rather than building a web. This timid and secretive spider rarely bites people, and then only if provoked a lot. You're most likely to see a tarantula in summer when it is out wandering the hills in search of a mate. At this time, it only has one thing on its mind, and it does not involve attacking people.

Scorpions, on the other hand, are less forgiving about human curiosity and can easily be provoked into stinging. Although the scorpions that live in and around the

Sandia Mountains do not have life-threatening venom, you will know it if you are stung. In the wild, most scorpions live under rocks, fallen branches, plants, or anything else that it can scoot beneath. During the night, these little creatures are particularly well-known for finding their way into buildings—or hiding in shoes that are left unattended.

Unlike the previous two creatures, centipedes are found throughout the United States. New Mexico's species are big but nonaggressive. The giant desert centipede, which is the largest variety in North America, grows to an average of seven inches long and successfully hunts larger prey such as lizards and mice. Only mildly venomous, their bites are painful but not lethal.

If you happen to be unfortunate enough to receive a sting or bite, wash the site with soap and water and apply a cold compress and an antiseptic. The site may be painful for a day or two and will likely become red and swollen. For a centipede bite, consult your physician about getting a tetanus shot. If your symptoms persist or worsen, seek medical care.

you stay calm and seek medical attention as quickly as possible. All Albuquerque medical centers are prepared to treat snakebites. If you have to walk a distance to your car, move slowly and carefully, keeping your heart rate low. Use of tourniquets, ice, or the old suction strategies are now discouraged. If it is safe to do so, observe the snake for later identification, but do not try to catch it.

Plant Concerns

Two types of plants can cause a problem for local hikers: prickly species such as cacti and yuccas, and poison ivy. The cacti and yuccas grow throughout the city, foothills, and lower mountains. Although

most people know to avoid them, if you are unfortunate enough to brush against one while on a hike, simply pull the spines out and be on your way. A pair of tweezers from a Swiss Army knife can be a great help. If you sit on a cactus or the spines break off under the skin and can't be removed, monitor the location for signs of infection over the next few days.

Poison ivy is the other plant to be aware of. Hikers should be prepared to encounter it in every canyon in the foothills, and the patches can be quite extensive if there is an active spring nearby. Generally in New Mexico the plants are on the ground and relatively easy to identify, with three leaves together on one stem. The leaves are shiny and smooth and are usually dark green in color, but can have a red tinge along the edges. New growths may be light green. The leaves turn a brilliant red in the fall. The easiest way to avoid exposure is to wear long pants on a hike that could include ivy. If you bring a dog on your hikes, remember that the resin containing the allergen is on both the leaves and stems and can be transferred to you if the dog brushes against the plants.

An estimated 75 percent of the population is sensitive to poison ivy and will develop a rash if exposed. If you have touched a plant, wash the affected skin with soap as soon as possible and monitor it for developing rashes. Avoid touching your eyes or mouth until you are certain the resin is off your hands, and wash your hiking clothes immediately to avoid contaminating items at home. Rashes generally surface within twelve to seventy-two hours; the skin will be red, swollen, and itchy, and sometimes blisters will form. Mild reactions may last

from one to two weeks and can be easily treated at home with soothing lotions and over-the-counter medicines. More extreme reactions, especially if the rash is in a sensitive area, may need medical treatment.

When in doubt about whether a plant is poison ivy, remember the old saying: *Leaves of three, leave it be.*

HIKING EQUIPMENT

Clothing and Shoes

What to wear is always a good question to ponder before going outdoors. Clothing will naturally range from lightweight in the summer to heavier and warmer fabrics in the winter. Because the trails described in this guide do not climb into the high mountains, the air temperature should be the same as it is where you exit your car: if you are comfortable at the start, you should be good for the hike. Regardless of air temperature, consider wearing long trousers and a hat

year-round. Long pants have the distinct advantage of keeping prickly plants and rocks from scraping your legs, which is particularly nice on small trails filled with vegetation. Hats are also a good idea for the longer hikes and during the summer, as they keep the sun off your head and reduce the risk of sunburn and heat exhaustion.

Keep in mind that extra clothing may be needed in two situations: evenings and thunderstorms. When the New Mexico sun goes down, the air temperature can drop quickly, especially in late fall to early spring. If you are planning to be out close to sunset, take an extra layer along for warmth. In the summer (April through November), rapid temperature shifts also happen during thunderstorms. It may be 95°F (30°C) when the storm starts, but it can drop to a chilly 65°F (18°C) in ten minutes. It might seem like strange advice for New Mexico, but if going on a long summer hike, a rain jacket could be a heaven-sent addition to your pack.

Which pair of shoes to wear is also something to consider. At a minimum, they must have a closed toe: open-toed shoes such as flip-flops or sandals will quickly collect sand and cause blisters. For the longer walks, high-quality athletic shoes or boots are recommended, while for the steeper or rockier trails, a good pair of hiking boots is your best option.

Hiking Packs

A backpack is likely going to be bigger than you need for many of short routes described in this guide. You will be close to both your car and civilization. A small fanny pack with a water-bottle holder or a small bag with a few convenience items slung over your shoulder will make your short hike a little bit nicer. Items to take on short hikes include water (a must-have), a charged cell phone, sunscreen, sunglasses, a little food, some adhesive bandages, a small pocketknife, and, if you have a dog, some poop bags.

For the longer hikes and the routes that lead into the lower mountains, a small backpack should work well for the additional items that you will want: extra water (one quart/liter per person per hour of hiking), extra clothing or a raincoat, a map of the hike, and a good-sized snack or lunch.

Electronic Hiking Tools

This guide and all of its map data can be taken on the trail digitally if you have a smartphone. If you've purchased the book in hard copy, you can download the digital route data at http://unmpress.com/books/massong-60-short-hikes-sandia-foothills/hikes. Each hike has its own file with the main trail data in Keyhole Markup Language (KML) format. These data are easily viewed and used in free phone apps such as Google Earth or Map Plus. See appendix C for more details on how to use the downloadable trail KML data.

Other geospatial data (also known as waypoints) are provided at the end of each hike description for use with a GPS unit. The waypoints can also be used with a smartphone that has a GPS application.

Beyond its ability to process digital KML data, a cell phone is one of the most important tools you can take on these short hikes. In a single lightweight unit, you have maps, a camera, a flashlight, and, of course, a means of communication. Because the foothills are next to Albuquerque, high-quality phone service is available nearly everywhere on these hikes. If you find yourself in one of the rare locations where there is no reception, climb a nearby hill or exit the canyon to get a view of the city, which should do the trick.

IF YOU LOSE YOUR WAY OR ARE SERIOUSLY INJURED

Some of the smaller trails described in this book fade in and out or turn abruptly, so losing them is easy to do. However, it is unlikely that you will get lost for very long; these hikes have such great views that you should be able to find your way with a little exploring.

If you lose the trail or discover that you chose the wrong path, work hard to self-rescue. The first step is to retrace your previous route and go back to where you lost the trail. Do not cut across a slope or hill, as this may result in your getting more lost or injured in extreme terrain. If you find yourself in a truly dangerous situation that you cannot get out of by yourself or if you are seriously injured, use your phone to call for help. If you do so, do not expect a helicopter; rather, expect to wait for many hours for the rescue team to gather and then hike up to you. If you are injured, they may transport you down the mountain on a litter.

To request help, dial 911 on your cell phone and ask for the New Mexico State Police Division. The police will need information from you such as your name, personal information, why you are calling (are you lost or hurt?), where you are, and a phone number to call you back. If you are lost, the operator may be able to triangulate your cell signal, but you need to be prepared to give information about your location. A latitude and longitude from a GPS or an app is the best information you can give them, but you should also know the name of a nearby ridge or the trail you were hiking when you got lost. Without this information, the team will have trouble finding you, which translates into a long, delayed rescue.

TRAIL RULES, DOGS, AND ETIQUETTE

Posted at each official trailhead is a set of trail rules that outline the official dos and don'ts. Generally they are: no motor vehicles, no shooting or hunting, no fires or camping (City Open Space only), no litter, no glass, no alcohol, and keep dogs on leashes and clean up their waste. Walking your dog is a wonderful activity in the foothills, but unfortunately a few owners do not follow the rules, which has led to a disproportionate number of dog-related complaints. Having your dog off-leash could result in a ticket, but the reality is that dog rules protect other trail users and the wildlife that live in the area. Therefore, these rules and the others need to be adhered to regardless of the threat of a fine: after all, nobody wants to see a dog chasing a deer through the foothills.

Signs at all the trailheads also designate a pecking order for trail users, also known as trail etiquette: bike riders yield to

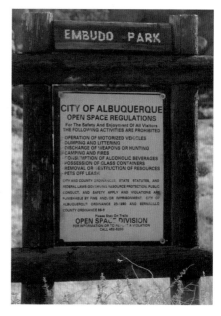

everyone, and everyone yields to horses. Although this seems clear-cut, there are no rules posted for how hikers should yield to other hikers. The most common trail users are on foot, all with different walking speeds and needs. Large groups often make frequent stops and go slowly. Families with children may have strollers. Runners tend to go faster, while hikers with dogs have leashes that could get tangled. A good rule of etiquette is to yield to the faster user or the one who is working harder (as, for example, when climbing up a steep path). If a runner approaches, a hiker should step aside and let him or her pass; this rule can also be applied to bikers as they zip by. Slow-moving groups should be prepared to move out of the way for the rest of the trail users. Hikers with dogs should also be prepared to yield to everyone else.

PRESERVE THE SANDIA FOOTHILLS

Although not pristine, the Sandia Mountains and its foothills are special; they were set aside for us. When Albuquerque was founded in the 1600s, the city was miles and miles away from the mountains, and a huge area of foothill space was available for recreation, cattle grazing, hunting, and the like. As the city expanded east, the public area of the foothills shrank and shrank and shrank. The public lands that we have today are all that is left. Although there are two large agencies whose job it is to manage these public lands, we as users also have a role in their care.

John Muir said it best: "Take nothing but pictures, leave nothing but footprints, kill nothing but time." The vegetation in this heavily used area grows slowly and erosion happens quickly, so your role as a hiker is to minimize your impact on the environment as you explore. Take every piece of trash with you, no matter how small it is. Even better, if you find a piece of litter, pick it up. Avoid damaging the trees and other vegetation. Don't step on the cacti. Leave the wildflowers for the next visitor to enjoy. Don't spray-paint or carve your initials into the rocks or push over any of the precariously balanced boulders. Don't purposely make new trails, and adhere to trail and land restoration activities and associated closures.

FIRES

Between 2010 and 2014, after multiple years of extreme drought, wildfires burned over a million acres of New Mexico's forests. During that same time frame, the fire risk in the Sandia Mountains and the foothills reached beyond extreme levels, causing the USFS and Open Space to close all public lands for long periods of time. Many local residents feel lucky to have avoided a wildfire so far, and we want to keep it that way.

Camping is not allowed in the Open Space lands. However, backcountry camping (a.k.a. backpacking) is permitted in the Wilderness Area of the Forest Service lands. There are no designated campgrounds, so only camping via backpacking is allowed. Although campfires are technically permitted, given how close these trails are to civilization, there is never a good reason to kindle one in this dry forest. If you really, really want a fire in the backwoods, be extra careful and have enough water on hand to drown it out, dead.

Barbequing is allowed in dedicated barbeque grills, such as the ones at the Elena Gallegos picnic sites; however, in particularly dry years these grills may be closed due to extreme fire danger. If they are closed, signs will be displayed.

THE TEN ESSENTIALS

If you've never heard of the "Ten Essentials" in reference to hiking in the backcountry, then you are probably fairly new to this activity, as this discussion has been ongoing for decades. Generally speaking, this list of ten essential items was originally drawn up to help hikers prepare for travel through the great outdoors: map, compass, extra clothing, matches, headlamp, first aid, knife, extra food, sunglasses, and sunscreen. In particular, the items would help a stranded or lost hiker to survive for a day or two in the woods. For hikers who walk five to ten miles into the wilderness, where there are many opportunities to get lost, having a supply of items to help an unexpected overnight stay is definitely a good idea. Although it is extremely unlikely that any person taking this book's short hikes would experience an unplanned overnight stay, it would definitely be a good idea to carry some of these items on the longer hikes into the lower-mountain areas.

As with so many things, the somewhat simple classic list has been updated with a new series of items by Steven M. Cox and Kris Fulsaas in their book *Mountaineering: The Freedom of the Hills*, 7th ed. (Seattle, WA: Mountaineers Books, 2003). Although the lists are similar, the new one acknowledges that a hiker might need one or more of several items under a general theme. For example, under the theme of "navigation," hikers might consider not only the map and compass but also a GPS unit and an altimeter. Additionally, the new list specifically recommends bringing a tool kit, emergency shelter, and extra water.

HOW TO USE THIS GUIDE

This guide is divided into three sections:

NORTHERN TRAILS: trails located north of the Sandia Peak Tram

CENTRAL TRAILS: trails located between the Sandia Peak Tram and the Embudito Trailhead

SOUTH CENTRAL TRAILS: trails south of the Embudito Trailhead to I-40

Each hike includes a description and summary of the route, a map, a picture or two, and a table with pertinent data concerning hiking difficulty, distances, estimated hiking time, trail conditions, land ownership, trail users, fees (if any), and special information about the area. Additionally, there are detailed hike directions, information about similar hikes, and a box with nonessential information such as details about a plant or animal that you might find in the area. For those hikers who carry GPS units, each section includes GPS point data (waypoints) for major intersections/features along the hike. There are also KML data intended to be used on smartphones with apps such as Google Earth. These data display the whole route as a line in the geospatial app.

Difficulty is rated on a scale of 1 (easy) to 5 (hard). For the harder hikes, descriptive information about the difficulty is located in the introductory paragraphs.

THE EVER-CHANGING TRAIL CONDITIONS

All trails and routes described in this book were digitized by the author and are displayed on the maps provided, as well as given in KML data form for use in geospatial phone apps. Although great effort was made to only develop routes on trails that were at least fairly well-established, the ones in the foothills are always evolving. Two major forms of change are official trail maintenance by one of the managing agencies, and natural forces that either wash away the trail or bury it under sediment. The latter natural changes are the most problematic on small trails. These routes are as correct as possible at the time of publication, but understand that the trails may change over time, and that these changes may not be reflected in either the printed descriptions or the digital data. Hikers should expect the small trails, in particular, to change over time and be prepared to do a little route-finding if they encounter a washed-out trail.

REFERENCE INFORMATION

Traditionally, guidebooks are the best places to find specific information about New Mexico's plants, animals, geology, history, Native cultures, and the like. The best are those that have gone through some sort of review process for accuracy and completeness. Below is a short list of some of the many books available that give background information about the Sandia Mountains or the surrounding area.

The Internet is another excellent source of information. However, because there are no "web police" making sure that the information is accurate, the most reliable online information is from reputable sites such as the USFS and other official government agencies or formal clubs such as the Albuquerque Mountain Rescue Council. The beginner's list below includes some reference material and sites for hikers in the Sandia Mountains.

Books and Other Print Materials
Coltrin, Mike. *Sandia Mountain Hiking*

Guide. Albuquerque: University of New Mexico Press, 2005.

deBuys, William. *Enchantment and Exploitation: The Life and Hard Times of a New Mexico Mountain Range*. Albuquerque: University of New Mexico Press, 2015.

Gray, Mary Taylor. *Watchable Birds of the Southwest*. Missoula, MT: Mountain Press, 1995.

Julyan, Robert, and Mary Stuever. *Field Guide to the Sandia Mountains*. Albuquerque: University of New Mexico Press, 2005.

Littlefield, Larry J., and Pearl M. Burns. *Wildflowers of the Northern and Central Mountains of New Mexico: Sangre de Cristo, Jemez, Sandia, and Manzano*. Albuquerque: University of New Mexico Press, 2015.

Melzer, Richard. *Coming of Age in the Great Depression: The Civilian Conservation Corps of New Mexico, 1933–1942*. Las Cruces, NM: Yucca Tree Press, 2000.

Shields, Helen. *Desert Plants: Recipes and Remedies*. Tularosa, NM: Okesa Publications, 1989.

Websites
Since websites change regularly, searching by organization name may be more useful.

Albuquerque Metropolitan Arroyo Flood Control Authority: http://www.amafca.org

Cibola National Forest and National Grasslands: http://www.fs.usda.gov/detail/cibola/

City of Albuquerque, Open Space Division: https://www.cabq.gov/parksandrecreation/open-space

New Mexico Game and Fish: http://www.wildlife.state.nm.us

New Mexico Office of the State Historian,

History of the Elena Gallegos Land
Grant: http://dev.newmexicohistory.org
/filedetails.php?fileID=24399
US Department of Agriculture–Forest
Service: http://www.fs.fed.us/
USDA Plants Database: http://plants
.usda.gov/about_plants.html

**HIKES IN THIS BOOK ACCORDING
TO CHARACTERISTICS**

Five Most Challenging Hikes
(in order from most to least challenging)
47. Piedra Lisa–Sunset Canyon Loop
46. Piedra Lisa Ridge Overlook Loop
40. Embudito South Ridge Trail to Boulder Cave
39. Embudito North Ridge Trail Loop
1. Upper La Cueva Overlook via La Luz Trail

Five Least Challenging Hikes
(in order from least to most challenging)
57. Hilldale Mound Loop
10. Juan Tabo Cabin (ruins) and Adjacent Arroyo Trail
8. Old 333 Road Trail
54. U-Mound Perimeter Loop
34. Lower Bear Arroyo Loop from John B. Robert Dam

Five Hikes Most Likely to See Large Wildlife
20. Northern Elena Gallegos Boundary Loop from Sandia Peak Tram
31. Academy Camp Loop
44. Candelaria Bench Loop
46. Piedra Lisa Ridge Overlook Loop
53. Embudo–U-Mound Overlook Loop

Five Hikes with Springs
5. Hidden Falls Canyon Route
7. Waterfall Canyon via Piedra Lisa Trail
21. Cañon Domingo Baca Trail
38. Embudito Canyon Route/Loop

51. Embudo Trail Loop to Upper Watershed/Headwall

Five Hikes with Large Falls
5. Hidden Falls Canyon Route
7. Waterfall Canyon via Piedra Lisa Trail
45. Piedra Lisa Falls and Bench Loop
48. Narrow Falls
55. Old Man Canyon Loop

Five Hikes with Cabins/Ruins
4. Juan Tabo Picnic Area
10. Juan Tabo Cabin (Ruins) and Adjacent Arroyo Trail
12. La Cueva Picnic Area and Valley Hike
13. Ruins Loop from La Cueva Picnic Area
21. Cañon Domingo Baca Trail

Five Best Large-Trail Mountain Hikes
1. Upper La Cueva Overlook via La Luz Trail
6. El Rincon via Piedra Lisa Trail
17. Tram Trail (a.k.a. Tramway Trail)
22. Pino Trail to the Dead Trees
51. Embudo Trail Loop to Upper Watershed/Headwall

Five Best Small-Trail Mountain Hikes
9. Jaral Watershed Loop
32. Bear Canyon Overlook
40. Embudito South Ridge Trail to Boulder Cave
46. Piedra Lisa Ridge Overlook Loop
59. Tijeras Canyon–Four Hills Overlook Loop

Five Classic Foothills Hikes
24. Grassy Hills Loop
28. Elena Gallegos Inner Trail Loop
29. North Levee/Trail 305 Loop
31. Academy Camp Loop
33. Middle Bear Arroyo Loops from Michial Emery Trailhead

NORTHERN

TRAILS

THE NORTHERN TRAILS area is popular for its mountainous hiking with beautiful forested landscapes and amazing views of both the city and the northern Sandia Mountains. Given the arid climate of Albuquerque, exploring a mountain forest is a special treat, and Sandia's forests are easiest to access from this area. Those near the roads are piñon-juniper, but dense pine/fir forests are easily found by hiking further up into the mountains. Fantastic views of the city and the surrounding terrain can be had everywhere in this northern area. Together with the forests and views, these trails draw visitors from all over. The most popular is the La Luz Trail, which has become an icon for hiking in Albuquerque. However, the crowds can be daunting for hikers seeking a more natural outdoor experience. Luckily, there are numerous other places to explore in this area that embody the same attributes that made the La Luz Trail so popular.

In 1931, this area and all of the public lands of the Sandia Mountains (formerly part of the Manzano National Forest) were made part of the newly established Cibola National Forest. At about the same time, the US Forest Service intensified its efforts to increase public use of these lands. For the Northern Trails area, the USFS focused on new public recreational facilities and trails, employing the Civilian Conservation Corps (CCC) to construct several buildings in the Sandia Mountains, including picnic facilities at the Juan Tabo and La Cueva Picnic Areas. Starting in about 1935, a temporary base camp, Juan Tabo Cabin, was established near FR 333 and Tramway Road to support the larger and more permanent construction of the recreational buildings. The two picnic areas were completed in

1936 and were described as ideal CCC construction in the "rustic architecture" that made the project's buildings distinct and durable. (See appendix B for more historical information.) In fact, the buildings at both picnic areas are still fully functional and intact, having needed only moderate amounts of maintenance over the years.

The mountains and their trails, tight, brush-filled canyons, old roads turned into trails, old buildings, wildlife, wide-open views, and picnic sites are densely packed into this area, spawning numerous outdoor opportunities. Most trails lead through open areas that have amazing views of the mountains, the city, West Mesa, and beyond for a hundred miles. Although the views on the large trails are likely the single most important factor that make this area so popular, some of the other less-popular trails have outdoor experiences that are just as amazing. These "other" trails are more spread out, yielding better opportunities for wildlife viewing and some peace and quiet. The hikes described in this section range from easy to hike and navigate to very strenuous, with a few requiring climbing and trail-finding skills.

BEST TIME TO VISIT

Spring and fall are the best times to visit this area. Although it is open year-round, spring and fall have cool but typically not cold air temperatures, and if the previous season had a lot of rain, then the wildflowers might be out. Winter is a great time here, too, but only a few trails are clear of snow and ice during the winter months. The routes in the higher elevations or in excessive shade—for example, La Luz Trail, La Cueva Canyon, and Waterfall Canyon—usually have snow and ice accumulation, making them dangerous. Summers are hot and dry with ovenlike afternoons and evenings for the canyon or southwest-facing trails, such as La Luz Trail, Juan Tabo Canyon, and Tram Trail.

SPECIAL INFORMATION FOR THIS AREA

The vast majority of the Northern Trails area is owned and operated by the USFS; however, there are several private holdings within its boundaries. Please be aware of posted private properties and respect the landowners.

The entire Juan Tabo Canyon–La Cueva area is a USFS Fee Area. A Sandia Mountain Annual Permit or National Parks Pass covers this recreation fee: just put the pass on your car's dashboard, with the expiration date visible. A daily permit can be obtained at one of the many USFS self-serve fee stations. The daily fee at this writing is $3; bring exact change.

The Sandia Peak Tram parking area is also a fee area: $2 per car per day at the time this book was printed.

USFS parking areas have posted closing times. If a gate is present at the lot area or on the access road, it may be closed after posted hours.

Know your abilities and stay safe. The hike descriptions in this book have information about difficulty and recommendations for skill levels. Beyond skills, the Northern Trails area is wild and can be unpredictable, with loose rocks, house-sized boulders, ice in the winter, heat in the summer, and steep drop-offs (cliffs). Rescue crews know this area well and have helped any number of lost, stranded, or unprepared day hikers. A modest amount of preparation will keep you safe and greatly improve your hiking experience.

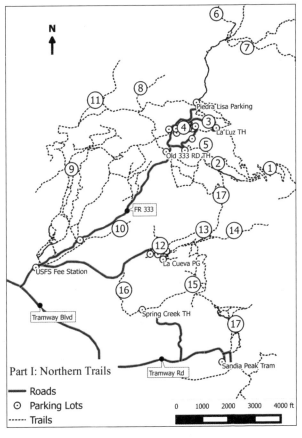

Part I: Northern Trails

— Roads
⊙ Parking Lots
----- Trails

0 1000 2000 3000 4000 ft

DIRECTIONS TO THE AREA

This general area is located at the far northeastern corner of the Albuquerque metropolitan area, with Forest Road (FR) 333 providing access to almost all of the trailheads and parking lots. The few routes not located off of FR 333 are accessed from Tramway Road, which leads to the Sandia Peak Tram.

FROM I-25, follow Tramway Road east from the Sandia Casino area, then turn left onto FR 333. From I-40, take the Tramway Boulevard exit and then take this road north for about ten miles as it follows along the base of the mountains. Continue past the stop sign at the Bernalillo–Sandoval County line to FR 333. For hikes near Sandia Peak Tram, turn onto Tramway Road at the stop sign, then turn left and follow the signs to the Tram.

UPPER LA CUEVA OVERLOOK VIA LA LUZ TRAIL

Difficulty	5	Long distance, high elevation, steep trail
Distance	5 mi (8 km) round-trip	
Hiking Time	2–4 hours	
Elevation	1,000 ft. gain (304 m)	Peak elevation: 8,000 ft. (2,438 m); Low elevation: 7,040 ft. (2,146 m) at parking
Trail Condition	Excellent	USFS-owned and -maintained
Trail Users	Hikers and horses	Horses are rare
Best Time	Late spring and fall	Winter has snow/ice and summer is very hot
Parking Lot	La Luz Trailhead	
Fees	$3 per vehicle	

SPECIAL INFORMATION: Crowded, especially on weekends and holidays.

OTHER HIKING OPTIONS

1. La Luz to Tram Trail (shorter option)
Difficulty: 4
Distance: 2 miles round-trip
Hiking Time: 40–60 minutes round-trip
Elevation: 360 ft. gain

2. La Luz to Sandia Mountain Crest Trail (longer option)
Difficulty: 5 due to length and steepness
Distance: 14 miles round-trip
Hiking Time: 6–12 hours round-trip
Elevation: 3,240 ft. gain (crest elevation is 10,280 ft.)
Special Note: After La Cueva Ridge, this trail gets steeper and has mountainous terrain and weather conditions. Hikers should be prepared for mountain conditions if planning to hike the full length of the La Luz Trail. Snow and ice cover large sections of the upper trail late into the spring season (sometimes until late April), creating dangerous hiking conditions for unprepared hikers. If hiking in the winter or spring, consult the USFS for current trail conditions.

ALTERNATE PARKING

Juan Tabo Picnic Area
(6,920 ft. elevation) via a 0.5 mile road walk
Piedra Lisa Trailhead parking lot
(6,960 ft. elevation) via La Luz–Piedra Lisa Trail (0.5 mile)

THE LA LUZ TRAIL is an amazing, well-maintained trail with fantastic scenery and views from start to finish. This USFS trail climbs swiftly from the parking lot to the Sandia Crest with magnificent views of the mountains and valleys and the city along most of its length. As might be expected, the scenery changes as you travel up the mountain: the first three miles of the trail leading into La Cueva Watershed are full of incredible views of Albuquerque, small canyons, and the very tops of the mountains. Once in La Cueva Watershed and along the upper part of the trail, lovely views of the alpine forests, upper mountains, cliffs, and deep valleys are everywhere. You will begin to feel how far up you are as it ascends into a high-elevation terrain that is slightly cooler in the summer, with grand views of the upper mountains. The La Luz Trail has been popular for decades. Given all the foot traffic, there are numerous side "trails" along the way (e.g., the La Cueva Watershed Overlook trail), creating countless great intermediate stopping points.

Accordingly, this trail is popular and usually busy. The main parking lot fills early on weekends, and parked cars often extend down the road, making this whole area highly congested on busy days. If you want to see what all the fuss is about but don't like excessive crowds, try the trail at midweek; there will still be people around, but not as many. The cooler seasons (late spring and early fall) are best for this trail, as the lower slopes face to the west and have almost no shade. In winter, the lower portion of the trail, up to La Cueva Ridge, is often but not always snow-free; consult with local USFS rangers for current trail information. Summer afternoons are crazy hot on this trail; therefore, it is recommended to avoid hiking there at that time. The upper portion of the trail (beyond the La Cueva Ridge) really must be considered a mountain trail, and preparedness is mandatory. If the crest is your destination, refer to *Sandia Mountain Hiking Guide* by Mike Coltrin for more specific hiking information about the upper La Luz Trail.

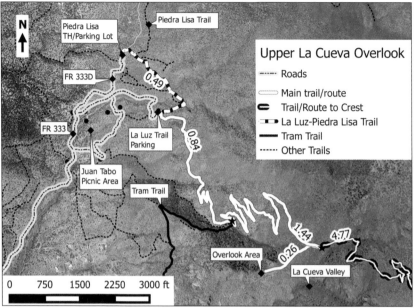

Upper La Cueva Overlook

----- Roads

⊂⊃ Main trail/route

⊂ Trail/Route to Crest

⊏⊐■ La Luz-Piedra Lisa Trail

▬ Tram Trail

----- Other Trails

N

Piedra Lisa TH/Parking Lot

Piedra Lisa Trail

FR 333D

0.49

FR 333

La Luz Trail Parking

0.84

Juan Tabo Picnic Area

Tram Trail

1.44 4.77

Overlook Area 0.26

La Cueva Valley

0   750   1500   2250   3000 ft

Abandoned Mine near the La Luz Trail

In 1540, the Spanish conquistador Coronado trekked through New Mexico and beyond in search of the fabled Seven Cities of Gold. Although he never found them, he was convinced they existed, as the area was obviously rich in metals and other precious resources. Other explorers came seeking riches, and although there were no cities made of gold, mining for precious metals became and continues to be popular and profitable today. At one time, numerous small but active mines were located in the Sandia Mountains; the La Luz Mine was the last of these, closing in the 1970s.

Today the once-active gold mine is simply a blocked tunnel, a few local trails, and the ruins of a cabin. Although the relic mining items are somewhat unspectacular, a geocache site is nearby and the nostalgia of the "good ol' days" draws many hikers each year to this area. Many websites and hiking books describe this location and specifically the geocache site near the mine. A small, unmarked trail is located to the north of the La Luz Trail just before the last major set of switchbacks leading to the crest. However, before trying to find this site, note that it is a fair distance beyond the Overlook hike, and the small trail leading to the mine is quite rugged, so a little preparation is needed. A good map or set of directions can be found in other guidebooks and on the Internet; the web page for the geocache "Lost Mine at the Rockpile" site has coordinates that help. As always, getting a US Geological Survey topographic map (hard copy or digital) is advised.

■ THE HIKE

Start at the La Luz Trailhead parking area.

Walk on the La Luz Trail past the Tram Trail intersection at 0.8 mile.

After another 1.5 miles and the second set of switchbacks, the trail crosses into the La Cueva Watershed; this ridge is marked by a gray post where the old La Luz Trail rejoins the current trail.

Turn right at the gray post to follow a well-worn, but unmarked trail that leads out onto the ridgeline to the right of the La Luz Trail. This ridgeline extends about a quarter of a mile and then ends.

Return to the parking area on the same trail.

IF YOU LIKED THIS LARGE-TRAIL MOUNTAIN HIKE, try HIKE 6: El Rincon via Piedra Lisa Trail, which feels a little easier, or HIKE 22: Pino Trail to the Dead Trees.

FOR THOSE USING GPS DATA

(DATUM: WGS 84)

Intersection of the La Luz Trail and the Tram Trail: –106.475544, 35.213597

Intersection of the La Luz Trail and the trail leading to the Overlook Area: –106.46912, 35.212179

LA LUZ SWITCHBACK OVERLOOK FROM TRAM TRAIL

Difficulty	4	Medium length, relatively steep trail
Distance	2.5 mi (4 km) round-trip	
Hiking Time	1–2 hours	
Elevation	400 ft. gain (60 m)	Peak elevation: 7,440 ft. (2,207 m); Low elevation: 7,040 ft. (2,146 m) at parking
Trail Condition	Excellent	USFS-owned and -maintained
Trail Users	Hikers and horses	Horses are rare
Best Time	Fall through spring	Winter may have snow and summer is very hot
Parking Lot	La Luz Trailhead	
Fees	$3 per vehicle	National Parks Pass or Sandia Mountains Pass

SPECIAL INFORMATION: Crowded, especially on weekends and holidays. See **HIKE 1: Upper La Cueva Overlook via La Luz Trail** for other trail information.

THIS IS A GREAT HIKE for those who want to get out into the mountains and get some exercise without going too far. After climbing a short distance up the La Luz Trail, hikers descend into a small wooded valley, home to the Tram Trail junction. Popular sites for a quick rest stop line this part of the trail, which passes through a dense forest of piñon and a few ponderosa pine trees, creating an atmosphere with deep shade and cooler temperatures. At the furthest point on this route, hikers walk along a sharp ridgeline that overlooks Hidden Falls Canyon and the first set of switchbacks on the La Luz Trail. Sitting and watching birds fly over the canyon or the many La Luz Trail hikers ascend and descend the switchbacks is a fun resting activity. Those who prefer can turn their back to the canyon and switchbacks and look out over the city and the West Mesa. On clear days, Mt. Taylor can easily be seen to the west, Ladron Peak to the southwest, and Cabezon Peak, a vertical rock, to the northwest. For hikers with binoculars, exploring the entirety of this view can take hours.

Because this area is close to the La Luz Trail, solitude is unlikely on this hike. Even if there are no hikers on the Tram Trail with you, voices from the La Luz Trail carry across the Hidden Falls

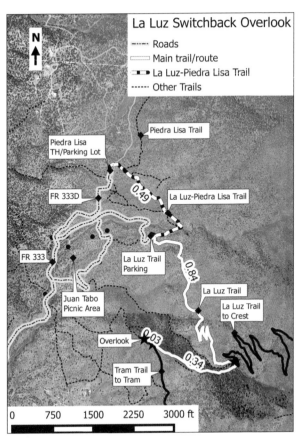

La Luz Switchback Overlook

---- Roads
===== Main trail/route
━■━■ La Luz–Piedra Lisa Trail
······ Other Trails

Piedra Lisa Trail

Piedra Lisa TH/Parking Lot

FR 333D

0.49

La Luz–Piedra Lisa Trail

FR 333

La Luz Trail Parking

0.84

Juan Tabo Picnic Area

La Luz Trail

La Luz Trail to Crest

Overlook

0.03

Tram Trail to Tram

0.34

0   750   1500   2250   3000 ft

ALTERNATE PARKING

Juan Tabo Picnic Area (6,920 ft. elevation) via a 0.5-mile road walk

Piedra Lisa Trailhead parking lot (6,960 ft. elevation) via a walk up the La Luz–Piedra Lisa Trail (0.5 mile)

Canyon; in fact, from the overlook area, the louder conversations are easily overheard. If you desire solitude, rather than going to the overlook area stay on Tram Trail for a little further. After it turns sharply to the left (near the overlook area), you will immediately stop hearing hikers on the La Luz Trail and will

The Old La Luz Trail

As is common with old trails, the La Luz Trail was originally an old mining route that led straight up the mountains to the La Luz Mine. Using the original track, the distance to the mine was about 4.5 miles—a very steep 4.5 miles. In the 1960s the USFS rerouted the lower section of the original trail, adding an extra 1.5 miles to reduce its slope, with most of the new distance added in the form of switchbacks. These reduce the grade in the steeper sections from about 20 percent on the old path to about 12 percent on the new. Although longer, the new trail is a significant improvement over the old one in terms of quality and overall steepness, making this the preferred route.

But if you really want to experience the hike the way the miners did, the old trail section is easy enough to find with just a little looking along the way. In fact, there seems to be a club of hikers who prefer the old trail to the new and thus keep the abandoned section open and in decent condition. The easiest way to find the old trail is to climb the first mile of the La Luz Trail, turn onto the Tram Trail, and follow it for about a quarter of a mile. The unmarked old section of the La Luz Trail is located to the left, just before the Tram Trail makes a sharp turn to the left (south) and reaches the Switchback Overlook area. Finding a map that denotes the old trail is a little difficult, but if you're committed to locating one, there are user-created versions on the Internet.

gain a different perspective as the route changes to a southerly direction. Surprisingly few hikers go beyond the overlook area, which means that a short distance past the left turn usually leads to peace and quiet and a more wild-feeling trail experience.

▪ THE HIKE

Proceed from the La Luz Trailhead parking area onto the La Luz Trail.

Continue on to the Tram Trail intersection at 0.8 mile.

Turn right onto the Tram Trail and hike a short distance into the forest for deep shade. Continue on this trail beyond the forest to where it turns sharply to the left (0.3 mile).

Rather than turning left with the Tram Trail, stay straight along the small ridgeline trail for a short distance (0.1 mile). The La Luz Trail and the first set of switchbacks are on the neighboring hill just beyond the deep canyon.

Return along the same route.

IF YOU LIKED THIS LARGE-TRAIL MOUNTAIN HIKE, try **HIKE 37: Embudito Canyon Overlook Loop,** which is about the same difficulty, or **HIKE 1: Upper La Cueva Overlook via La Luz Trail,** which is a little harder.

FOR THOSE USING GPS DATA
(DATUM: WGS 84)
Intersection of the La Luz Trail and the Tram Trail: –106.475544, 35.213597
Intersection of the Tram Trail and the small trail leading to the overlook area: –106.480677, 35.214381

LA LUZ–PIEDRA LISA TRAIL

LA LUZ–PIEDRA LISA TRAIL

Difficulty	3	Steep sections with some trail-finding required
Distance	1 mi	Round trip from either parking lot
Hiking Time	10–20 minutes	
Elevation	240 ft. gain (74 m)	Peak elevation: 7,200 ft. (2,195 m); Low elevation: 6,960 ft. (2,121 m) at parking
Trail Condition	Moderate	USFS-owned but not -maintained
Trail Users	Hikers and horses	Horses are rare
Best Time	Spring	Great year-round, may have flowers in spring. Winter can have snow and ice
Parking Lot	Piedra Lisa Trailhead	
Fees	$3 per vehicle	National Parks Pass or Sandia Mountains Pass

SPECIAL INFORMATION: Can be crowded on weekends and holidays. This trail is a great option for La Luz hikers who find the La Luz parking area full. It is also a wonderful side trail for exploring the La Luz area while avoiding crowds at that parking area.

A **GROWING TREND** at many public lands access points, and especially in the greater La Luz area, is for hikers to stay local, exploring the landscape around the parking area. Although most people who visit the greater La Luz Trail area do intend to hike it, an increasing number discover that they are unprepared for the main trail because they don't have enough water or physical stamina. Many find that they are content with simply exploring the small canyon and boulder-covered slopes to the east of the La Luz parking area. Consequently, numerous user-created trails now exist that lead to a variety of places, all of which are fun to explore. There are unexpected curiosities for everyone who likes to look into rock crevices, sneak around large boulders looking for critters, climb up on top of these rounded giants, look for wildflowers, or simply enjoy the trees that grow in the small, pleasantly shady

niches. During the summer months, many local hikers seek out the small canyon area to the northeast of the La Luz parking area, which is full of nooks and crannies with some shade thanks to trees and tall mountain bushes.

The best access for this area is via the La Luz–Piedra Lisa Trail, with parking at the Piedra Lisa parking lot. This short trail connects the La Luz parking area with the Piedra Lisa parking area and serves two types of hikers: those who want to hike the La Luz Trail, but can't get a spot in its small parking lot, and those who want to hike and explore the local area. It has surprising views of the mountains and hillside in and around the La Luz Trailhead. With the higher density of trees producing shade and the north aspect of the landscape, this trail and the entire area are slightly cooler than the La Luz Trail, so if you find yourself in the area on a sunny June afternoon, the La Luz–Piedra Lisa Trail and general area are recommended over the main trail.

ALTERNATE PARKING

La Luz Trailhead parking lot (7,040 ft. elevation)

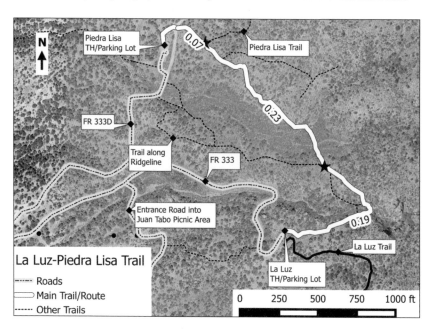

Piedra Lisa
TH/Parking Lot

0.07

Piedra Lisa Trail

N

FR 333D

0.23

Trail along
Ridgeline

FR 333

Entrance Road into
Juan Tabo Picnic Area

0.19

La Luz Trail

La Luz-Piedra Lisa Trail

---- Roads
⊃ Main Trail/Route
------ Other Trails

La Luz
TH/Parking Lot

0   250   500   750   1000 ft

■ THE HIKE

Park at Piedra Lisa Trailhead parking area.

Start on the Piedra Lisa Trail. After a short distance (about 0.1 mile), the Piedra Lisa Trail veers to the left (east) and the marked La Luz–Piedra Lisa Trail turns to the right (south) and begins to climb a small hill.

The La Luz–Piedra Lisa Trail follows along a wide arroyo valley bottom (the headwaters of Sandy Arroyo), then crosses it at about 0.25 mile from the Piedra Lisa Trail.

The trail climbs a small hill where it joins up with an old version of the La Luz–Piedra Lisa Trail. From this hill, it drops into another arroyo channel, then turns right (west). The trail ends next to the toilets in the La Luz Trailhead parking area.

The return trip is along the same route, but in reverse.

IF YOU LIKED THIS HIKE, try **HIKE 8: Old 333 Road Trail**, which is a little easier, or **HIKE 9: Jaral Watershed Loop**, which is a little harder.

FOR THOSE USING GPS DATA
(DATUM: WGS 84)
Intersection of the new Piedra Lisa Trail
    segment and the La Luz–Piedra Lisa Trail:
    –106.48262, 35.22293
Intersection of the new La Luz–Piedra Lisa Trail
    and the old ridgeline trail:
    –106.48002, 35.22087

Slope Aspect and Vegetation

If you hike both the La Luz–Piedra Lisa Trail and the lower La Luz Trail, you will invariably notice the difference between them in amount of vegetation. As neighbors, at similar elevations, and with a common management history, one would think that their vegetation would be alike. But with a cursory visual inspection, even a person with little to no plant knowledge can tell that there is a lot more vegetation along the La Luz–Piedra Lisa Trail. The key to this difference is hillslope direction: south- and west-facing hills are hotter and the vegetation doesn't grow as well, while north- and east-facing hills do not get the direct sun, so they stay just a little cooler. The hills along the La Luz–Piedra Lisa Trail generally face northeast, which means they get the early morning sun during the cool time of the day. The hills along the La Luz Trail generally face southwest, which translates into direct sun from late morning until sunset, during the hottest time of the day. If you've ever walked the La Luz Trail on a sunny summer afternoon, you know it feels like an oven, with heat blasting you from every direction. This difference in sun exposure causes relatively more moisture to evaporate from the soil on south- and west-facing slopes, thus making it harder for vegetation to grow.

JUAN TABO PICNIC AREA

Difficulty	1	Short trails crisscross with the road
Distance	Varies	
Hiking Time	Varies	
Elevation	Varies	Lot elevation: 6,920 ft. (2,109 m)
Trail Condition	Moderate	USFS-owned but not -maintained
Trail Users	Hikers	
Best Time	Summer	Picnic area road is open from May 15 to Oct 15
Parking Lot	Juan Tabo Picnic Area	
Fees	$3 per vehicle	National Parks Pass or Sandia Mountains Pass

SPECIAL INFORMATION: A vastly underutilized area most of the time, but can be crowded on summer holidays. This area is a great option for La Luz hikers who find the La Luz parking area full.

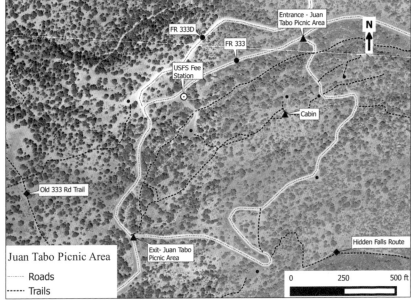

Juan Tabo Picnic Area

‑‑‑‑‑ Roads
‑‑‑‑‑ Trails

ALTHOUGH THE MOST obvious and popular features in this area are the Civilian Conservation Corps (CCC) structures, the Juan Tabo Picnic Area might better be named the "Juan Tabo Hidden Picnic Area," as nearly all the picnic tables are conccaled from the road. The CCC construction crews who built this picnic area obviously spent a lot of time carefully placing the tables with privacy in mind. To improve local recreation, the CCC also constructed the outdoor toilets, the picnic shelter, the roads, and other picnic items such as concrete pads for garbage cans.

The large CCC-built picnic shelter located at the top of the loop road is likely the most popular feature. This rustic-style building, as well as the toilets, blend well with the local topography and landscape; their locations were well-chosen, and they were assembled using the local rock (Sandia granite) and large timbers (known locally as vigas), with cement to fill the crevices. The large shelter is the ultimate covered picnic building, with thick rock walls and windows that seem to funnel air inside for a comfortable atmosphere. The building also has a smooth concrete floor, a bench, and a nice little fire pit in one corner. All of the CCC buildings provide an effective armor from the summer sun for visitors and picnickers, even on the hottest days.

Although the picnic shelter can be seen from FR 333 and easily draws people into the area, don't forget about the picnic tables. Several concrete picnic tables were placed in and among the boulders, trees, and little hills of the picnic area and must be looked for, as they are all concealed from the road. Most of the tables have privacy rather than shade. The trails between them range from good to poor, sometimes requiring climbing steps or squeezing between trees and boulders. Most of the tables are well-spaced, with views of the surrounding area. In a few cases, they were carefully placed among a group of large boulders, creating an interestingly cozy space, if a bit cramped. The

fun lies in finding all the different tables, and in doing so, leaving the road area to explore the hills, boulders, and nooks and crannies. Undoubtedly, finding them all will take multiple trips, as they are located throughout the loop and the central picnicking area. A good place to start looking for the tables is from the loop road, on the hill across the street from the picnic shelter and toilets.

The Juan Tabo Picnic Area has two road components: the central parking/fee area and the loop road that arcs fully around it. The loop road is paved, but

closed for much of the year (October 15 to May 15). A great short hiking opportunity during the winter is to walk this road and enjoy the solitude without the summer crowds; to complete the loop, meander through the picnic area, exploring the small hills for the hidden picnic tables. The central parking area, connected to FR 333, is located next to the fee station, and is open year-round.

IF YOU LIKED THIS PICNIC AREA, try HIKE 12: La Cueva Picnic Area and Valley Hike, HIKE 13: Ruins Loop from La Cueva Picnic Area, and HIKE 28: Elena Gallegos Inner Trail Loop, which also include great picnic areas.

FOR THOSE USING GPS DATA
(DATUM: WGS 84)
Cabin in the Juan Tabo Picnic Area:
   –106.48456, 35.2193

CCC Rustic Architecture

The Civilian Conservation Corps (CCC) was implemented in 1933 as part of President Franklin D. Roosevelt's New Deal. This new agency put men to work doing environmental conservation on public lands; in Albuquerque this meant building Forest Service trails and recreation structures throughout the Sandia Mountains. The buildings used a rustic architecture style and were designed to be particularly hardy. In fact, the style of the Juan Tabo and La Cueva Picnic Area buildings was revered by the USFS as ideal for standard CCC construction. The CCC's primary philosophy, in concert with that of the USFS, was to construct features of utility in harmony with the environment, all while using natural materials. Their rustic architecture used a strong horizontal emphasis, complimentary colors, and extensive wood and stone, and was flexible enough to remain in accord with local styles.

Wood products have always been limited in New Mexico compared to other parts of the

United States. The CCC buildings here made extensive use of rock and were designed in a pueblo style unique to New Mexico's culture. In both the Juan Tabo and La Cueva Picnic Areas, great care was taken during construction to shape the native rock (or find the already perfectly shaped rocks) to create a tight fit for the picnic shelters' walls and the door and window arch frames. Using this method ensured that the structures relied on the rock rather than the cement for integrity. Here, the cement is more like a filler material placed between the fitted rocks that hold the weight of the buildings. Two dominant features of the pueblo style are found in the picnic shelters in this area: projecting vigas in the front and rear, and flat roofs. Vigas are very large, minimally processed timbers, which provide major support to the roof. In both of these buildings, the original vigas were the weak points in the structures, and they have been replaced with metal beams.

HIDDEN FALLS CANYON ROUTE

Difficulty	3	To base of falls
Distance	1 mi (1.6 km) round-trip	
Hiking Time	1–1.5 hours	
Elevation	440 ft. gain (135 m)	Peak elevation: 7,200 ft. (2,195 m) at base of falls; Low elevation: 6,760 ft. (2,060 m) at beginning of channel
Trail Condition	Fair in canyon	USFS-owned but not -maintained
Trail Users	Hikers	
Best Time	Spring through fall	
Parking Lot	Juan Tabo Picnic Area loop road (at last switchback area)	
Fees	$3 per vehicle	National Parks Pass or Sandia Mountains Pass

SPECIAL INFORMATION: Two small tributaries drain into Hidden Falls canyon after they cross the La Luz Trail; these side canyons can be used to exit the main canyon. Both get steep near the La Luz Trail.

AN INTERESTING and little-explored area is the small canyon to the south of the Juan Tabo Picnic Area, an unnamed watershed that drains the landscape along the lower La Luz Trail. About half a mile from the picnic area, the canyon turns sharply, the walls narrow, and a tall bedrock falls comes into view. In early spring, a small spring often emerges in the channel bottom near the falls. This dry falls cannot be seen from any vantage point from the La Luz Trail, the Tram Trail, or even from within the canyon, except at very close range. With the steep canyon walls and sharp turns, this falls area can really only be seen by walking up to its base, which is a fun hike. Although there are hikers all around this area, this little valley is truly hidden with a high aspect of solitude.

Vegetation in the valley bottom is dense: chamisa and Apache plume fill the wider sections and cottonwoods the narrower sections. This interesting combination of high-desert vegetation coupled with the larger, lush riparian trees is a magnet for wildlife, despite the La Luz area's high population. With the dense valley and channel vegetation, this canyon walk is brushy and scratchy and sometimes, especially near the picnic area, overgrown by the vegetation. Trails on the slope leading to the canyon from the picnic area are particularly small and are prone to washing out. Please preserve this area for the next visitors by traversing it carefully to avoid disturbing the vegetation.

This hike should be avoided during inclement weather of any kind, as it is within a tightly confined canyon. Slippery bedrock and flash floods could make this area extremely dangerous.

■ THE HIKE

Park along the paved rectangular Juan Tabo Picnic Area loop road parking area, located just after the tight switchback near the exit. If the loop road is closed,

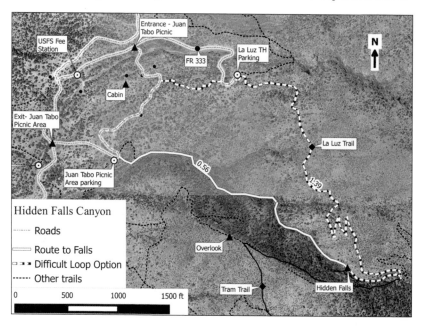

Hidden Falls Canyon
- - - - Roads
═══ Route to Falls
□ ▪ ▪ Difficult Loop Option
----- Other trails

0   500   1000   1500 ft

Sandia granite

Don't Drink the Water

Although natural springs deliver beautiful clear, cold water, it is not necessarily safe for humans to drink straight from the spring. At many of these locations, hikers will find the ruins of some neglected cabin, pieces of old farm equipment, remnants of pioneer gardening efforts (such as grapevines or fruit trees) or even a livestock trough like the one often buried by sand at the entrance to Embudito Canyon. These items remind us that these springs are not pristine: they have been used by humans (and often cows) for hundreds of years. The water could contain bacteria that are harmful to humans, and should always be treated before drinking. With today's extensive technology, there are several easy methods—chemicals such as bleach or iodine and a combination of ultraviolet light and filters—to make spring water drinkable.

Although the bleach/iodine method is probably the easiest for everyone, the chemicals leave behind their own distinctive and undesirable flavor. It also requires a fair bit of time. However, if you're willing to wait, it is very effective. The National Park Service in the Grand Canyon recommends adding two drops of household bleach or five drops of tincture of iodine to each gallon of water. Give the water bottle a good shaking and wait for at least thirty minutes before drinking.

Ultraviolet lights and filters can be expensive but preserve the natural flavor of the spring water. They come in a large variety of makes and models and can be purchased at most large outdoor equipment/camping stores. This method is extremely fast: in general, the water is drinkable after only a couple of minutes. Follow the instructions that come with your specific model.

park at the exit and walk the short distance up the road.

From the loop road, several small local trails lead to the canyon bottom, none of which are very good or preferred. Once at the bottom, hike up the arroyo channel about 0.5 mile to the base of the falls. From the falls, turn around and return along the channel to the picnic area. For those who choose to climb the falls, follow the valley bottom uphill until it intersects the Tram Trail. Turn left on the trail and then return along the La Luz Trail to FR 333 and the Juan Tabo Picnic Area.

IF YOU LIKED THIS HIKE, TRY **HIKE 7: Waterfall Canyon via Piedra Lisa Trail**, which is a little easier, or **HIKE 55: Old Man Canyon Loop**, which is similar.

FOR THOSE USING GPS DATA (DATUM: WGS 84)
Parking Area within the Juan Tabo Picnic Area: −106.48499, 35.21696
Large falls along route: −106.47737, 35.21372
Intersection of the La Luz Trail and the Tram Trail: −106.475544, 35.213597

HIDDEN FALLS ASCENSION–LA LUZ LOOP OPTION

Difficulty: 5
Distance: 2-mile loop with return leg on the La Luz Trail
Hiking Time: 1–2 hours loop trip
Elevation: 7,400 ft. gain along the La Luz Trail
Special Note: This route includes a very difficult climb up Hidden Falls and should only be completed by experienced climbers. If you climb the falls, do not try to climb down them; instead, continue upstream a short distance to return along the La Luz Trail.

EL RINCON VIA PIEDRA LISA TRAIL

Difficulty	3	
Distance	4 mi (6.4 km) round-trip	
Hiking Time	2–4 hours	
Elevation	1,240 ft. gain (378 m)	Peak elevation: 8,200 ft. (2,499 m) at El Rincon; Low elevation: 6,960 ft. (2,121 m) at parking
Trail Condition	Excellent	USFS-owned and -maintained
Trail Users	Hikers and horses	
Best Time	Early spring through fall	Winter can have snow
Parking Lot	Piedra Lisa Trailhead near Albuquerque	
Fees	$3 per vehicle	National Parks Pass or Sandia Mountains Pass

SPECIAL INFORMATION: El Rincon Spur Trail is a great side adventure at the watershed divide for hikers who want to explore the ridgeline.

ALTHOUGH NOT QUITE AS POPULAR as the La Luz Trail, the Piedra Lisa Trail is probably a close second. It passes through a dense forest in the far northern area of the Sandia Mountains. One distinct landscape feature sets this route apart from the La Luz Trail area, making it very appealing to hikers: it abounds with shade from the beginning of the route to El Rincon. The wide, well-maintained trail, the northern aspect, and the abundant shade make this route a friendly one to all hikers, especially on a bright, sunny summer afternoon.

The Piedra Lisa Trail follows the Juan Tabo ridge, leading up to the watershed divide (El Rincon) with drainages that flow to the north into Placitas and Bernalillo. After El Rincon, the highest elevation on this hike, the Piedra Lisa Trail continues down the other side and into the del Agua Watershed to a trailhead near Placitas, New Mexico.

The hike described in this guide stops at El Rincon, which is only the first half of the full trail. Along the way, this route passes by several small side trails that provide access to popular rock-climbing areas in the northern Sandia Mountains. Views of these rock faces, especially "The Shield," are outstanding from this trail. Several side canyons are also waiting to be explored, making this trail a wonderful access for exploring this great landscape.

HIKING OPTION: FULL LENGTH OF THE PIEDRA LISA TRAIL

Difficulty: 4

Distance: 6 miles between the two trailheads (12 miles round-trip)

Hiking Time: 2–4 hours (4–8 hours round-trip)

Elevation: 1,340 ft. gain (3,340 ft. round-trip)

Special Note: Trail conditions are moderate between El Rincon and the trailhead near Placitas.

ALTERNATE PARKING

Piedra Lisa northern trailhead parking lot near Placitas, NM (6,040 ft. elevation)

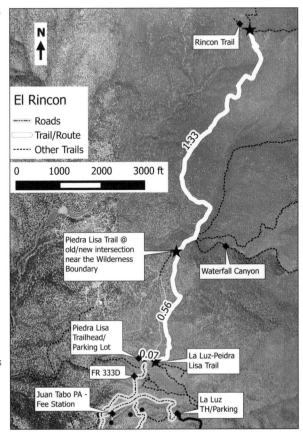

N

El Rincon
--- Roads
⬭ Trail/Route
----- Other Trails

0   1000   2000   3000 ft

Rincon Trail

1.33

Piedra Lisa Trail @ old/new intersection near the Wilderness Boundary

Waterfall Canyon

0.56

Piedra Lisa Trailhead/ Parking Lot

0.07

La Luz-Peidra Lisa Trail

FR 333D

Juan Tabo PA - Fee Station

La Luz TH/Parking

Transition Life Zone

Aspect and elevation create a unique vegetation experience on the Piedra Lisa Trail. Even though this route reaches the lower-elevation band of the Canadian life zone, the vegetation continues to be dominated by Transition zone piñon and ponderosa pine trees. In the Sandia Mountains, the life zone descriptions, which are systematically tied to elevation, confidently and accurately predict where different species grow. But along this route, the plants, and particularly the trees, seem have their own opinions on where to grow: the Upper Sonoran and Transition zones blur together and extend well above their normal elevation range.

The Transition life zone is characterized by ponderosa pines and typically extends up to about 7,800 feet, but here, at just above eight thousand feet, ponderosas are still dominant. As the Piedra Lisa Trail climbs up from the parking area, these pines slowly emerge as junipers and evergreen oaks fade out. Ponderosa pines are large coniferous evergreens that have blackish-brown bark as young trees (also known as "blackjacks" by loggers). As the tree ages, the trunk expands and the bark develops plates and valleys, with the plates turning to brown and orange hues while the deeper valleys lighten to shades of yellow and orange. The deep valleys in some of the very old ponderosa pines can develop a faint vanilla smell, so when you find one of these old-timers, take a minute to smell the cracks in the bark.

If you can find an open place without trees, fantastic 360-degree views can be had. The El Rincon spur trail is one such place; it runs along the watershed ridgeline, leading to better views both to the west and the east of the saddle from which the Piedra Lisa Trail crosses the divide. The west spur leads to wonderful views of the Rio Grande Valley and the whole western landscape, while the east spur leads to beautiful views of the Sandia Crest and North Peak.

Prior to 2016, the first part of this USFS trail began on Road 333D, but a new route built in 2015 now takes hikers across the road and onto a nicely built path that leads into the small watersheds to the south. The La Luz–Piedra Lisa Trail was also rerouted along this new trail; its junction is about 0.1 mile up the Piedra Lisa Trail. The best part of this new trail is that it feels as though it's been there for years, weaving its way through the mature piñon forest. The new trail meets the old Piedra Lisa Trail near the Wilderness boundary. Although the old trail is still available, this old segment will likely be retired in the future. At the junction of the new and old trails, turn right to continue the route into the Wilderness Area and to El Rincon. After entering the Wilderness, the trail dips to cross the creek, then heads north into the deeper forests of the Sandia Mountains. Just as it reaches the watershed divide at about two miles from the parking area, the trail gets a bit steeper, as it ascends the last hill to the divide. As is the case with all of the longer USFS trails, this guide does not have details for the full length of trail hiking. If the full length of the Piedra Lisa Trail is your choice, check out the *Sandia Mountain Hiking Guide* by Mike Coltrin for more specific hiking information about the second half.

■ THE HIKE

Park at the Piedra Lisa Trailhead parking area on FR 333D.

Follow the signs to start the hike at the northeastern end of the parking area. Cross the road and start on the trail as it turns to the east. Pass by (stay left at) the La Luz–Piedra Lisa Trail junction at about 0.1 mile. This intersection is marked with a sign. Hike along the new trail for 0.6 mile to where it intersects with the old trail, and turn right. The trail is well-marked and is next to the Wilderness Boundary, which is also marked with a sign that provides information about Sensitive Species land closures when in effect. Continue along the trail until reaching the watershed divide, about 2 miles from the parking area. Return route is along the same path.

IF YOU LIKED THIS LARGE-TRAIL MOUNTAIN HIKE, try **HIKE 37: Embudito Canyon Overlook Loop**, which is about the same difficulty, or **hike 1: Upper La Cueva Overlook via La Luz Trail**, which feels a little harder.

FOR THOSE USING GPS DATA
(DATUM: WGS 84)
Intersection of the new Piedra Lisa Trail
    segment and the La Luz–Piedra Lisa Trail:
    –106.48262, 35.22293
Intersection of the new Piedra Lisa Trail
    segment with the old trail:
    –106.48105, 35.22978
El Rincon Ridge:
    –106.47553, 35.2436

WATERFALL CANYON VIA PIEDRA LISA TRAIL

Difficulty	4	
Distance	2 mi (3.2 km) round-trip	To and from first set of waterfalls
Hiking Time	2–4 hours round-trip	
Elevation	640 ft. gain (195 m)	Peak elevation: 7,600 ft. (2,316 m) in canyon; Low elevation: 6,960 ft. (2,121 m) at parking
Trail Condition	Good at beginning, but degrades after first waterfall.	USFS-owned but not -maintained
Trail Users	Hikers	
Best Time	Spring and early summer	Winter can have snow
Parking Lot	Piedra Lisa Trailhead near Albuquerque	
Fees	$3 per vehicle	National Parks Pass or Sandia Mountains Pass

SPECIAL INFORMATION: A trip to the first waterfall is a great family hike with lots of shade year-round. Spring is the best time to visit, as the canyon springs are most likely to be flowing at this time.

THE WATERFALL CANYON route is a small, unmaintained side or spur trail and quite inconspicuous; if you are not paying attention, it is easy to miss this hidden gem. This is a beautiful canyon to explore, with tall trees, several springs, rocks to climb, and, as the name suggests, waterfalls. The lower section of Waterfall Canyon is an easy-to-moderate hike with a defined route, some rocky-channel hiking, and short falls/steps to climb over. As with many canyons in New Mexico, the valley bottom is filled with tall deciduous trees, a variety of brush, and grasses. (Also present is the dreaded poison ivy, but not typically in vast quantities.) These features combine to make this canyon a wonderful introduction to canyon hiking for inexperienced hikers and children. However, the further that hikers travel up the canyon, the more the route intensifies in difficulty. As the falls get taller, hikers are forced to go around them, making short but steep climbs up the sides of the canyon or over large bedrock outcrops.

The coniferous forests have crept down to the edge of the channel in many locations, creating a beautiful mixture of riparian and upland species. Since this is an out-and-back hike, go as far as desired and then turn around for the return trip.

Waterfall Canyon is the first, and probably the most popular side trail off the Piedra Lisa Trail. Day hikers readily explore it year-round. Rock climbers have used this trail as an access route to the large, near-vertical rock faces to the east of the Piedra Lisa Trail, and in fact they probably created it decades ago. Several climbing side trails depart from the Piedra Lisa Trail in this general area (see map for **HIKE 6: El Rincon via Piedra Lisa Trail**) and are great adventures even if they are a bit steep and unmaintained. The large cliffs not only draw human visitors, but also a variety of birds that use them as habitat. Consequently, many of these spur trails are closed for a portion of the year (March 1 through August 15) to allow nesting by rare and sensitive species. Signs

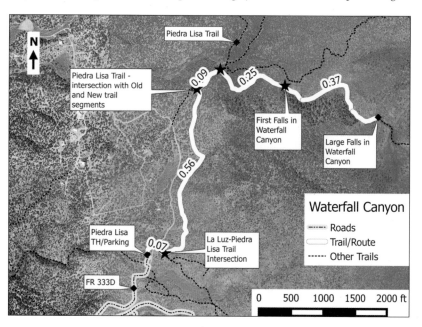

N

Piedra Lisa Trail

Piedra Lisa Trail - intersection with Old and New trail segments

0.09

0.25

0.37

First Falls in Waterfall Canyon

Large Falls in Waterfall Canyon

0.56

Piedra Lisa TH/Parking

0.07

La Luz-Piedra Lisa Trail Intersection

FR 333D

Waterfall Canyon

----- Roads
⬭ Trail/Route
······ Other Trails

0   500   1000   1500   2000 ft

are posted by the USFS along the Piedra Lisa Trail advising recreationists of this closure when it is in effect. Luckily, the Waterfall Canyon route is located just outside of the closure area and is thus open to recreation year-round. Being outside of the closure area is also true of the landscape and any trails to the west (left) side of the Piedra Lisa Trail.

Because this hike is within a canyon, the route should be avoided during inclement weather. Although not a slot canyon, it is

Closures Due to Nesting of Sensitive Bird Species

In the area to the right of the Piedra Lisa Trail, a large section of the Sandia Mountains is closed to hikers and climbers from March 1 through August 15 each year. Signs along the trail, especially at small junctions, indicate the locations of this closure. Luckily, Waterfall Canyon is just outside of this seasonal (nesting) closure area. Lucky hikers on the Piedra Lisa and Waterfall Canyon routes can see one of the protected species, peregrine falcons, soaring through the area as they hunt for food.

Peregrine falcons were once one of the most endangered birds in the United States. Although they are still a sensitive species, they were removed from the Endangered

Species list in 1999. These small predatory birds have long, pointed wings like other falcons, are roughly the size of a crow, and are slate gray on the head and back with pale undersides and distinguishing "sideburns" or stripes on the sides of their faces. They use ledges on high, remote cliff walls for nesting and feed primarily on smaller birds, often catching prey in mid-flight. When diving, peregrine falcons can reach speeds in excess of two hundred miles per hour. These falcons have one of the longest migrations of any North American bird, traveling up to fifteen thousand miles a year from the Arctic tundra to Patagonia.

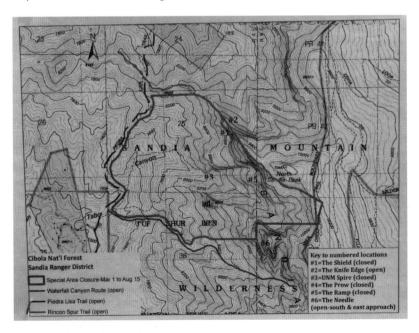

still a very dangerous location during and after a rainstorm, due to slippery bedrock and the potential for flash floods. Be smart and avoid this hike if rain is on the way.

■ **THE HIKE**

Park at the Piedra Lisa parking area. Start by crossing the road and hiking along the Piedra Lisa Trail, 0.6 mile. After the USFS Wilderness boundary, the trail descends into the Waterfall Canyon Watershed and crosses the channel less than 0.25 mile from the boundary. The Waterfall Canyon route is the unmarked trail to the right (east) just before the Piedra Lisa Trail crosses the stream, which is the first channel/drainage after the boundary sign. The canyon's trail begins by contouring a short distance along the hillside before Piedra Lisa crosses the channel.

The canyon route is sometimes on a trail and at others simply walking up the channel. At about 0.3 mile, the canyon bottom steepens, going up and over bedrock steps and small waterfalls. The first set of waterfalls is the most popular destination for day hikers.

For more experienced hikers, a larger set of waterfalls is another 0.4 mile upstream. Beyond these larger falls, the trail continues upstream through an area where the valley/canyon opens up before climbing steeply again to the base of several rock-climbing routes/faces. Return is along the same route.

IF YOU LIKED THIS HIKE, try **HIKE 48: Narrow Falls**, which is easier, or **HIKE 38: Embudito Canyon Route/Loop**, which has more distance and a loop option.

FOR THOSE USING GPS DATA
(DATUM: WGS 84)
Intersection of the new Piedra Lisa Trail
    segment and the La Luz–Piedra Lisa Trail:
    –106.48262, 35.22293
Intersection of the new Piedra Lisa Trail
    segment with the old trail:
    –106.48105, 35.22978
Intersection of the Piedra Lisa Trail with the
    small, unmarked trail into Waterfall Canyon:
    –106.47985, 35.230595
The first waterfall in the canyon:
    –106.47644, 35.229985

OLD 333 ROAD TRAIL

Difficulty	1	Gentle slopes on an abandoned road section
Distance	2 mi (3.2 km) round-trip	1 mi from trailhead to housing area
Hiking Time	less than 1 hour round-trip	
Elevation	220 ft. gain (67 m)	Peak elevation: 6,880 ft. (2,097 m) at end of trail
		Low elevation: 6,660 ft. (2,030 m) at Sandy Arroyo
Trail Condition	Good but unmaintained	USFS-owned, not -maintained
Trail Users	Hikers	
Best Time	Late summer through fall	Great year-round, but has abundant summer shade
Parking Lot	Old 333 Road Trailhead	
Fees	$3 per vehicle	National Parks Pass or Sandia Mountains Pass

SPECIAL INFORMATION: The old road provides a wide path, which is perfect for groups or families.

THE OLD 333 ROAD TRAIL is an easy, unmarked, one-mile, one-way hike. This abandoned section of FR 333 is dirt covered, weathered, and eroded where arroyos cross it, but generally the road base is intact, creating a nice wide surface for walking. The trail winds its way up and over small hills and through a mature piñon-juniper forest full of lizards and rabbits. Several side trails off the old road take hikers to overlooks of the city, Juan Tabo Canyon, and the mountains. Although abandoned as a road, it is a perfect trail: wide and mostly double-track, which is great for families or groups of people. The appeals of the Old 333 Road Trail are its shade, its wide and well-graded nature, the relative solitude, and the quiet woods that surround it. It is a sweet trail that you can blast along, stretching your legs by speed-walking or running, or stroll along, getting your fill of fresh air and the feel of nature and the woods. With shade available and the north-facing aspect of most of the route, this is a better option for summer afternoons than those trails with a southern aspect (e.g., the La Luz Trail), but it can still be quite hot. Its elevation is similar to that found at the parking area.

About halfway along this trail, the large Sandy Arroyo crosses the old road, creating a "dogleg" in the trail. To the left (downstream), Sandy Arroyo leads to the

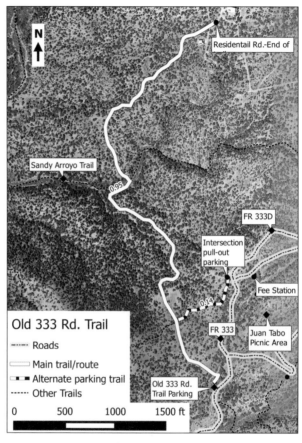

Old 333 Rd. Trail
- - - - Roads
▭ Main trail/route
■-■ Alternate parking trail
⋯⋯ Other Trails

0   500   1000   1500 ft

Sandy Arroyo Trail

Residentail Rd.-End of

FR 333D

Intersection pull-out parking

Fee Station

FR 333

Juan Tabo Picnic Area

Old 333 Rd. Trail Parking

SHORTER HIKING OPTION

To Sandy Arroyo
Difficulty: 1
Distance: 1 mile round-trip
Hiking Time: 10–20 minutes round-trip
Elevation: 120 ft. gain (Sandy Arroyo is the lowest elevation: 6,600 ft.)

ALTERNATE PARKING

Juan Tabo picnic parking lot at fee station (~6,800 ft. elevation)

Juan Tabo canyon bottom. To the right (upstream), it leads to the Piedra Lisa parking area. About one mile from the parking lot, the trail approaches the back

Piñon-Juniper Forests and the Changing Climate

Piñon and juniper trees are native to the Southwest and are found throughout the Sandia Mountains and its foothills. When conditions are right, they grow densely, forming a beautiful forest environment with plenty of shade. Today, piñon -juniper woodlands generally occur between an elevation of 4,500 to 7,500 ft. (1,370–2,290 m), with juniper more abundant at lower elevations and piñon predominating higher up. These trees are able to grow in just about any soil type, but they are best suited for those that are moisture- and nutrient-limited. Once established, they improve their local soil condition and moisture content by concentrating organic material and nutrients beneath their canopies over time, creating "islands" of better soil.

Although this forest is composed of hardy species, the changing climate in the Southwest has already affected it, as can be seen by the dead and dying trees along the Old Road 333 Route. Recent drought, warming temperatures, and the notably longer summers (hot seasons) have led to noticeable tree mortality and forest dieback in the piñon-juniper forests of the Sandia Mountains. Here, drought weakened some of the piñon pines enough to make them an easy target for insects such as the piñon ips bark beetle. Without enough water throughout the year, these trees were not able to repel attacking beetles with increased flows of pitch. Once insect populations are large enough, they are able to successfully attack healthy trees, thus potentially affecting an entire forest.

side of the residential area and meets up with the current 333 road system within it. Although it is possible to walk back along FR 333D and FR 333, it is actually a shorter distance with less elevation change on the trail, not to mention a nicer, more scenic experience.

■ THE HIKE

Park at the Old 333 Road Trail parking area. If this small lot is full, park at the FR 333/333D Intersection parking area or the Juan Tabo Picnic Area, next to the fee station.

From the Old 333 Road parking area, the trail first dips, then gently climbs as it skirts to the northwest of several small hills. (The 333/333D Intersection parking area is on the other side of these hills.)

The trail winds its way through a hilly landscape. About halfway, it doglegs as it crosses Sandy Arroyo. The trail ends at the residential area.

Return to the starting point using the same trail.

IF YOU LIKED THIS HIKE, try HIKE 34: **Lower Bear Arroyo Loops** from John B. Robert Dam, which is little bit easier but has a longer trail option, or **HIKE 54: U-Mound Perimeter Loop,** which has more hills and a loop option.

FOR THOSE USING GPS DATA
(DATUM: WGS 84)
Pull-out parking area at start of hike:
   –106.48739, 35.21678
End of trail, at housing area: –106.48772,
   35.22617

JARAL WATERSHED LOOP

Difficulty	4	Unmarked trails may require some route-finding; steep hills	
Distance	2.5 mi (4 km) round-trip		
Hiking Time	1–2 hours round-trip		
Elevation	520 ft. gain (159 m)	Peak elevation: 6,600 ft. (2,012 m)	
		Low elevation: 6,080 ft. (1,853 m) at parking	
Trail Condition	Good but unmaintained	USFS-owned, not -maintained	
Trail Users	Hikers, horses, and bikes		
Best Time	Winter	Usually snow-free in winter	
Parking Lot	USFS Fee Station		
Fees	$3 per vehicle	National Parks Pass or Sandia Mountains Pass	

THIS AREA IS KNOWN FOR ITS WIDE- open, easily visible hiking options, trails that wind their way in, around, and all over the lower mountains without losing the fantastic views. This hiking area covers the lower Rincon Ridge, which has a different geology from the rest of the mountains. Here, mica schist is the bedrock; it has been treated relatively better by the elements, creating a rolling hill terrain that is much less steep than the larger mountains to the east and can be more appealing to the casual hikers, trail runners, and families so commonly seen here.

The Jaral Canyon Watershed is the main feature in these lower mountains; it drains most of the area and offers an easily accessed ridgeline walk or a walk along the valley bottom. The main hike described follows the outline of the watershed as it climbs up Jaral Canyon's west fork ridge to the divide between the Juan Tabo Canyon and Jaral Canyon, then loops around the headwaters before descending along the outside of Jaral Canyon's east fork. Even though the many trails might be confusing to inexperienced hikers, the whole watershed is close to FR 333, reducing the possibility of getting lost.

None of the many trails in this area are named, signposted, or maintained, but none of that seems essential because the trails have wide-open views and are generally in good condition. The terrain is relatively unadorned: vegetation is best described as sparse and, in particular, trees are rare. Consequently, shade is also infrequent. For more vegetation, consider leaving the ridge trails and hiking along the valley bottom trail, where riparian vegetation grows more thickly than on the hillsides.

Not far from the Jaral Canyon route and scattered throughout the Sandia Mountains are abandoned mines and mine shafts. Many of these mines were test pits that were deemed unprofitable. Unfortunately, many of them were simply abandoned and remain as uncovered holes in the ground. These shafts typically drop straight down and would easily injure a hiker who fell in; the walls aren't easily scaled, as they are often vertical. It's best to stay away from these features, but if you approach one, remember to keep your distance, as the side walls can also collapse.

The main route that follows the divide has several steep hills that can be somewhat slippery with loose rocks and pea gravel. It is easier to follow the channel route back to the car from about the halfway point. However, if there is inclement weather on the horizon or it is already raining, stay out of the canyon/channel bottom to avoid flash flooding.

■ **THE HIKE**

Park in the parking area of the first USFS fee station on FR 333 (the first parking area after turning off Tramway Road).

Walk across the road and climb up the first (and closest) well-worn path that climbs the hills to the north of the road. At the top of this hill, the trail leads into the Jaral Canyon Watershed.

Once up this first hill, the trail divides into two main trails. Take the one that goes straight ahead, descends a few feet into Jaral Canyon, then veers right as it hugs the hillside. This trail crosses the channel within the canyon, then begins to climb up to a western ridge and follows it to a small saddle that marks the Juan Tabo/Jaral Canyon Watershed divide (0.9 mile).

From the saddle, turn right and follow

Alternate Parking

Juan Tabo picnic parking
lot at fee station
(~6,800 ft. elevation)

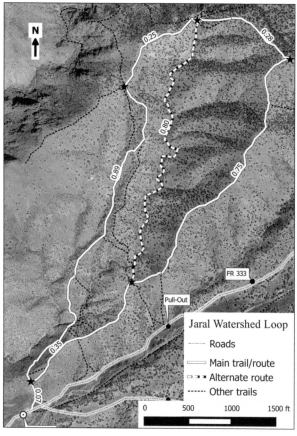

N

Jaral Watershed Loop
------- Roads
══════ Main trail/route
▫ ▪ ▪ Alternate route
------ Other trails

FR 333

Pull-Out

0.25   0.28   0.80   0.75   0.89   0.35   0.07

| 0 | 500 | 1000 | 1500 ft |

the ridgeline about 0.25 mile to the next saddle and trail junction area. If you wish to return along the canyon, make a sharp right at this junction to descend to the valley bottom. Jaral Canyon becomes steep downstream of where the western and eastern forks join, so exit before this point on one of the many trails that cross the canyon.

For the main route, the watershed divide trail, veer right at this junction, choosing the trail that stays on the ridgeline. Follow this ridgeline for 0.25 mile to another trail junction and saddle area.

Keep the Jaral Canyon on your right and stay on or near the ridgeline. Follow this trail for 1.1 miles to where it completes the loop by rejoining the first trail from FR 333.

Descend to FR 333 and return to the parking area.

IF YOU LIKED THIS HIKE, try **HIKE 31: Academy Camp Loop**, which also has an open landscape and a better likelihood of seeing wildlife, or **HIKE 44: Candelaria Bench Loop**, a slightly harder small-trail mountain hike.

Rincon Ridge and Mica Schist

According to Vince Kelley, the leading geologist of his time for the Sandia Mountains, Rincon Ridge, which extends from El Rincon to FR 333 at Jaral Watershed, is one of the most prominent features of the Sandia Mountains due to its different rock type. The Jaral Watershed and the Juan Tabo Canyon offer hikers a landscape composed of another Precambrian rock: mica schist. Although these rocks are slightly younger than the Sandia granite, they are still over a billion years in age. Schist is a medium-grade metamorphic rock containing mica, medium to large sheet-like crystals that lie flat against each other. This rock also contains a fair bit of quartzite and feldspar. Schist forms deep underground where there are moderately high temperatures and a moderate amount of pressure, hence the alignment of the minerals. Mica is characteristically foliated, meaning that the individual mineral grains split off easily into flakes or slabs, often with no more than a scratch from a fingernail. The best exposures of the schist are in Juan Tabo Canyon. However, a quick exploration of rocky trail sections or outcrops in the Jaral creek bed or simply seeing the sparkles in the soils/sands on a sunny day will confirm that these rounded hills are different from the rest of the Sandia Mountains.

FOR THOSE USING GPS DATA (DATUM: WGS 84)
First trail intersection along route (stay left to hike along ridge to headwaters): –106.503869, 35.203824
Watershed divide between the Jaral and Juan Tabo Watersheds (veer right to stay on ridge and follow Jaral Watershed route): –106.500271, 35.214807

Intersection at ridgeline trail and channel route option: –106.497467, 35.217285
Two additional Jaral Watershed ridgeline trail points leading back to parking area: –106.49389, 35.21586; –106.499972; 35.207548

JUAN TABO CABIN (RUINS) AND ADJACENT ARROYO TRAIL

Difficulty	1	Unmarked trails require some route-finding
Distance	2 mi (3.2 km) round-trip	
Hiking Time	Less than 1 hour round-trip	
Elevation	320 ft. gain (97 m)	Peak elevation: 6,400 ft. (1,950 m); Low elevation: 6,080 ft. (1,853 m) at parking
Trail Condition	Fair, with arroyo walking	USFS-owned, not -maintained
Trail Users	Hikers, horses, and bikes	
Best Time	Fall through spring	Usually snow-free in winter
Parking Lot	USFS Fee Station	
Fees	$3 per vehicle	National Parks Pass or Sandia Mountains Pass

SPECIAL INFORMATION: The map only shows the largest trails in this area. Several small side trails exist through this flatter landscape.

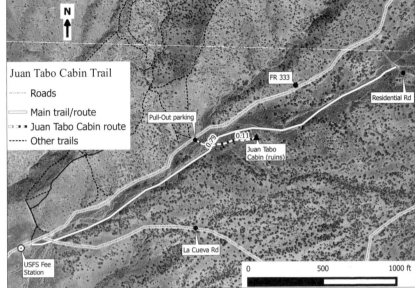

Juan Tabo Cabin Trail
- ----- Roads
- ===== Main trail/route
- ▫ ■■ Juan Tabo Cabin route
- ------ Other trails

N ↑

FR 333

Residential Rd

Pull-Out parking

079

0.11

Juan Tabo Cabin (ruins)

La Cueva Rd

USFS Fee Station

0   500   1000 ft

DURING OR JUST PRIOR TO the construction of recreation facilities at Juan Tabo Picnic Area and La Cueva Picnic Area in 1936, the Civilian Conservation Corps (CCC) built the Juan Tabo Cabin. This fairly large temporary base camp near FR 333 and Tramway Road supported two groups: the CCC crews working uphill in the picnic areas and other CCC crews from around the Albuquerque area during the winter months. At this writing, the cabin's roof and portions of its walls are missing (reportedly from a human-caused fire many years ago), but it is in good condition, with most of the walls standing firm. The rock structure encasing the well/spring is also still standing, although the spring no longer flows. A continuous short wall surrounds the cabin and well. It takes only a little bit of imagination to envision a garden in this space, or perhaps it was filled with tents for the work crews.

Exploring these ruins and the arroyo walk is one of the easiest hikes described in this guide and is particularly suited

for hikers looking for a short adventure. Given that the hike parallels FR 333, from the road's first USFS Fee Station parking area to the residential road FR 333C, the route is extremely easy to find and follow. Several small paths lead away from the ruins but tend to fade out after a few hundred yards, while the arroyo route is a relatively large path.

The Juan Tabo Cabin ruins are located about halfway between the fee station and the residential road. You may catch a glimpse of the cabin from the road at the pull-out parking (second pull-out from fee station), but otherwise it is hidden from view even though it is close to FR 333.

Arroyo hiking is never safe when the channel is flowing. If you see that it contains water, or if a thunderstorm is brewing, simply walk the road back to your vehicle.

■ **THE HIKE**

Park at the first USFS Fee Station parking area on FR 333.

Hike into the arroyo channel just south of the lot. Turn toward the mountains, cross La Cueva Road, and follow the arroyo upstream for about 0.4 mile.

The Juan Tabo Cabin ruins are on the small hill to the south of the arroyo. Several well-worn side trails lead to this structure.

The arroyo route continues east and up the channel another 0.4 mile to where the arroyo crosses FR 333C, marking the end of the route.

Return along the same route.

IF YOU LIKED THIS HIKE, try **HIKE 15: Spring Creek Trail (a.k.a. Jaral Cabin Trail)**, which also has an arroyo trail and ruins, or **HIKE 38: Embudito Canyon Route/Loop**, a somewhat harder arroyo route.

FOR THOSE USING GPS DATA (DATUM: WGS 84)
Juan Tabo Cabin ruin location:
 −106.49660, 35.20600

ALTERNATE PARKING

Pull-out-style parking off FR 333 near the Juan Tabo Cabin (6,240 ft. elevation)

Camp Juan Tabo and the CCC

In response to the Great Depression, President Franklin D. Roosevelt implemented the CCC in 1933 as a public work relief program, a component of his New Deal. Employing unmarried men aged seventeen to twenty-eight, the CCC provided unskilled manual labor for the conservation and development of natural resources in rural lands owned by federal, state, and local governments. In New Mexico, the first CCC camps appeared in the 1930s, including Camp Juan Tabo along FR 333, which reportedly housed as many as two hundred men. These were similar in form to army barracks. The program contributed to New Mexico's economy by employing residents and purchasing local supplies and materials for the various work projects. Unlike many CCC camps, Camp Juan Tabo was active year-round and served as a winter operations center for other nearby units, such as Sulphur Camp at Sandia Park.

CCC construction evolved quickly and was defined by national standards to ensure that its buildings had consistent quality and character. Its design is typically referred to as "Rustic Style" and was committed to maintaining a natural and nonintrusive quality of design. Principles emphasized under the Rustic Style included

- emphasis on horizontal form and avoidance of hard, straight lines;
- combinations of harmonious exterior textures and colors;
- use of local natural materials;
- appearance of pioneer building methods;
- strong incorporation of handcrafted elements.

The CCC was never intended to be a permanent agency. The program was disbanded in the early 1940s and shut down completely by 1942, to allow the country to focus its energy and resources on World War II.

JUAN TABO CANYON VIA SANDY ARROYO/OLD 333 ROAD TRAILS

Difficulty	3	Poor trail conditions and route-finding
Distance	2 mi (3.2 km) round-trip	
Hiking Time	1–2 hours round-trip	
Elevation	320 ft. loss (98 m)	Peak elevation: 6,720 ft. (2,048 m) at parking; Low elevation: 6,400 ft. (1,950 m) in canyon
Trail Condition	Poor, with arroyo walking	USFS-owned, not -maintained
Trail Users	Hikers and horses	
Best Time	Fall through early spring	Often snow-free in winter
Parking Lot	Old 333 Rd Trail	
Fees	$3 per vehicle	National Parks Pass or Sandia Mountains Pass

SPECIAL INFORMATION: A couple of warnings for lower Juan Tabo Canyon: Do not attempt to bushwhack up the canyon wall because you missed the exit trail; the two access trails in this guide are the best options for this canyon. It is recommended that a hiker exit the canyon using the same access trail.

JUAN TABO CANYON is one of those places that isn't really hidden, but if you aren't looking for it, you simply will not find it. There are no marked routes to the canyon, only some less-beaten paths. From the hillsides, it is obviously a rocky canyon with steep, almost sheer walls, but it has a lovely valley bottom, which is wider than expected and filled with natural curiosities. It is a magnificent feature that feels remote, with sounds of nature echoing between the canyon walls.

Although there are no designated trails, Juan Tabo Canyon is located due west of several popular areas in the Juan Tabo/La Cueva USFS area. The best route is to follow the Sandy Arroyo Trail from the Old FR 333 Road Trail. Another option is to use the trails in the Jaral Watershed to reach the edge of Juan Tabo Canyon, then follow a small rocky trail that leads down to the canyon floor. Either way, this canyon is a fun place to explore and has a surprisingly nice valley bottom covered in sand, rocks, and vegetation.

During mountain rains, this canyon could be especially dangerous due to its large size; a flash flood could sweep through it without a single drop of rain falling in the canyon. Hikers in the lower sections of the canyon would have a difficult time climbing the steep walls to a safe location. Be smart and avoid this hike if mountain thunderstorms are in the forecast or you see rain clouds on the way.

GETTING TO THE CANYON VIA SANDY ARROYO TRAIL

Using the Sandy Arroyo drainage channel to access the Juan Tabo Canyon is a great option, as it is well-defined and a clear landmark to follow into and out of the canyon. The easiest hiking route is to access Sandy Arroyo Trail from the Old

ALTERNATE CANYON ACCESS

1. Piedra Lisa Parking Lot to Canyon via Sandy Arroyo Channel
Difficulty: 4 due to sand and brush
Distance: 2 miles round-trip
Hiking Time: 1.5–2 hours round-trip
Elevation: 520 ft. loss

2. First USFS Fee Station Parking Lot
Difficulty: 4 due to increased length, route-finding, and steep trail into canyon
Distance: 4 miles round-trip
Hiking Time: 1–2 hours round-trip
Elevation: 520 ft. gain, then 320 ft. loss into canyon

ALTERNATE PARKING

Piedra Lisa Trailhead parking lot (6,960 ft. elevation)
USFS Fee Area Parking off FR 333 (6,080 ft. elevation)

FR 333 Road Trail. Sandy Arroyo can also be accessed from the Piedra Lisa Trailhead parking area, although this channel walk is more brushy and difficult than the lower portion of Sandy Arroyo. Once in Juan Tabo Canyon, a hiker can turn left and explore the tighter portion of the lower canyon (about half a mile of terrain) or turn right and follow the canyon for about a mile up to the edge of the residential area.

From the Old 333 Road Trail Parking Area

Park at the Old 333 Road Trail parking area. If this small lot is full, park at the FR 333/333D Intersection parking area or at the Juan Tabo Picnic Area.

Follow the Old 333 Road Trail to Sandy Arroyo, about 0.5 mile from the parking area. The arroyo is easy to identify, as it is the only drainage that has completely washed out the old road. Although there used to be signs at this intersection, there were none as of late 2016.

Turn left at the arroyo and follow its well-defined sand-bed channel about 0.5 mile downstream to the canyon.

From Piedra Lisa Trailhead Parking Area

Park at the Piedra Lisa parking area.

Find Sandy Arroyo (the small drainage that crosses the road at the entrance to the parking area) and walk 0.5 mile to the Old 333 Road Trail.

Follow this drainage another 0.5 mile to the canyon.

GETTING TO THE
CANYON VIA THE
JARAL WATERSHED AREA

Juan Tabo Canyon

------- Roads

▬▬ Juan Tabo Canyon

═══ Best Access Route

□ ■ ■ Jaral Access Route

═ ═ ═ U. Sandy Arroyo Route

------ Other trails

0 500 1000 1500 2000 ft

Hikers can meander along the western edge of the Jaral Watershed to find the small trail that leads into lower Juan Tabo Canyon. This route is less desirable, due mostly to the longer distance, but also to the greater risk of missing the access trail into the canyon area. Also, note that the canyon is deeper in this area, with nearly sheer walls. The actual trail down is quite steep, with several areas of loose rock; however, it is the best trail for accessing this part of the canyon. Once at the bottom, a hiker can go either upstream or downstream: both directions offer a fun adventure. A fence crosses the canyon

about 0.25 mile downstream of this access point, identifying the USFS–Pueblo of Sandia land boundary. Turn around and come back when you reach it.

Park in the parking area of the first USFS fee station on FR 333.

Walk across the road and take the closest well-worn path that climbs the hills to the north of the road. At the top of this hill, the trail leads into the Jaral Canyon Watershed.

Once up this first hill, the trail divides. Take the branch that goes straight ahead, descends a few feet into Jaral Canyon, then veers right as it hugs the hillside. This trail crosses the channel within the canyon, then begins to climb up to a western ridge and follows it to a small saddle that marks the Juan Tabo/Jaral Canyon Watershed divide (0.9 mile).

Continue straight at the saddle. After a short descent into the Juan Tabo Canyon Watershed, the trail veers right (north) as it reaches a small ridgeline and follows it for a short distance to a canyon overlook. Near the overlook, a small trail veers off to the right. It is small, poorly defined, steep, and loaded with loose rocks. This small trail descends into the canyon near a spring that has a well-established thicket of vegetation.

Turn left to descend into the tighter part of the canyon or right to hike upstream into the wider part of the canyon.

The return route is the same as the hike in. Remember to use the same small, steep trail to climb out of the canyon.

IF YOU LIKED THIS HIKE, try **HIKE 38: Embudito Canyon Route/Loop**, another easy canyon route, or **HIKE 14: La Cueva Canyon Route**, a harder canyon route.

FOR THOSE USING GPS DATA
(DATUM: WGS 84)
Intersection of Old 333 Road Trail and Sandy Creek Trail: –106.49051, 35.22187
Juan Tabo Canyon at end of Sandy Creek Trail: –106.49865, 35.22029

Echoes

If you've never heard the echo produced in a narrow canyon by a chirping rock squirrel, Juan Tabo Canyon should be on your bucket list. In the tighter section of the canyon, near the property boundary fence, the steep rock walls are just right for creating echoes that travel readily up and down the valley. Technically, an echo is the repetition of sound produced by the reflection of sound waves from a wall, mountain, or other obstruction. The sound is heard more than once because of the time difference between its initial production and the sound waves' return from the reflecting surface. Although a perfect echo is nearly identical to the original sound, here in Juan Tabo Canyon, the undulating valley walls slightly distort the returning sounds, adding a little eeriness to the whole experience.

Some animals use echoes in canyons to transmit their voices a great distance, as their own special loudspeaker. For example, rock squirrels chirp loudly when they see a predator such as a dog or when a hawk circles overhead. In Juan Tabo Canyon, it is not uncommon to hear these creatures' chirps at the upstream end, only to walk to the boundary fence and never feel as though you have passed by the squirrel's perch. On rare occasions, coyotes in the Sandia Mountains and elsewhere have been observed barking in canyons, locating themselves in the perfect spot for their voices to echo. These animals seem to purposefully use echoes to broadcast their voices as a means to help locate their pack.

LA CUEVA PICNIC AREA AND VALLEY HIKE

Difficulty	2	
Distance	0.8 mi (1.3 km)	
Hiking Time	30–60 minutes	
Elevation	200 ft. gain (61 m)	Peak elevation: 6,720 ft. (2,048 m) at Tram Trail; Low elevation: 6,520 ft. (1,987 m) at parking
Trail Condition	Unmaintained local trails	USFS-owned, not -maintained
Trail Users	Hikers and horses	
Best Time	Summer	Access road is closed Oct 15 – May 15
Parking Lot	La Cueva Picnic Area	
Fees	$3 per vehicle	National Parks Pass or Sandia Mountains Pass

THE LA CUEVA PICNIC AREA has better day-user features than any other in the region; it is a quiet surprise for those seeking fewer people, a shady picnic spot, hiking with access to a major trail, a CCC building, a chance to explore the small, secluded local arroyos, or space to just sit and listen to nature. Along with plenty of parking there are two toilet buildings, a group picnic site, and numerous individual picnic tables. Most of the tables are under cover, with the trees providing a healthy dose of shade. If you're not into hiking, a large, flat area at the end of the road is perfect for a family baseball game. If you can reach it, this recreational area is one of the nicest in the foothills area.

The major drawback here is that the USFS access road leading to the La Cueva Picnic Area is closed most of the year, from mid-October to mid-May. Although the road can be walked or biked year-round, it is a continuous uphill walk that feels much longer than its 1.25 miles. When the USFS access road is closed, the easiest route is to walk (or bike) the paved access road from FR 333. However, the shortest and least steep hiking route (about 1 mile) is via **HIKE 1: Upper La Cueva Overlook via La Luz Trail.**

Similar to the Juan Tabo Picnic Area, a large CCC picnic shelter exists at the La Cueva Picnic Area. However, unlike the other shelter, this rustic-style building is somewhat hidden, and it seems that most visitors don't even know it is there. The shelter is slightly offset from the road, just before the last parking area, with a narrow but thick patch of forest blocking sight of it. Thick rock walls offer deep shade and cool temperatures year-round. The CCC constructed this building, along with the rock-fashioned toilets and the numerous picnic tables, in

SPECIAL INFORMATION

Hiking Options to the La Cueva Picnic Area When the Road Is Closed

From FR 333 on La Cueva Road: 1.25 miles, 20–45 minutes, easy.

From Spring Creek parking–lower Spring Creek route: 1 mile, 20–40 minutes, easy-to-moderate difficulty due to trail-finding.

From Spring Creek parking via the Tram Trail: 2 miles, 40–90 minutes, easy-to-moderate difficulty due to length.

From Sandia Peak Tram parking: 2 miles, 40–90 minutes, easy-to-moderate difficulty due to length.

From La Luz parking: about 2.5 miles, 1–2 hours, moderate difficulty due to length and elevation changes.

ALTERNATE PARKING

USFS Fee Area Parking (6,080 ft. elevation)
Spring Creek parking lot (6,240 ft. elevation)
Sandia Peak Tram parking lot (6,520 ft. elevation)
La Luz Trailhead parking lot (7,040 ft. elevation)

the mid-1930s. For more historical information, see appendix B or the sidebars on pages 17 and 39.

■ **THE HIKE**

As a short afternoon excursion (or after a picnic), hikers can explore the loop route around the La Cueva Valley. This 0.8 mile loop includes a scenic and somewhat exploratory hike on a small trail that leads hikers into and up the La Cueva arroyo valley. The trail within the valley is easy to follow near the picnic area and toilets, but it deteriorates before becoming intermittent and reforming on the small ridgeline to the left (north) of the channel. Just downstream from La Cueva Canyon, this

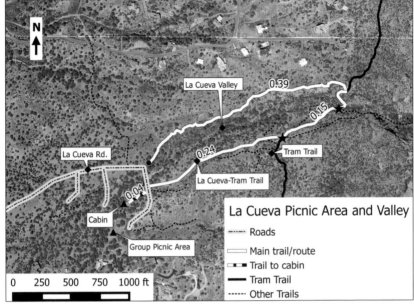

La Cueva Valley 0.39

La Cueva Rd.

0.15

0.24 Tram Trail

La Cueva-Tram Trail

0.04

Cabin

Group Picnic Area

0 250 500 750 1000 ft

La Cueva Picnic Area and Valley

----- Roads

▭ Main trail/route

▭▬ Trail to cabin

▬ Tram Trail

······ Other Trails

Birds: The Wildlife That May Come to You

Just about every hiker wants to see wildlife when they are out on a trail, but spotting a mammal such as a deer or coyote, the most likely large animals, is truly rare, and even less likely in this northern section of the Sandia Mountains, because it is so popular with humans. One of the most overlooked but watchable wildlife groups in the Sandia Mountains is birds. And the best part about them is that they sometimes come to you.

In the summer, hummingbird experiences are fun for all hikers wearing red or orange hats: thinking perhaps that you are a flower, these brave little birds will fly right up to your face. If you sit quietly, the resident birds will often accept your intrusion in just a few minutes and flit around in the trees and cacti as if you have simply become a part of the l andscape. In high-visitor areas, scrub jays and ravens often seek people out in their never-ending search for food. Recognizing these airborne creatures as wildlife to watch will greatly enrich your hiking experiences.

While sitting, you are more likely to see smaller

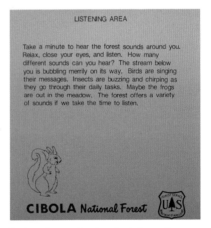

LISTENING AREA

Take a minute to hear the forest sounds around you. Relax, close your eyes, and listen. How many different sounds can you hear? The stream below you is bubbling merrily on its way. Birds are singing their messages. Insects are buzzing and chirping as they go through their daily tasks. Maybe the frogs are out in the meadow. The forest offers a variety of sounds if we take the time to listen.

CIBOLA National Forest

birds such as nuthatches, bushtits, towhees, bluebirds, finches, sparrows, and robins, to name a few. These birds, which are focused on searching the ground and vegetation for their food, also seem to be accepting and will go about their business once you get settled.

While hiking, you are more likely to come upon or scare up roadrunners chasing lizards, see quail as they scurry between bushes, or see a variety of predatory birds circling overhead, such as Cooper's hawks, ravens, and scrub jays.

route intersects the Tram Trail. Turning right onto the Tram Trail and right again at the La Cueva–Tram Trail brings hikers back to the picnic area on popular and easy-to-follow trails. Because this short route follows a distinct valley uphill to the well-worn and unmistakable Tram Trail, it is the perfect chance for new hikers to develop basic route-finding skills. This small trail starts to the left of the pay station and toilets, where the paved road turns sharply to the right (south).

IF YOU LIKED THIS PICNIC AREA, also visit the Juan Tabo Picnic Area, the Elena Gallegos Picnic Area, and the picnic area at the Embudo Trailhead–Menaul Blvd. parking lot.

IF YOU LIKED THIS SMALL-TRAIL VALLEY HIKE, try HIKE 10: Juan Tabo Cabin (Ruins) and Adjacent Arroyo Trail, an easy arroyo route, or HIKE 9: Jaral Watershed Loop, using the shorter option for exploring the channel/canyon.

FOR THOSE USING GPS DATA (DATUM: WGS 84)
Intersection of the unmarked La Cueva
  Valley Trail and the Tram Trail:
  –106.481658, 35.206656
Intersection of La Cueva Parking Lot Trail
  with Tram Trail: –
106.483437, 35.205601

RUINS LOOP FROM LA CUEVA PICNIC AREA

Difficulty	3	Fair trail conditions, unmarked
Distance	1.5 m (2.4 km) round-trip	
Hiking Time	45 minutes – 1.5 hours round-trip	
Elevation	240 ft. gain (73 m)	Peak elevation: 6,720 ft. (2,048 m) at LC/Tram Trail; Low elevation: 6,480 ft. (1,975 m) at ruins
Trail Condition	Fair	USFS-owned, parts not maintained
Trail Users	Hikers and horses	
Best Time	Fall through early spring	Great year-round and is usually snow-free in winter
Parking Lot	La Cueva Picnic Area	
Fees	$3 per vehicle	National Parks Pass or Sandia Mountains Pass

SPECIAL INFORMATION: A nice walk from either the La Cueva Picnic Area or the Sandia Peak Tram.

THE RUINS OF THE HISTORICAL Jaral Ranger Cabin, with a still-functioning spring/well, is an interesting place to visit. But this is one of those neat places that most hikers just breeze by, focused on the larger or longer Tram Trail hike. Three obvious routes lead to this location: Tram Trail from the La Cueva Picnic Area, Spring Creek Trail, and the Tram Trail from Sandia Peak Tram. The picnic area is probably the best of these, but it is closed for most of the year. Although Spring Creek Trail joins with the Tram Trail near the ruin, Spring Creek Trailhead is not marked, and the trail itself passes by residential yards that appear to have encroached on the trail, making it difficult to find and the hike uncomfortable. Hiking from the Sandia Peak Tram is the most reliable track, but with so many other features on this popular trail, most people tend to overlook the ruins.

ALTERNATE PARKING

USFS Fee Area Parking on FR 333 (6,080 ft. elevation)

Spring Creek parking lot (6,240 ft. elevation)

Sandia Peak Tram parking lot (6,520 ft. elevation)

La Luz Trailhead parking lot (7,040 ft. elevation)

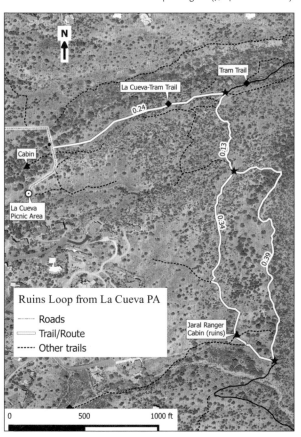

Ruins Loop from La Cueva PA
- - - - Roads
═══ Trail/Route
· · · · · Other trails

The history of the Jaral Ranger Cabin is not precisely documented, but the USFS says that this pre-CCC building was constructed in the early 1900s and used for decades as a ranger station. Although in ruins today, the foundation, lower walls, and front steps are quite visible. Unlike the CCC structures in the nearby picnic areas, this building made use of concrete in the walls, which fully encase local large rocks, making them more like filler material than the primary structural component. The concrete at Jaral Ranger Cabin is visibly deteriorated and rubble conceals much of the floor and outer foundation. (USFS documents indicate, sadly, that the damage was done by vandals with explosives in the 1970s.) Despite this, the general shape and entrance of the building are still present, making this old cabin an interesting spot to take a break and listen to the still-functioning spring/well.

■ THE HIKE

Park at the La Cueva Picnic Area parking lot.

Start on the La Cueva–Tram Trail. This unmarked trail is a little hard to find. It is easiest to access next to the cabin, just after the upper paved road turns south, leading toward the group picnic site and last parking area. The trail starts next to the picnic table in the middle of this paved section and climbs quickly.

Follow this trail 0.25 mile to the Tram Trail.

Turn right onto the Tram Trail and follow 0.5 mile to the Spring Creek Trail.

To find the ruins, turn west off of the Tram Trail and onto the Spring Creek Trail, a USFS marked intersection. A few hundred yards down this trail, the ruins of the Jaral Ranger Cabin are on the right. A small spring ruin still flows into a rock/concrete basin that is perfect drinking water for a dog but is *not* potable for humans.

From the spring/well, continue straight (north) to follow the side trail that leads back uphill. This trail weaves around some hills and boulders but veers to the right and then rejoins the Tram Trail, 0.33 mile from the ruins.

Turn left onto Tram Trail and return to the parking area via the La Cueva–Tram Trail, 0.4 mile.

IF YOU LIKED THIS MIX OF LARGE-TRAIL AND SMALL-TRAIL MOUNTAIN HIKING, try **HIKE 21: Cañon Domingo Baca Trail**, which is slightly longer and also leads to ruins and springs. The shorter version of **HIKE 9: Jaral Watershed Loop** also explores a beautiful valley and watershed and is nearby.

FOR THOSE USING GPS DATA
(DATUM: WGS 84)
Intersection of La Cueva Parking Lot Trail with
  Tram Trail: –106.483437, 35.205601
Intersection of Tram and Spring Creek Trails:
  –106.48236, 35.19980
Intersection of unmarked trail with Tram Trail
  for the Loop option: –106.48326, 35.20391
Jaral Ranger Cabin ruins location:
–106.48320, 35.20039

Jaral Ranger Cabin Ruins

As is often the case in the Sandia Mountains, this station was constructed near a spring, which functioned as its water source. Exact construction information about the Jaral Ranger Station does not seem to exist, but USFS spring improvement documents from the 1930s indicate that it was already fully functional by this time. Other USFS documents suggest that this station was built in 1917, if not earlier. The full station consisted of the cabin (resident quarters), a water fountain, a modern surface water catchment, an outhouse, an outbuilding near the corral, a fence, and a road. Today, the most obvious features are the ruined cabin and the spring. Remnants of the road and fence exist, with most of the fence fallen and lying on the ground.

The big draw to this location is the cabin ruins. The USFS first documented this historical building in 1981, a few years after its destruction, presumably by dynamite. The building was made of Sandia granite and concrete and consisted of one room. The walls were an average of one-and-a-half feet thick and were covered on the inside with a thin coat of mortar, all of which can still be observed in the ruins today. The water fountain next to the building is also made of cement and Sandia granite rocks and has a small water catchment basin. This fountain is still functioning today, but the water is untreated and should be presumed unpotable.

LA CUEVA CANYON ROUTE

Difficulty	5	Gets more difficult farther up the canyon
Distance	2 mi (3.2 km) round-trip	Varies on distance traveled up the canyon
Hiking Time	2–4 hours round-trip	
Elevation	680 ft gain (208 m)	Peak elevation: 7,200 ft. (2,195 m) or higher; Low elevation: 6,520 ft. (1,987 m) at parking
Trail Condition	Poor	USFS-owned, not -maintained; Unmarked canyon route
Trail Users	Hikers	
Best Time	Spring and fall	Summer can be very hot
Parking Lot	La Cueva Picnic Area	
Fees	$3 per vehicle	National Parks Pass or Sandia Mountains Pass

SPECIAL INFORMATION: The canyon requires climbing over boulders (a.k.a. bouldering).

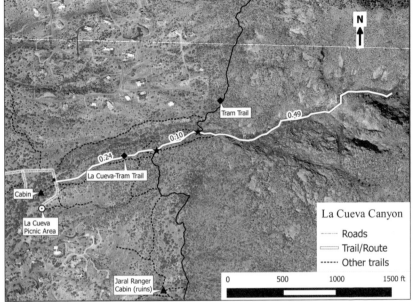

La Cueva Canyon

- - - - Roads
===== Trail/Route
· · · · · Other trails

0   500   1000   1500 ft

THE STARKLY BEAUTIFUL La Cueva Canyon is the first major drainage to the north of the La Cueva–Tram Trail, about 0.25 mile from the junction. Rock climbers like this canyon because it offers several climbing opportunities up the steeply sloping granitic rock faces. If solitude and exploring is your thing, La Cueva Canyon is the right trek for you. The "trail" in this canyon is quite rough, though: hiking up this canyon requires a little bouldering, rock-sliding, bushwhacking, cactus avoidance, and, above all, route-finding. It's a great adventure, but expect it to be slow going.

The La Cueva Canyon trail starts out as moderately difficult, then quickly turns into a difficult bushwhacking trek once in the tighter valley. As the valley narrows, the trail climbs over haphazardly placed boulders and through a valley bottom filled with brush, trees, and cacti. The trail degrades quickly and is best described as "intermittent," traversing

ALTERNATE PARKING

USFS Fee Area Parking (6,080 ft. elevation)
Spring Creek parking lot (6,240 ft. elevation)
Sandia Peak Tram parking lot (6,520 ft. elevation)
La Luz Trailhead parking lot (7,040 ft. elevation)

through vegetation and over boulders as it follows the valley bottom upstream. A spring is located about half a mile up the canyon, but this does not necessarily have surface flow year-round. This canyon does not meet up with any other trails, so go as far upstream as desired, have a water break, enjoy the scenery, then turn around and head back down the valley. Remember, bushwhacking usually takes as long going down the valley as it did to go up, so plan your time accordingly.

Per canyon safety, this hike should be avoided during inclement weather, especially when there are mountain thunderstorms brewing. La Cueva Canyon has a large watershed, such that storms in the mountains can create flash floods that travel through this hiking area. The valley/canyon walls are also unusually sheer, making it extremely difficult to climb out if a flood comes or if the bedrock is wet. Be smart and avoid this hike during rainy weather.

Also, canyons typically heat up quickly with the sun; with all the exposed light-colored granitic bedrock, the sun seems to glare brightly here even during the winter. The best time to visit it is a cool, non-rainy day. Use a little extra sunscreen and wear a good hat.

■ **THE HIKE**

Park at the La Cueva Picnic Area parking area.

Hike 0.25 mile up the La Cueva–Tram Trail to access the Tram Trail.

Turn left (north) and follow the Tram Trail 0.1 mile to the La Cueva Canyon.

Turn right (east) onto the small trail that heads up La Cueva Canyon.

Go as far as desired up the canyon. The return route is the same as the outgoing route. Remember, the return hike will likely take a similar amount of time.

IF YOU LIKED THIS CANYON, try **HIKE 7: Waterfall Canyon via Piedra Lisa Trail**, an easier canyon route with small waterfalls, or **HIKE 5: Hidden Falls Canyon Route**, which has a steep waterfall and loop option.

FOR THOSE USING GPS DATA
(DATUM: WGS 84)
Intersection of La Cueva Parking Lot Trail with Tram Trail: –106.483437, 35.205601
Intersection of Tram Trail with La Cueva Canyon Trail: –106.48185, 35.20625
Upper waterfall location: –106.46902, 35.21039

Climbing in the Sandia Mountains

The long, exposed rock cliffs along the northwestern front of the Sandia Mountains are a rock-climber's dream come true. Several local climbing books describe in detail the routes up these cliffs, many of which have fantastic names such as Mexican Breakfast Crack, Miss Piggy, Zonker's Folly, Crankenstein, and Increasingly Dred. Throughout La Cueva Canyon, large slabs of the Sandia granite are exposed on both sides of the valley, making this a popular climbing location. Lower La Cueva Canyon is accessed from the La Cueva Picnic Area, while the upper canyon area is accessed either from Sandia Crest or from the La Luz parking area.

Three major climbing areas are popular

in the lower La Cueva Canyon: Lower La Cueva Domes, Gemstone West Slabs, and Gemstone East Slabs. In the upper La Cueva Canyon, there are more than thirty climbing areas, all of which can be reached starting on the La Luz Trail. Each of these has numerous routes to explore, making for hundreds of climbs in this one rich valley.

If climbing is your goal, bring along all the correct equipment and detailed knowledge of the routes you intend to explore. For those with no experience, it is advised to take a rock-climbing class to learn about rope and climbing safety and to try it out with experienced climbers. After all, one fall can end it all.

SPRING CREEK TRAIL (A.K.A. JARAL CABIN TRAIL)

Difficulty	2	
Distance	1.1 mi (1.8 km) round-trip	
Hiking Time	Less than 1 hour round-trip	
Elevation	280 ft. gain (85 m)	Peak elevation: 6,520 ft. (1,987 m) at Tram Trail; Low elevation: 6,240 ft. (1,902 m) at parking
Trail Condition	Fair	USFS-owned, not -maintained; Unmarked arroyo route
Trail Users	Hikers and horses	
Best Time	Fall through spring	
Parking Lot	Spring Creek	
Fees	None	

SPECIAL INFORMATION: The trailhead is unmarked and can be difficult to find. USFS signs mark the arroyo path about 0.25 miles from the parking area.

THIS IS A LESSER-KNOWN, no-fee USFS access point for the Sandia Mountains via the cute Spring Creek Valley. There are several obvious reasons why it is not as popular as the other nearby USFS access points. First, the parking area is difficult to find and is not marked with USFS signs. Second, the arroyo section of the trail is brushy and not well-defined. The third and maybe most important reason is that residential yards appear to encroach on the arroyo valley. Although there are USFS signs and lumber marking the trail route in the tightest areas, the arroyo has a private feel to it.

Although these unreceptive features might make even the most avid hiker question using this access point, venturing up Spring Creek Arroyo is a nice hike that explores an arroyo valley filled with typical chamisa and Apache plume bushes and weaves through a mature cottonwood patch before leading to the still-functioning spring at the Jaral Ranger Cabin ruins. If that isn't enough, it also accesses several side trails and the larger and quite popular Tram Trail. Because this trail is harder to find and a little less tempting at the start, there is a greater sense of solitude and inquiry once in the Wilderness area. If hikers want to explore the La Cueva Picnic Area, valley, or canyon, this is the closest parking when the access road to the picnic area is closed.

This route hikes directly up an arroyo, so it should be avoided when thunderstorms are in the area. Fast-flowing water and flash floods are particularly dangerous, as even shallow flows of one foot of water can sweep people away.

∎ THE HIKE

Park in the pull-out area at Spring Creek.

Hike up the arroyo/valley. The valley bottom is quite brushy, but typically it is less so at the far right (south), where the main channel flows.

Make your way through the small braided channels and brush, always

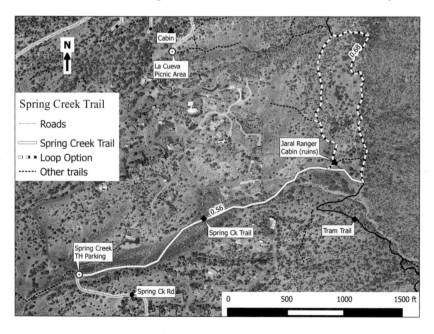

N

Cabin

La Cueva
Picnic Area

Spring Creek Trail
------ Roads
▭ Spring Creek Trail
▫ ⇥ ⋗ Loop Option
------ Other trails

0.68

Jaral Ranger
Cabin (ruins)

0.56

Spring Ck Trail

Tram Trail

Spring Creek
TH Parking

Spring Ck Rd

0   500   1000   1500 ft

heading upstream and staying in the main valley, which soon tightens into an obvious arroyo channel. As the valley tightens, trees form a beautiful riparian forest. The trail hugs the southern valley wall, while houses line the northern slopes. Once through this narrow patch of USFS land, the arroyo widens, the valley opens up, and USFS signs mark the well-formed pathway up to the Tram Trail.

The ruins of the Jaral Ranger Cabin and its spring are on the left, just before reaching the Tram Trail intersection. Several local trails have formed around the ruins; the most direct route to the Tram Trail is on the south side of the ruins. A side trail to the north of the cabin/spring parallels the Tram Trail before intersecting with it about 0.3 mile to the north, making a short loop option.

Return to the parking area along the same path.

IF YOU LIKED THIS HIKE, try **HIKE 19: Water Tank Canyon Route–Local Trails** at Sandia Peak Tram, an easier/shorter canyon route or,

HIKE 38: Embudito Canyon Route/Loop, which has a slightly harder channel route.

FOR MORE CABIN RUINS, try either **HIKE 10: Juan Tabo Cabin (Ruins) and Adjacent Arroyo Trail**, an easy hike, or **HIKE 21: Cañon Domingo Baca Trail**, a harder hike into a canyon with ruins and springs.

FOR THOSE USING GPS DATA
(DATUM: WGS 84)
Intersection of Tram and Spring Creek Trails:
    −106.48236, 35.19980
Intersection of unmarked trail with Tram Trail
    for the Loop option: −106.48326, 35.20391
Jaral Ranger Cabin ruins location:
    −106.48320, 35.20039

ALTERNATE HIKE: NORTH LOOP

Difficulty: 3
Distance: Additional 0.7 mile to main trail,
    slightly more difficult
Hiking Time: Additional 30–45 minutes
Elevation: Highest point: 6,680 ft., side trail/
    Tram Trail intersection, additional 160 ft. gain

Narrow Bands of Public Access

There are a couple of places in the foothills where established trails pass next to a house or private fence line, and the Spring Creek Trail is one of these. The Spring Creek Trail, also known as the Jaral Cabin Trail, is a primary access route to the remains of the Jaral Ranger Cabin. Historical documents indicate that the cabin was constructed in or before 1917 and served as a residential ranger cabin. As such, it is likely that this access point has been around just as long, if not longer. However, as is often the case, the land downhill from the cabin is not in the public domain, and the private landowners have built homes and other buildings on their privately held land.

Today, Spring Creek Trail follows the arroyo uphill to the cabin ruins and the Tram Trail, providing a sliver of public access through a patch of private property. The continued success of this trail lies in the trail users' hands. Hikers need to be respectful of the surrounding private property, follow the USFS directional signs, and stay on the route. Additionally, pay attention to parking to avoid blocking any private properties, and don't linger on the trail when it passes close to a private dwelling. If you desire to cross private property, ask the landowner for permission beforehand.

LOWER SPRING CREEK ROUTE AND LOOP

Difficulty	3	
Distance	3 mi (4.8 km), loop option	
Hiking Time	1–2 hours, loop option	
Elevation	520 ft. gain (158 m)	Peak elevation: 6,720 ft. (2,048 m) at LC/Tram Trail; Low elevation: 6,200 ft. (1,890 m) at fence trail
Trail Condition	Fair	USFS-owned, not -maintained; Unmarked arroyo routes
Trail Users	Hikers and horses	
Best Time	Winter	
Parking Lot	Spring Creek	
Fees	None	

SPECIAL INFORMATION: This route utilizes the USFS lands to the west of the parking area. The trails are unmarked and require a little bit of route-finding.

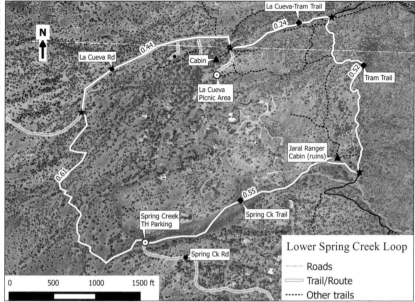

La Cueva-Tram Trail

0.24

N

La Cueva Rd

0.44

Cabin

Tram Trail

0.52

La Cueva
Picnic Area

Jaral Ranger
Cabin (ruins)

0.61

0.55

Spring Creek
TH Parking

Spring Ck Trail

Lower Spring Creek Loop

Spring Ck Rd

0   500   1000   1500 ft

----- Roads
===== Trail/Route
····· Other trails

This hiking loop is a wonderful way to see a variety of landscapes. It provides access to the La Cueva Picnic Area and to the Tram Trail, all the while staying off the beaten path. It starts at the Spring Creek parking area and is routed through the lesser-used sliver of USFS land just downstream. A series of small trails crisscross through this small piece of public land in and around the various small drainages that flow across the landscape.

This portion of USFS land is an outwash fan created by the local sediment deposition from several uphill drainages and thus has a landscape character similar to that found on the Domingo Baca outwash fan. Here, the landscape is composed of rolling hills of rocks and boulders intermixed with arroyo channels. In addition to multiple grass species, the vegetation includes a variety of trees, bushes, bear grass, cacti, and yuccas. This loop option is an interesting adventure, especially during the October-to-May time frame, when the La Cueva parking lot

access road is closed and there is often nobody around.

All of the small trails downstream from the Spring Creek parking area meet at the fence along the Sandia Pueblo land boundary, then turn north toward the La Cueva Road and picnic area. From the La Cueva Picnic Area and Tram Trail, a nice loop option presents itself by returning along the Spring Creek Trail to the parking area. This loop is about three miles and can be easily completed in one to two hours. This is a great introductory hike for beginners improving their route-finding skills, as the terrain is not to difficult to walk and the probability of getting lost is low. Hiking in this relatively unused area is a nice afternoon's exploration that includes high-desert vegetation, trees, boulders, solitude, and great views of the city and mountains.

■ THE HIKE

Park in the pull-out area at Spring Creek. Hike down the arroyo/valley. A short distance downstream from the road, a well-worn path forms and leads to the property boundary fence between USFS and Pueblo of Sandia land.

Turn right (north) to follow the fence-line trail for a short distance. Although this north-trending path starts out fairly well-defined, after it passes through a couple of small arroyos it starts to branch into ever-smaller trails, becoming something closer to a deer trail just before reaching the La Cueva Road. Regardless of the trail, if you continue north you will find the La Cueva access road (about 0.6 mile from the Spring Creek parking area).

Once at the La Cueva Road, turn right and continue on the road for about 0.4 mile (uphill) to the picnic area, where toilets and picnic tables are available. From here, a hiker can return on the same path or on another path through the foothills, or hike up the La Cueva–Tram Trail to the Tram Trail.

For the loop, take the La Cueva–Tram Trail (starts uphill from the CCC Cabin) up to the Tram Trail (0.25 mile), turn

right (south), and hike another 0.5 mile to the Spring Creek Trail (USFS marked intersection).

Turn right onto the Spring Creek Trail and follow it about 0.5 mile back to parking area.

IF YOU LIKED THIS SMALL-TRAIL MOUNTAIN HIKE, try HIKE 8: Old 333 Road Trail, an easier and shorter route on an unmaintained old road, or HIKE 20: Northern Elena Gallegos Boundary Loop from Sandia Peak Tram, which has a little more of an exploratory/remote feel to it.

FOR THOSE USING GPS DATA (DATUM: WGS 84)

Approximate location of Lower Spring Creek route intersection with FR 333A: –106.49308,35.20202

Start location for the La Cueva Parking Lot Trail to the Tram Trail –106.48733,35.20444

Intersection of La Cueva Parking Lot Trail with the Tram Trail: –106.483437, 35.205601

Intersection of the Tram and Spring Creek Trails: –106.48236, 35.19980

Pueblo of Sandia Property Boundary

On the far western edge of this hike, the trail parallels a fence line that marks the boundary between the USFS and the property of the Pueblo of Sandia. The pueblo lands, also called a reservation, are managed by the pueblo with assistance from the US Bureau of Indian Affairs. Because tribes possess tribal sovereignty, albeit limited, laws on tribal lands may vary from the surrounding area. For example, Pueblo of Sandia laws allow for legal casinos on their reservations, even though they are not generally legal under New Mexico state laws. Even though these reservation lands look just like the public USFS land, they are closed to the public unless the tribe has indicated explicitly that they are open. Hikers on this route should remember that the pueblo lands have the same rules as other

private property. Please respect their land by not damaging any of the vegetation at the boundary, and do not cross the fence.

The Pueblo of Sandia is one of nineteen pueblos located throughout New Mexico. Although this pueblo's official lands extend from this hiking area down to the Rio Grande, the Sandia people have a long history within the greater Albuquerque area. Since about AD 1300 the present village site has been home to the Sandia people, who cultivate the land and raise their families there. As with many pueblos, the Sandia Mountains provide the source of their spirituality as well as plant and animal resources that have been critical to their survival in this desert region. Once the largest pueblo in the area, with over three thousand people, they currently have just under five hundred members.

TRAM TRAIL (A.K.A. TRAMWAY TRAIL)

TRAM TRAIL (A.K.A. TRAMWAY TRAIL)

Difficulty	4	
Distance	5 mi (8 km) round-trip	
Hiking Time	2–4 hours round-trip	
Elevation	920 ft. gain (280 m)	Peak elevation: 7,400 ft. (2,256 m) near the La Luz Trail; Low elevation: 6,480 ft. (1,975 m) near the Spring Creek Trail
Trail Condition	Good	USFS-owned and -maintained
Trail Users	Hikers and horses	
Best Time	Fall and spring	
Parking Lot	Sandia Peak Tram parking	
Fees	$1 at the Tram	

SPECIAL INFORMATION: The Tram trail can be accessed in several locations, as it connects the La Luz trail with the Sandia Peak Tram.

THE TRAM TRAIL is a great USFS trail that connects the La Luz Trail with the Sandia Peak Tram parking lot. This is a surprisingly spirited trail with a variety of terrain, hills, and forests, without ever climbing up the mountains. It follows along the lower edge of the Sandia Mountains, occasionally dipping down along the upper edge of the outwash plain. Views of the city are especially good— as are views into the residential housing units that border the public lands.

As the trail meanders north it crosses several mountain drainages, creating several short but steep climbs that then drop down into the next valley bottom. As it rolls with the little canyons, it gradually gains elevation, ending in a beautiful forest at the La Luz Trail. Hikers can start either from the Sandia Peak Tram parking area or the La Luz Trailhead parking area. Generally, the southern portion of the Tram Trail has more features and is less steep. Although fewer people generally start at the Sandia Peak Tram than at the La Luz Trailhead, this is a popular trail that rarely provides a solitary hike experience. The Tram Trail can be hiked round-trip for most of the year from either parking lot, or as a one-way if you have two cars.

The trailhead is well-marked and immediately climbs. This trail is easy to follow, and it is the largest in the area, making it easy to distinguish from the many side trails that join it.

After the immediate ascent, the trail descends into the Spring Creek Watershed, crossing the channel at 0.8 mile from the parking area.

At 0.9 mile, the Tram Trail passes the Spring Creek Trail.

At 1.4 miles, the trail passes the La Cueva–Tram Trail, then crosses the La Cueva Valley.

At 2.2 miles, the trail turns sharply to the right and passes by the Hidden Valley/ La Luz Switchback Overlook area.

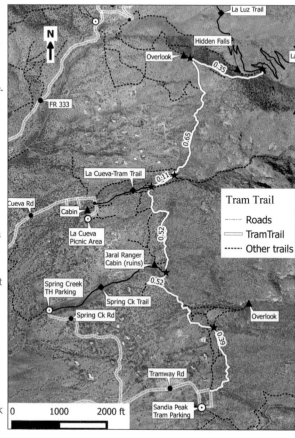

■ **THE HIKE**

Park at the northeastern corner of the Sandia Peak Tram parking lot.

At about 2.5 miles, the Tram Trail ends at the La Luz Trail. For an out-and-back, turn around at the La Luz Trail and return to the parking area. If you have a second car parked at the La Luz Trailhead, turn left onto the La Luz Trail and follow it to the parking area, about 1 mile.

If you liked this mountain hike, try **HIKE 23: Domingo Baca Outwash Fan–North EGPA Loop**, which explores the rolling hills of the Cañon Domingo Baca outwash fan, or **HIKE 30: Mountain Base Loop from Michial Emery Trailhead**, which has great views of the central foothills as it traverses the base of the mountains.

FOR THOSE USING GPS DATA (DATUM: WGS 84)
Intersection of the Tram and Spring Creek Trails: –106.48236, 35.19980
Intersection of the La Cueva Parking Lot Trail with the Tram Trail: –106.483437, 35.205601

Intersection of the La Luz Trail and the Tram Trail: –106.475544, 35.213597

SHORTER HIKING OPTIONS

1. Sandia Peak Tram to the Jaral Ranger Cabin (Ruins)
Difficulty: 3
Distance: 1.8 miles round-trip, easier route
Hiking Time: 45–60 minutes round-trip
Elevation: 120 ft. loss; peak elevation at parking lot: 6,600 ft.

2. Sandia Peak Tram to the La Cueva Valley
Difficulty: 3
Distance: 3 miles round-trip, easier route
Time 1–1.5 hours round-trip
Elevation: 240 ft. gain; peak elevation at valley: 6,720 ft.

ALTERNATE PARKING

La Luz Trailhead parking lot (7,040 ft. elevation)
La Cueva Picnic Area (6,520 ft. elevation)
Spring Creek parking lot (6,240 ft. elevation)

Sandia Peak Tram

Inspired by trams in Europe, Robert Nordhaus partnered with Ben Abruzzo to build the Sandia Peak Tram in the 1960s. Located at the northeastern edge of Albuquerque, it connects the foothills with the crest of the Sandia Mountains, 10,378 ft. at the top tram terminal. Its primary purpose was to transport skiers from Albuquerque to the top of the Sandia Peak Ski Company's ski slope on the eastern side of the Sandia Mountains. But, of course, visitors of all backgrounds and recreational desires enjoy this easy and breathtaking ride, as well as the restaurants, small shops, and trails at either end. The snow at the top, a major feature for much of the year, draws not only alpine skiers but also cross-country skiers, snowshoers, and people who simply want to play in the snow.

It took many years for Nordhaus and Abruzzo to gather the financial resources they needed, another two years to complete design and permitting, two years for construction, and then two full months of rigorous testing before the tram transported its first passengers on May 7, 1966. One of the more difficult design features to implement was the extra-long span between Tower 2 and the mountain crest: an impressive 7,720 feet (2,353 m), the third-longest aerial tram leg in the world. An estimated ten million passengers have ridden the Sandia Peak Tram in the years since. The whole trip takes about fifteen minutes, ascending about four thousand feet over a straight distance of 2.7 miles. Views from the summit and all along the Crest Trail match the scene that you would expect from an airplane when looking out over the city.

PART TWO

CENTRAL

TRAILS

2

THE CENTRAL TRAILS AREA is the embodiment of what most people envision when they think of Albuquerque's foothills: wide-open, easily walked rolling hills covered in desert grasses. Trail users come alone and as couples, groups, and sometimes multiple packs to enjoy the easy trails, hoping to see a deer and, of course, to enjoy the views that stretch as far as the eyes can see.

Without a doubt, of the three areas described in this guide, the Central Trails area, and especially the Elena Gallegos Picnic Area (EGPA) and the Bear Arroyo/floodplain area, have the largest connected grassy foothills territory available for public use. Miles and miles of trails crisscross this beautifully timeless landscape and are visited by thousands of trail users each year. Surprisingly, these areas are also the most likely areas to see wildlife, in particular deer, coyotes, birds, and rabbits.

This popular countryside has been created through a simple geologic process of erosion of the mountains with alluvial plain/fan development at their base. Here, rocks and sand that wash down from the larger Sandia Mountains create thick and expansive deposits that make a gently sloping outwash plain. This slopes away from the edge of the steep mountain front and extends to the Rio Grande valley bottom. The surface of the outwash plain was somewhat uniform when formed; however, the building and modification of the plain is ongoing, with mountain streams continuing to bring more sediment while the arroyos rework and redistribute it as they cross the plain on their journey to the Rio Grande. This continual movement of sediments is important for hikers, as the channels continually reshape the plain's surface, creating valleys and hills and, of course, reshaping trail sections that cross these features. Technically, the outwash plain extends from the mountains to the Rio Grande Valley; however, the lower-elevation surfaces are easy to build houses on, and over the years they have been developed as Albuquerque has expanded eastward. Luckily, this large area near the mountains remains undeveloped and is open to the public.

Trail 365, the principal trail in this area, leads through the heart of the foothills; it cuts across the outwash plain, up and over fans and hills, and twists its way through valleys and arroyos. Starting at the Sandia Peak Tram, Trail 365 travels south across the Domingo Baca fan (an outwash fan on steroids), skirts the edge of the EGPA, crosses through the large foothills landscape east of the Michial Emery Trailhead, and ends, unbroken, at the Embudito Trailhead. This well-worn trail is the most popular in the area, and just about every foothills hike either starts on it or uses it to get somewhere. Its rolling terrain also attracts bike riders. (Although sometimes at odds, cyclists and hikers usually coexist quite nicely in this open space where there are numerous trails to be used.)

A large variety of animals use this area, despite the constant flow of trail users and a solid line of residential communities adjacent to the Open Space area. Although the grassy hills are themselves home to many animals, their juxtaposition with the lower-mountain slopes and the arroyo channels/floodplains creates a desirable mix of habitats used by other species. This area has the normal array of desert grasses, cacti, yuccas, and a few trees, but because it also has several active arroyos with large floodplain areas, dense riparian vegetation

corridors are filled with an expansive array of plant species growing in and around the channels. Keen-eyed hikers may spot deer, coyotes, bobcats, snakes, lizards, rabbits, roadrunners, quail, hawks, ravens, and a large variety of smaller birds that live in the cacti, bushes, and trees. Occasionally, more often in drought-stricken summers, black bears roam the lower mountains and foothills searching the valley bottoms for food.

The most heavily used area in this section is in and around the Elena Gallegos Picnic Area. On weekends, in particular, large groups of people congregate at this park for family reunions, class field trips, and the like, and hike together en masse on

its large, well-marked trails. Luckily, the city's Open Space Division has prepared a detailed trail map, so if you find yourself surrounded by a class of eighth-graders investigating the plants along the Pino Trail, you can quickly locate all of the trail options available elsewhere.

The second most popular destination for hikers and cyclists is the trail system within the Bear Arroyo Watershed. Luckily, this is an extensive corridor with enough trails for all users. This swath of open space extends relatively uninterrupted from the John B. Robert Dam at Juan Tabo Boulevard to the crest. Three parking lots feed this area and its associated trails. If you would like to contend with smaller crowds, visit this watershed on a weekday.

The Bear Arroyo Watershed and its extensive, undeveloped corridor are also popular with wildlife. Deer browse its long grasslands and thickly vegetated arroyos. With ample rodents living in the valley bottom, coyotes also frequent this watershed as they hunt for rabbits, mice, and prairie dogs. A stormwater runoff "pond" is located near the Embudito Trailhead parking area, one of the few areas in the foothills where water is retained for a large portion of the year. All of the local wildlife seem to know about this water source; searching for deer prints in the mud surrounding the pond is a wonderful morning excursion.

Although the foothills are the dominant landform in the Central Trails area, a variety of other landscapes are waiting to be explored, from deep canyons with springs to steep, mountainous ridges that lead into lush pine forests. Luckily, there are trails that lead into each of these different landscapes, allowing hikers of every skill level and endurance level to enjoy this area.

Trees are such a treat in New Mexico that many hikers specifically seek out forests to trek through. Above the canyons, trees in this portion of the Sandia Mountains generally begin growing at an elevation of about 7,600 feet; because most of the parking areas are at or lower than 6,400 feet, it can be a long hike to reach the wonderful shade of our mountain forests. In recent years, the lower-elevation conifers (piñon, junipers, and other pine and fir trees) have suffered a notable mortality rate, not here and there, but grouped in specific areas. Reports from the USFS place the blame on a combination of drought and insects. Most trails that climb into the mountains pass through sections of dead trees before ascending into the healthy higher-elevation forests. These dead and dying trees sometimes form a ring around the lower edge of the thicker forests, with piñon trees the most common casualties. However, there are definitely

lower areas where juniper trees have suffered greatly, especially in the Jaral Watershed. Even though ponderosa pines have mainly been spared, the most extreme case of tree mortality actually occurred in Pino Canyon, where a significant portion of these tall evergreens perished within the last ten years.

BEST TIME TO VISIT

Spring and fall are the prime times to get out and visit these hills. However, this area is full of options in the winter and summer as well. In winter, the central mountain trails have the same issues as those in the northern section: snow and ice can definitely be a problem in the higher elevations. In the summer months, the afternoons and evenings are quite hot, even in the higher elevations, but especially in canyons or trails that trend east–west, such as the Embudito Trail.

The foothill trails, however, are a bit different. Winter can be a little muddy, but snow and ice rarely prevent their use, as it often melts away within a few days. Summer afternoon hikes can be quite hot in the foothills. But with so many trail options, hikers can explore there for hours and never get too far from their

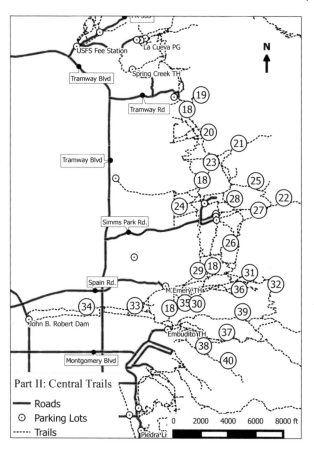

cars. The main beauty of this low level of commitment in the foothills is that hikers need far less preparation and can leave at any time.

SPECIAL INFORMATION FOR THIS AREA

The vast majority of this area is owned and operated by either the City of Albuquerque's Open Space Division or the USFS; however, there are some private in-holdings. Please be aware of posted private properties and respect the landowners.

There is a $2 per car fee for using the Sandia Peak Tram parking area. The

Elena Gallegos Picnic Area is also a fee area, charging $1 per car on weekdays and $2 on weekends.

Wildlife abounds here. Deer, bears, coyotes, bobcats, birds, snakes, and many types of rodents roam this area regularly. Mornings are the best time to spot the larger animals.

Know your abilities and stay safe, especially on the mountainous trails. Although the routes described are short, typically less than four miles, the hills are steep, the trails are small with lots of loose rocks, and anyone—yes, even *you*— can trip and fall.

DIRECTIONS TO THE AREA

This general area is located east of Tramway Boulevard, in the foothills/ mountains between the Sandia Peak Tram and the Embudito Trailhead near the end of Montgomery Boulevard. Four primary parking areas are available: from north to south, Sandia Peak Tram, Elena Gallegos Picnic Area (end of Simms Park Road), Michial Emery Trailhead parking lot (near end of Spain Road), and Embudito Trailhead parking lot (near end of Montgomery Boulevard). All parking lots have specific directions from Tramway Boulevard in appendix A.

TRAIL 365–SANDIA PEAK TRAM TO EMBUDITO TRAILHEAD

Difficulty	3	Northern area has steeper/rockier trails
Distance	5.78 mi (9.3 km) one-way	
Hiking Time	2–3.5 hours one-way	
Elevation	440 ft. gain (134 m)	Peak elevation: 6,680 ft. (2,036 m) at the Tram; Low elevation: 6,240 ft. (1,902 m) at Embudito Trailhead
Trail Condition	Excellent	Open Space– and USFS-owned and -maintained; Rolling foothill trails
Trail Users	Hikers, bikers, horses	
Best Time	Year-round	
Parking Lots	Sandia Peak Tram or Embudito Trailhead	
Fees	$1 at the Tram	

SPECIAL INFORMATION: This primary foothills trail is easily accessed from two other locations, creating numerous opportunities to create one-way trips or longer round-trips.

TRAIL 365 IS THE premier foothills trail in the Central Trails area and is extremely popular for hiking, trail running, and bike riding. It is a wide, well-maintained trail that seamlessly snakes its way through USFS property and City of Albuquerque Open Space, with the occasional section bordering private lands. Although it connects all the public land from the Tram in the north to the Embudito Trail in the south, the most important connection is the middle area: the Elena Gallegos Picnic Area (EGPA). Without a doubt, EGPA is the most heavily used area in the Central Trails section, and it seems that most trails, including Trail 365, lead to this great place.

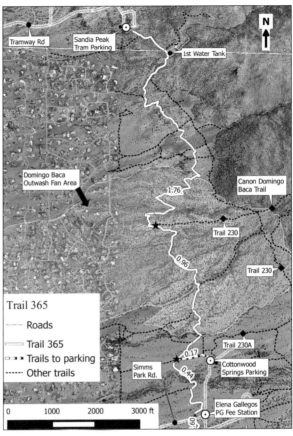

Trail 365
----- Roads
═══ Trail 365
▫ ▪ ▪ Trails to parking
----- Other trails

0   1000   2000   3000 ft

In the late 1990s and early 2000s, when the High Desert residential area was first being developed, the future of Trail 365, and especially its continuity, was unclear, for a notable portion of the original trail crossed portions of privately held lands. However, trail advocates fought valiantly to keep it open, or at least to keep its function viable. After much discussion, lots of planning, and some rerouting of the trail, it was kept intact and remains the primary trail in this portion of the foothills area. Good signage makes it easy to follow.

As with many trails in this area, the character of Trail 365 changes from its starting point at the Tram to where it ends at Embudito Trailhead. In the northern part of the trail, near the Tram, there are steeper hills and a rockier path. Trees, boulders, and tight turns are intermittently scattered between the longer stretches of grassy plains. With the exception of a short, confined segment where it was rerouted near the Embudito Trailhead, this trail crosses large tracts of wide-open land covered in grasses, desert fauna, and a few trees, which makes it an interesting landscape to explore. Trail 365 can be hiked all year long from any of the parking lots, or as a one-way if you have two cars.

Elena Gallegos Picnic Area–Cottonwood
    Springs parking lot (6,400 ft. elevation)
Michial Emery Trailhead parking lot (6,180 ft.
    elevation)
Embudito Trailhead parking lot (6,240 ft.
    elevation)

SPECIFIC TRAIL/HIKE DESCRIPTIONS

1. Sandia Peak Tram to Elena Gallegos Picnic Area–Cottonwood Springs Parking

The trailhead (marked with a USFS sign) is in
the southeast corner of the Sandia Peak Tram
parking lot. Trail 365 immediately climbs and
veers right (west) as it starts its trek to the water
tanks on the edge of the Tram/Forest Service
land boundary. At the water tanks, veer right and
descend into and cross the arroyo. From here,
the trail enters into a tree- and boulder-strewn
landscape with moderately steep hills and tight
turns. At about a mile from the parking area, it
crosses into a wide-open grassy plain with few
trees. Several trails have been created in this
area, creating several opportunities to explore or
to make a loop hike and return to the parking lot
on one of the smaller trails.

After the grassy plain, the trail ascends up
a notable hill covered in rocks and trees
(Domingo Baca outwash fan). A series of long
switchbacks climbs up this hill, crossing the
deep arroyos that cut into the outwash fan. In
approximately the middle of the outwash fan
(1.76 miles from the parking area), Trail 365

intersects with Trail 230, which is the most
direct trail to Domingo Baca Trail. Trail 230 also
marks the northern EGPA land boundary and is
another great option to use to form a loop trek
back to the Tram parking area.

From the Trail 230 intersection, Trail 365 continues into the EGPA as it crosses the southern
portion of the Domingo Baca outwash fan
for about another mile. As this trail leaves the
fan and nears the parking areas of the Elena
Gallegos Picnic Area, it travels across large
grassy plains and meets up with Trail 230A. Trail
230A leads to the northernmost parking area
of EGPA, Cottonwood Springs (about 0.2 mile
from Trail 365).

ONE-WAY HIKING DISTANCES BETWEEN PARKING LOTS

	Elena Gallegos Picnic Area–Cottonwood Springs	Michial Emery	Embudito Trailhead
Sandia Peak Tram	2.9 mi (60–75 minutes)	5.2 mi (2–3 hours)	5.8 mi (2–3.5 hours)
Elena Gallegos Picnic Area–Cottonwood Springs	—	2.65 mi (45–75 minutes)	3.25 mi (60–75 minutes)
Michial Emery	—	—	1.5 mi (30–60 minutes)

2. Elena Gallegos Picnic Area (EGPA) to Embudito Trailhead Parking Area

From the Trail 365/Trail 230A intersection near the EGPA–Cottonwood Springs parking area, Trail 365 descends into a deep arroyo/channel before meeting and crossing Simms Park Road, the access road for EGPA (0.44 mile). From there, it continues in a southerly direction across more wide-open grassy hills and sandy/gravelly arroyo crossings. The trail closely follows the residential/private lands boundary on the west side of EGPA through this area. As it crosses the EGPA's southern boundary and reenters Forest Service land, it passes by Trail 366 and Trail 305A, both of which lead back to the central area of EGPA, creating several wonderful loop opportunities for trail users.

At just over a mile beyond Simms Park Road, Trail 365 crosses a gravel private-access road for the Albuquerque Academy's mountain camp. From there it drops into the wide valley/floodplain of Bear Arroyo. As the trail leaves the valley bottom, it passes by Trail 305 (which leads back to EGPA) before meeting up with the Michial Emery Trail, the main access trail leading to the Michial Emery Trailhead parking area (0.44 mile from Trail 365 to parking lot).

From the Michial Emery Trail intersection, Trail 365 makes its way across a deep arroyo before entering into a tightly confined area. Here the trail winds and twists its way around large boulders, trees, and steep hillslopes, following the eastern edge of the private lands of the High Desert Homeowners Association. As it leaves this constricted section, it crosses Embudito Canyon Arroyo and ends at the Embudito Trailhead parking lot.

Trail 365

----- Roads
▭▭ Main trail
■▬■ Trails to parking
······ Other trails

Cottonwood Springs parking area
EGPA Fee Station
Loop Parking
Trail 366
Simms Park Rd.
Trail 305
Michial Emery TH parking
Spain Rd.
Trail 305
M. Emery Trail
Embudito TH parking
Trailhead Rd.

| 0 | 1500 | 3000 | 4500 | 6000 |

IF YOU LIKED THIS TRAIL, try **HIKE 41:** Trail 365–Comanche Road to I-40, or **HIKE 42:** Trail 401–Piedra Lisa Canyon to Hilldale Mound.

FOR THOSE USING GPS DATA (DATUM: WGS 84)

Intersection of Trail 365 and Trail 230:
   –106.477567, 35.175928
Intersection of Trail 365 and Trail 230A:
   –106.474543, 35.161674
Intersection of Trail 365 and Simms Park Road:
   –106.472198, 35.150808
Intersection of Trail 365 and Trail 305A:
   –106.473338, 35.146135
Intersection of Trail 365 and Trail 305: –106.4752, 35.145869
Intersection of Trail 365 and Michial Emery Trail:
   –106.475956, 35.165986

Rosy Finches in the Sandia Mountains

Three species of rosy finch make the Sandia Mountains their home for the winter months: the gray-crowned, black, and brown-capped varieties. As their names suggest, the three species have different-colored heads, but all have rosy or pink feathers on their wings and rumps. Widespread recognition of their presence in the late 1990s, followed by feeders placed at the Sandia Crest since 2002, has made the area a birder's dream location for seeing all three of these finches. Although the crest is the most popular location to see large flocks of rosy finches, they reportedly visit many winter feeders throughout the area, as they also winter in mountain valleys, open plains, and towns. Rosy finches are present in the Sandia Mountains from early November through late March, and all three species mix with the large flocks of other birds that roam the area.

For the summer, all of the finches migrate north to use high-mountain (above-timberline) habitats such as tundra, snowfields, and talus slopes. These elusive birds are infrequently observed when nesting, mostly because it is hard to get that high in the mountains, but also because they nest in challenging places such as mine shafts, cliff crevices, and between the rocks in talus slopes. Of all the finches, the gray-crowned rosy finch travels the furthest, nesting in western Alaska and British Columbia. The black rosy finch breeds high on mountaintops in the Great Basin, while the brown-capped rosy finch nests closest to Albuquerque, in the southern Rockies.

WATER TANK CANYON—LOCAL TRAILS AT SANDIA PEAK TRAM

Difficulty	3	
Distance	1.75 mi (2.8 km) round-trip/loop	
Hiking Time	1 hour round-trip	
Elevation	200 ft. gain (61 m)	Peak elevation: 6,880 ft. (2,097 m) at farthest point in canyon; Low elevation: 6,680 ft. (2,036 m) in parking area
Trail Condition	Fair	Privately and USFS-owned; Unmaintained canyon route
Trail Users	Hikers	
Best Time	Fall through spring	Summers can get very hot
Parking Lot	Sandia Peak Tram	
Fees	$1 at the Tram	

SPECIAL INFORMATION: This is a very small canyon route. The channel bottom is sandy, rocky, and brushy, with a few moderate-sized boulder steps.

WHEN CONSIDERING hiking from the Sandia Peak Tram, most people think about the popular Tram Trail, and honestly, this is a great option. However, on the south side of the parking lot is Trail 365, leading south into the premier foothills area, and it seems that few people go this direction. Even on busy Tram Trail days, heading south out of the parking area often leads to solitary hiking adventures such as the short, but very fun Water Tank Canyon. This hike explores the little valley just to the south of the water tanks, near the southern parking area. It is kind of narrow, kind of steep, has a fair bit of sand, includes a "boulder cave" to sit in, and offers interesting views of the tramcars as they pass over Tower 1.

Local Trails at Sandia Peak Tram
----- Roads
▭ Water Tank Canyon
▬▬ Spring Creek Canyon Overlook
▬ ▬ Tower Access road/trail
----- Other trails

If you are new to exploring canyons, this is a great starter trip. This short, easy-to-reach canyon feels isolated, but most important for beginners, it follows the water tank hill, which has an easy exit. This hill (and the road that ascends it) is an easy and quick option for returning to the parking area. With the tramcars regularly humming by, this is far from wilderness, but few canyons are as easy to walk up as this one. Hikers can go as far as they like and then turn around. The little "boulder cave" about a quarter-mile from Trail 365 is a great destination on a hot summer day, as the haphazard boulders create a deeply shaded room ideal for a lunch break. Continuing upchannel from the cave is still fun: the boulder steps get a little bigger, then the valley widens, giving hikers great views of the rocky slopes leading up and into the upper mountains.

Because this is a canyon, even a very small one, water collects here and then runs downstream. Consequently, this is a dangerous place during a rainstorm. As discussed earlier, a short scramble up the northern bank leads to the Tower/Water Tank access road, and this is the recommended route if caught in a thunderstorm while on this hike.

■ THE HIKE

Park near the Trail 365 trailhead, marked

with a USFS sign, in the southeast corner of the Sandia Peak Tram parking lot.

Start on Trail 365, which immediately climbs and veers right (south) as it starts its trek to the water tanks on the edge of the Tram/Forest Service land boundary.

At the water tanks, veer right again and descend into the arroyo. At the arroyo, turn left (east) to go upstream into Water Tank Canyon, about 0.25 mile from the parking area.

Hike as far as desired up this channel. The boulder/bedrock steps get a little bigger after the "boulder cave." The valley walls widen as the channel heads into its upper watershed.

Return along the channel or look for one of the small trails up the hill leading to the second water tank. The best of these side trails is located downstream

from the cave, and just downstream from a long section of channel bottom that is smooth bedrock (very easy walking). If you miss this tiny trail, don't worry: it is a short distance back to Trail 365 along the arroyo.

IF YOU LIKED THIS CANYON HIKE, try HIKE 48: Narrow Falls for another short canyon hike, or HIKE 45: Piedra Lisa Falls and Bench Loop for a trail up one of the waterfalls and a lower-mountain loop option.

FOR THOSE USING GPS DATA
(DATUM: WGS 84)
Crossing of Trail 365 with Water Tank Canyon:
   –106.47659, 35.18845
Approximate location of cave:
   –106.47473, 35.19075

Tramcars and Towers

Situated at 7,010 feet, Tower 1 overlooks a small canyon; hikers there can relax and watch the cars pass by, which happens about every fifteen minutes. Tower 1 is the taller of the two towers at 232 feet. If it looks a little off, that's because it is tilted on purpose. With an inclination of eighteen degrees, this tower is perfectly designed for the tram cables to evenly support the cars and provide the smoothest, safest ride possible for passengers. Each tramcar is capable of carrying fifty passengers or ten thousand pounds up the mountain at a maximum rate of two hundred passengers per hour. On the average, the tram makes 10,500 trips per year.

Tower 2, which is not visible from this canyon, is a mere eighty feet tall, but is situated uphill at an elevation of 8,750 feet. It sits on the edge of the Domingo Baca Watershed and is very difficult to get to on foot. Although there is a rough trail leading to the base of the tower, the landscape is steep and too rocky to build a road. Because of this

extremely difficult terrain, helicopters were used during construction rather than cars to transport the building materials.

Given the concern over customer safety on the tram, extra cables and specific protocols are in place in case of an emergency. Both tramcars are attached to hauling cables and the cars' movements are linked; the weight of the downhill tramcar helps to pull the other uphill to the top. The tramcars were designed with track cable brakes that automatically close and hold the car firmly in place in an emergency or haul cable failure. In case of a power failure, the tramcars can be returned to the terminals with a backup engine.

NORTHERN ELENA GALLEGOS BOUNDARY LOOP FROM SANDIA PEAK TRAM

Difficulty	3	
Distance	3.6 mi (5.8 km) round-trip	
Hiking Time	1–2.5 hours round-trip	
Elevation	280 ft. gain (86 m)	Peak elevation: 6,680 ft. (2,036 m)
		Low elevation: 6,400 ft. (1,950 m)
Trail Condition	Excellent/Good	Open Space– and USFS-owned. Trail 365 maintained; Rolling foothill trails.
Trail Users	Hikers, bikers, horses	
Best Time	Spring	Year-round; Wildflowers may be present in spring
Parking Lot	Sandia Peak Tram	
Fees	$1 at the Tram	

ALTERNATE TRAIL

Add-on Arroyo Loop

Difficulty: 3

Distance: Adds 0.5 mile to larger loop; same difficulty

Hiking Time: Additional 20–30 minutes

Elevation: 280 ft. gain

This route follows a small arroyo valley toward the eastern residential area, then loops back on the other side of the arroyo.

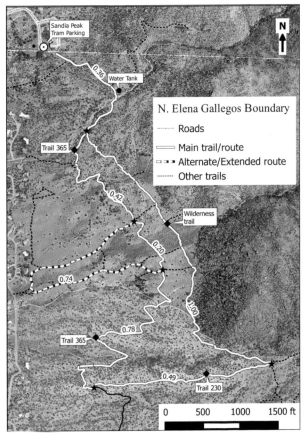

THE NORTHERN Elena Gallegos Boundary Loop uses Trail 365 to reach the northern edge of the Elena Gallegos Picnic Area (EGPA) at Trail 230. This hike is probably the least-used portion of Trail 365, where the trail itself is relatively small and narrow, giving it the feel of a mountainside trail, even though it is within the main foothills. Adding to this theme, the hills are a little bit steeper, the turns are a little bit tighter, and the path is a little bit rockier than other sections of Trail 365. With so few people around, this hike can also feel deserted, which in combination with everything else translates into a wonderful urban hike where it is easy to forget how close the city really is.

The native residents, especially deer, also seem to forget how close the urban setting is as they wonder through the relatively thick vegetation: hikers are more likely to see them and other wild visitors such as coyotes closer to the mountains and more specifically in areas with lots of trees and tall bushes.

This route starts at the Tram and descends down to the Cañon Domingo Baca outwash fan before looping back along the base of the mountains. The route covers a variety of landscapes, including small mountain slopes, arroyo crossings, grassy plains, rocky hills, and brushy valleys. All these landscapes are found throughout the Central Trails area; however, there is no other place where they are all so tightly packed into such an easily accessed short loop hike.

■ THE HIKE

Park near the Trail 365 trailhead, marked with a USFS sign, in the southeast corner of the Sandia Peak Tram parking lot.

Start on Trail 365, which immediately climbs to the water tanks on the edge of the Tram/Forest Service land boundary. At the water tanks, veer right (south) and descend into the arroyo.

From the arroyo, the trail continues straight across the channel and enters into a tree- and boulder-strewn landscape with moderately steep hills and tight turns. At about a mile from the parking area, it crosses into a wide-open grassy plain with few trees.

After the grassy plain, the trail ascends up a notable hill covered in rocks and trees; this is the Domingo Baca outwash fan. Trail 365 has a series of long switchbacks as it climbs across the deep arroyos that cut into the outwash fan.

In approximately the middle of the outwash fan (1.76 miles from the parking area), Trail 365 intersects with Trail 230. Turn left (east) here onto Trail 230, which marks the boundary with EGPA and leads up the Domingo Baca outwash fan to the Domingo Baca Trail.

At the Trail 230–Domingo Baca trail intersection, turn left (north) to hike along the base of the mountains on a small, unnamed side trail. This part of the route is within the designated Sandia Mountain Wilderness Area and parallels Trail 365, which is to the west of this trail.

The small, unnamed trail along the base of the mountains climbs gently, leading hikers back to Trail 365 near the water tank, which returns to the parking area (1.36 miles from Trail 230 to the parking area).

IF YOU LIKED THIS HIKE, try **HIKE 23: Domingo Baca Outwash Fan–North EGPA Loop**, which crosses a larger portion of the Domingo Baca outwash fan, or **HIKE 26: Bear Arroyo Loop from Elena Gallegos Picnic Area**, which also has a more remote feel.

Common Large Mammals

When we think of wildlife in the Sandia Mountains, many people think first about the predatory species: bears, cougars, bobcats. Although these three species are full-time residents in this area, they are rarely seen, especially the elusive cougar (a.k.a. mountain lion). With that said, if you spend enough time in and near the mountains, especially in the morning or evening, you might see one of these animals. If it has been really dry in the mountains, bears and bobcats will venture down to the edge of the residential areas hunting rabbits and other rodents, looking for easy food and water at all times of the day. Homeowners in the foothills complain especially about bears getting into their trash, but also about bobcats hunting their housecats and beloved squirrels and rabbits.

For the regular hiker, the two most common large mammals seen in the foothills and lower mountains are deer and coyotes. Small herds and individual deer roam all around this hiking area, browsing on the various bushes, new tree growth, grasses, and unfenced residential gardens. Coyotes are typically loners, but every so often you will see them with a friend or mate. These clever hunters frequent parks and other open spaces near the mountains in search of their favorite food, rabbits. Unfortunately, or maybe fortunately, both of these species run from humans, with deer being the more skittish of the two. The most common encounters are from a distance as hikers watch them running away.

FOR THOSE USING GPS DATA
(DATUM: WGS 84)
Intersection of Trail 365 and the unnamed trail
at the base of the mountain: –106.477929,
35.187014
Cutoff trail intersection for shorter loop:
–106.474503, 35.180966

Intersection of Trail 365 and Trail 230:
–106.47761, 35.175877
Intersection of Trail 230 and the unnamed trail
at the base of the mountain: –106.469634,
35.176857

CAÑON DOMINGO BACA TRAIL

Difficulty	3	
Distance	3.9 mi (6.3 km) round-trip	
Hiking Time	1.5–3 hours round-trip	
Elevation	800 ft. gain (245 m)	Peak elevation: 7,200 ft. (2,195 m) in canyon; Low elevation: 6,400 ft. (1,950 m) in parking area
Trail Condition	Good–Excellent	Open Space– and USFS-owned and -maintained
Trail Users	Hikers and horses	Bikers are allowed on the Elena Gallegos Picnic Area trails leading to the canyon trail
Best Time	Early spring through summer	Spring is the best time for the springs, but the trail is open year-round
Parking Lot	Elena Gallegos Picnic Area– Cottonwood Springs	
Fees	$1 weekdays, $2 weekends	

SPECIAL INFORMATION: Poison ivy is common in this canyon.

THE CAÑON (canyon) Domingo Baca is a gem in the Sandia Mountains. It is one of the more popular trails, with a beautiful canyon, trees, ruins, and springs, and it ultimately leads to the site of a tragic 1955 TWA airplane crash. Its long-lasting water source, natural springs, makes this canyon a fun place to explore and increases the chance of seeing wildlife. Even when the water is not flowing, the vast amounts of shade provided by the tight canyon walls and the dense trees in the springs area makes this a cool place for all to enjoy. The vegetation here is thick and lush, including large groups

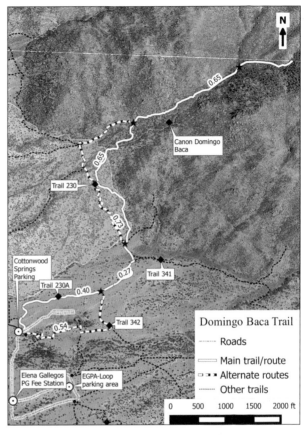

of trees, a seemingly never-ending line of brush along the valley bottom, and notable clumps of poison ivy, especially near the springs/creek area. When the valley widens, the large, beautiful trees use the space to spread out, creating perfect picnic sites, including comfortable places to rest and look for wildlife.

This area is relatively popular, so if you are seeking some private time in the canyon, start your hike early: by late morning, several groups will have found their way to this majestic place. The canyon is most often accessed from the Elena Gallegos Picnic Area (EGPA), but with a slightly longer walk it can also be reached

from the Sandia Peak Tram, which has fewer other trail users, especially if you stay in the wilderness area. (See previous hike.)

The canyon portion of this and other hikes should be avoided during inclement weather, especially when there are mountain thunderstorms brewing. Cañon Domingo Baca has a large watershed, so storms in the mountains can create flash floods that travel through this hiking area. Because this canyon is deep, with a riparian forest that obstructs the view of the sky, it may be difficult to see mountain storms or even storms coming from the direction of the city. Be smart and avoid this hike if you know mountain storms are on their way.

■ **THE HIKE**

Park at EGPA–Cottonwood Springs parking area. Start on Trail 230A, following it east, toward the mountains. After 0.4 mile, Trail 230A veers left (northeast) and becomes Trail 230. (Trail 342 heads south from this junction.)

Continue straight on Trail 230. After a short distance, the trail drops into an arroyo valley and Trail 341 veers off to the right (east). Continue straight on Trail 230 a little further (0.27 mile) to the Cañon Domingo Baca Trail junction. The Cañon Domingo Baca Trail veers right (east) off of Trail 230. A USFS sign welcomes hikers and clearly identifies the trail. The trail begins to climb as it enters the canyon area. After about 0.6 mile, it crosses the canyon bottom and

The TWA Crash and the Albuquerque Mountain Rescue Council

On February 19, 1955, Trans World Airlines (TWA) Flight 260 left the Albuquerque Airport, bound for Santa Fe. Shortly after takeoff, the plane, with its thirteen passengers and flight crew of three, crashed into the side of the cloudy Sandia Mountains, killing everyone onboard. Several members of the New Mexico Mountain Club and other volunteers assisting the State Police found the wreckage in the Domingo Baca Watershed the following day. During construction of the Tram, much of the plane wreckage was removed from the crash site, but some debris remains on the canyon floor today. A small memorial has been placed at the site to remember the sixteen lives that were lost in this awful accident.

This sad event led to the formation of the Albuquerque Mountain Rescue Council (AMRC), a voluntary organization still active today. The group filled a need for organized search and rescue capability in the Albuquerque area. The AMRC was formally incorporated as a nonprofit organization in 1959. Because it is exclusively voluntary, the membership is continually shifting and the group is always looking for volunteers. For more information, check out their website: http://www.abqmountainrescue.org.

To hike to the 1955 TWA crash site requires negotiating a steep and rugged path up the Cañon Domingo Baca, which leads into its headwaters area and ultimately to the memorial. This small, unmaintained trail extends another 1.6 miles from the end of this short hike, gaining about 1,400 feet as it reaches the crash site, located under the tram cables near the crest. To find the trail, follow the channel upstream about 0.25 mile from the ruins in the Cañon. From the main channel, veer right up a steep, raw path that leads up a twenty-foot bank/hillside. (Sometimes a small cairn marks this steep path/intersection, but not always.) Once up the crumbly, steep path and through some brush, a decent trail emerges to head uphill. The trail follows this "hill" and then a small valley as it climbs steeply to the site. The route is brushy and scratchy, with a small rock-climb of approximately fifteen feet up an outcrop just before reaching the site. Because this route is very steep and sometimes poorly defined, the 1.6 miles from the channel will feel like a very long distance. Hikers attempting this route (approximately 7.5 miles round-trip) should be prepared for mountain conditions (elevation of about 8,500 ft.) and have excellent physical endurance, perseverance, and route-finding skills. Plane debris is scattered, but the site is located at approximately GPS point –106.44253, 35.19493.

joins with another trail on the north side. Continue up the canyon (east), which becomes covered by large trees. Several springs bring water to the surface, especially during the springtime. Hike as far as desired up the canyon. The return route is the same as the outgoing route.

IF YOU LIKED THIS HIKE, try HIKE 38: Embudito Canyon Route/Loop, which has an easier canyon route with springs, or HIKE 7: Waterfall Canyon via Piedra Lisa Trail, a slightly more difficult canyon hike with springs.

FOR THOSE USING GPS DATA
(DATUM: WGS 84)
Intersection of Trail 230 and Domingo Baca Trail: –106.466863, 35.171032
Location where formal trail "ends" and a small trail leads off to crash site: –106.459883, 35.181384
TWA crash debris area: –106.4415, 35.194919

ALTERNATE TRAILS

1. Trail 230 Route
Difficulty: 3
Distance: Adds 0.1 mile to one-way distance; same difficulty
Hiking Time: Additional 10–20 minutes
Elevation: 800 ft. gain; peak elevation: 7,200 ft. (same as for main route)
Although Trail 230 is close to the Domingo Baca Trail, it crosses the outwash plain, a distinctly different landscape than that found along the Domingo Baca, which runs along the base of the mountains. This is a nice return route option.

2. Nature Trail via Trail 342 Route
Difficulty: 3
Distance: Adds 0.1 mile to one-way distance
Hiking Time: Additional 10–20 minutes
Elevation: 800 ft. gain; peak elevation: 7,200 ft. (same as for main route)
This option passes by the small wetland/pond area along the Nature Trail. A blind allows visitors to view wildlife in the wetland without being seen.

ALTERNATE PARKING

Elena Gallegos Picnic Area Loop parking lot (6,460 ft. elevation)
Sandia Peak Tram (6,680 ft. elevation)

PINO TRAIL TO THE DEAD TREES

Difficulty	4	
Distance	5 mi (8 km) round-trip	Hike to the dead tree section (halfway to Crest)
Hiking Time	2.5–4 hours round-trip	
Elevation	1,140 ft. gain (347 m)	Peak elevation: 7,600 ft. (2,316 m); Lowest elevation: 6,460 ft. (1,969 m) in parking area
Trail Condition	Good–Excellent	Open Space– and USFS-owned and -maintained
Trail Users	Hikers and horses*	No bikers are allowed on Pino Trail. *The Elena Gallegos Picnic Area trail portion is closed to horses, but alternate routes exist
Best Time	Spring through fall	Winter will have snow and ice
Parking Lot	Elena Gallegos Picnic Area	
Fees	$1 weekdays, $2 weekends	

SPECIAL INFORMATION: There is no obvious landscape feature such as an overlook or ridgeline along this trail for a halfway point, other than the Crest Trail. Recommend choosing a timeframe rather than a location for turning around (e.g., after one hour of hiking).

THIS IS ONE OF THE MORE popular trails in the Sandia Mountains; it ranks right up there with the La Luz and Piedra Lisa Trails. Three things make it so popular: it is easy to access from the EGPA, it is one of the few trails that reach the Crest Trail, and it is covered in trees for most of its distance. In fact, it enters a relatively dense forest at about 1.25 miles from the EGPA parking area. This deep shade makes this trail a delight for most of the year, including the summer. Every type of hiker will enjoy this trail, whether you want to ascend to the crest of the Sandia Mountains, hike through miles of beautiful forest, or simply stretch your legs for a few miles.

The Pino Trail through the EGPA is one of the widest trails around, easily fitting three to four people walking side by side; as this section is particularly popular, hikers often form groups taking up the whole width of the trail. Although its popularity doesn't decrease once inside the Wilderness area, the elbow

ALTERNATE ROUTE: PINO TRAIL TO CREST TRAIL

Difficulty: 5, due to length and steepness near Crest Trail

Distance: 10 miles round-trip

Hiking Time: 4–7 hours round-trip

Elevation: 2,740 ft. gain; peak elevation: 9,200 ft.

room does: large boulders, bushes, and trees force it to wind its way up the valley as a normal single-track trail. The trail climbs steadily toward the east, with the steepest section at the end as it climbs in switchbacks up the steep hillsides that lead directly to the crest. Because it is five miles one-way from parking to the crest, many hikers turn around a couple of miles prior to reaching the end.

Along the trail, there are numerous little forested hills where hikers could stop for a snack and call it their turn-around point. One such point occurs

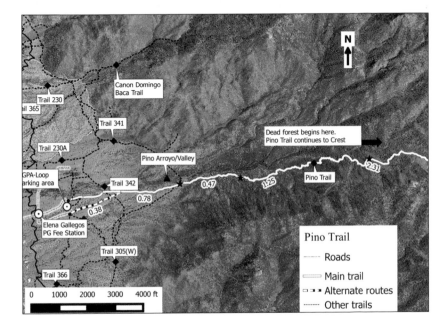

about 2.5 miles from the parking area, where the trail passes through a portion of forest where an insect infestation coupled with the drought from the early 2000s killed many trees. Most of these dead trees have lost their bark and many have fallen, creating long logs that are just begging to be sat on. Although not the most scenic of locations for those wanting a green forest, picnicking along one of these downed trees has a certain appeal. Hiking to the dead trees is about five miles round-trip and includes a little over two miles of forest hiking and some incredible trailside views of the Sandia Mountains and the city.

In the winter, this trail accumulates a fair bit of snow and ice within the forested area, creating dangerous hiking conditions for those unprepared for the conditions. For general hiking, late spring through fall is the best time for a visit. The trail itself is well-maintained, with plenty of signs so users don't get lost. As is the case with all of the truly mountainous trails, if the crest is your destination,

preparation for mountain conditions is a must, year-round. Refer to the *Sandia Mountain Hiking Guide* by Mike Coltrin for more specific hiking information about the upper Pino Trail.

■ THE HIKE

Head due east from the eastern edge of the loop road at EGPA on the well-worn Pino Trail (Trail 140).

For the first 0.75 mile, the trail gently climbs across a grassy desert plain with scattered vegetation as it reaches the Wilderness boundary, just after crossing Trail 341.

Once inside the Wilderness Area, the trail's width shrinks considerably, has steep sections, and becomes rockier, with boulder steps. Trees begin to overtake the desert vegetation, continuing to thicken with distance from the car. At about 1.25 miles from the parking area (0.46 mile from the Wilderness boundary), the trees become dense enough that most agree it is a forest.

Tree Hazards

Recently, Pino Canyon experienced a major tree kill event, with a large portion of the ponderosa pine forest dying in just a couple of years. Although these places can be a draw for their odd beauty, they also pose a hazard. The prolonged drought of the early 2000s greatly weakened the pine trees in this forest, and then insects such as the mountain pine beetle swooped in and killed the struggling trees. Although we highly value our mature forests, this is a natural process that ultimately regenerates them.

The mountain pine beetles are native to pine forests throughout North America. While laying groups of eggs, called galleries, they also introduce Blue Stain Fungus to the trees. In combination, the larvae and fungus attack and kill large groups of stressed trees, if not the entire forest. Healthy trees are able to withstand a beetle attack, and usually only the weakest trees succumb.

The large number of dead standing trees (a.k.a. snags or widowmakers) on this route create an interesting forest experience—and pose a substantial hazard. Hikers should always be aware of their surroundings when walking through or picnicking in a forest, and here, especially, they need to pay particular attention to the dead trees. The first rule for this hike is to avoid the dead tree area on windy days or during storms, as these are the times when snags are most likely to fall. Even when the weather is calm, avoid stopping in areas where dead trees are leaning or have started to fall, but are hung up on other trees. Never climb on standing or partially fallen dead trees.

From here, the trail continues to climb, following to the south side of the Pino Canyon. Along this section of trail, several small side trails lead hikers to clearings, overlooks and wonderful picnic locations. Starting at about 1.7 miles from the Wilderness boundary, about halfway to the Crest Trail junction, the trail enters into an area of the forest where many of the trees are dead. Although the trail is well-maintained, these dead trees fall year-round and sometimes cross the trail. For those hikers who are not necessarily interested in reaching the Crest Trail, this area is a good turnaround point.

The return route is the same as the inbound route, regardless of where the hiker turns around. If continuing to the crest (another 2.3 miles), the trail continues to climb, steepening as it approaches the final ascent—large switchbacks that ascend to the Crest Trail.

IF YOU LIKED THIS LARGE-TRAIL MOUNTAIN HIKE, try **HIKE 6: El Rincon via Piedra Lisa Trail** or **HIKE 1: Upper La Cueva Overlook via La Luz Trail**, which are similar in difficulty.

FOR THOSE USING GPS DATA
(DATUM: WGS 84)
Intersection of the Pino Trail with Trail 341:
    −106.45685, 35.16515
Approximate location where the Dead Forest
    begins: −106.43429, 35.16790

DOMINGO BACA OUTWASH FAN—NORTH EGPA LOOP

Difficulty	3	Trail has steep, rocky sections
Distance	2.8 mi (4.5 km) loop	
Hiking Time	45–90 minutes	
Elevation	280 ft. gain (86 m)	Peak elevation: 6,680 ft. (2,036 m) on N. Domingo Baca Trail; Low elevation: 6,400 ft. (1,950 m) at parking
Trail Condition	Good	Open Space–owned and -maintained; Rolling foothill trails
Trail Users	Hikers, bikers, and horses	
Best Time	Spring through fall	
Parking Lot	Elena Gallegos Picnic Area–Cottonwood Springs	
Fees	$1 weekdays, $2 weekends	

THIS IS A WONDERFUL route for exploring the Domingo Baca outwash fan from the Elena Gallegos Picnic Area (EGPA). Although outwash fans are somewhat common in New Mexico, this fan is especially easy to get to, has enough trees to provide shady spots, and is full of interesting arroyos, hills, tight turns, views, plants, and, of course, rocks. All these features, along with a relatively low use rate, allow hikers to get the feeling of getting out to the wilderness without having to climb into the mountains.

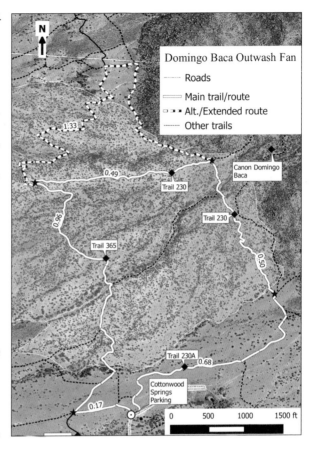

As is common on fans, the arroyos have cut deep channels into the outwash sediments, forming small, steep hills that the route crosses up and over. These hilly sections are particularly full of trees and bushes, including all those characteristic of the high-desert terrain, plus a variety of other small plants such as wildflowers. They are regularly mixed in with wide-open, flatter surfaces, creating an alternating trees versus grassy trail experience for the trail user.

This easy-to-follow route/loop utilizes the well-known Trail 365, along with several other named and maintained trails, to create a loop around a large portion of the Domingo Baca outwash fan. Although Trail 365 is popular in general, this section is not the most frequently used. The other trails on this loop, especially the

northern section of Trail 230 (along the property boundary) are also less used, improving the likelihood of solitude and seeing wildlife.

■ THE HIKE

Park at the EGPA–Cottonwood Springs parking area.

Start on Trail 230A, following it to the left (west), away from the mountains. After 0.2 mile, Trail 230A intersects Trail 365.

Turn right and follow Trail 365 for about 1 mile. The first major channel crossing is the southern Domingo Baca Arroyo; from here, the trail begins its climb up and across the western portion of the Domingo Baca outwash fan.

Turn right (east) onto Trail 230. This climbs up onto the middle of the outwash fan, then heads straight up it toward the Domingo Baca Trail (0.5 mile). (If the longer route option is desired, stay on Trail 365, continuing north and looping around the northern edge of the fan.)

At the USFS Wilderness boundary (north) Domingo Baca Trail, Trail 320 turns south and crosses the eastern area of the outwash fan (about 0.5 mile). As the trail leaves the fan, it passes by the southern Domingo Baca Trail and descends onto the more common foothills landscape of grass-covered rolling hills.

Continue south on Trail 230. Staying to the right, pass by two junction areas (Trails 341 and 342). At the junction with Trail 342, continue straight (west) onto Trail 230A to return to the parking lot on the left (0.68 mile).

IF YOU LIKED THIS HIKE, try **HIKE 20: Northern Elena Gallegos Boundary Loop from Sandia Peak Tram**, which is the other side of the fan. Or try **HIKE 30: Mountain Base Loop from Michial Emery Trailhead** or **HIKE 26: Bear Arroyo Loop from Elena Gallegos Picnic Area**, as these two hikes have a remote feel plus some small, tree-covered hills.

FOR THOSE USING GPS DATA (DATUM: WGS 84)
Intersection of Trail 230A and Trail 365: –106.47590, 35.16598
Intersection of Trail 365 and Trail 230: –106.47761, 35.175877
Intersection of Trail 230 and Domingo Baca Trail: –106.466863, 35.171032

ALTERNATE TRAIL: EXTENDED LOOP

Difficulty: 3
Distance: 3.6 miles round-trip
Hiking Time: 1–2 hours round-trip
Elevation: 280 ft. gain; peak elevation: 6,680 ft.
(same as for main route)
Use of the unmaintained mountain base trail owned by USFS.

ALTERNATE PARKING

Elena Gallegos Picnic Area Loop parking lot (6,460 ft. elevation)

Fan versus Plain

At first glance, hikers may not think too much about the difference between an outwash fan and an outwash plain, but the differences are obvious if you hike up and over the Domingo Baca fan. Simply stated, the reason for the differences comes down to sediment; lots of sediment is coming out of the Domingo Baca Watershed, and this is building up the fan to form a hill that sits on top of the outwash plain. The sediment difference isn't in the minerals, but rather in rock size: the fan sediments are larger gravels and cobbles, while the plain has more sands and smaller gravel. Beyond the physical hill and rock, the vegetation is also different: the fan is covered in trees, while the plain is blanketed by grasses.

Although they seem like very different landscapes, fans and plains are geologically intertwined. A fan is formed as one stream reaches a place in the landscape where it drops its sediment load, such as at the outlet of a canyon, or when a small stream joins a larger river, such as the Rio Grande. At these locations, the sediment piles up and forms a fan-shaped surface. When several fans join together and become so intermixed that you can't easily tell one from the other, they form an outwash plain.

GRASSY HILLS LOOP

Difficulty	2	
Distance	3.8 mi (6.1 km) loop	
Hiking Time	1–2 hours	
Elevation	300 ft. gain (91 m)	Peak elevation: 6,460 ft. (1,969 m) at pond; Low elevation: 6,160 ft. (1,878 m) at fence
Trail Condition	Good	USFS- and Open Space–owned; Some maintained
Trail Users	Hikers, bikers, and horses	
Best Time	Spring through fall	
Parking Lot	Elena Gallegos–Cottonwood Springs	
Fees	$1 weekdays, $2 weekends	

Elena Gallegos Picnic Area Loop parking lot
(6,460 ft. elevation)

AS IN SO MUCH of the foothills area,
there are many trail options for this section of the western Elena Gallegos Picnic
Area (EGPA). The route outlined here
explores the western trails where the
primary features are elongated, east-to-
west-trending ridges along the outwash
plain. These small "hills" were created by
the east–west arroyos cutting relatively
deep channels into the outwash plain, but
leaving the top surface uneroded. These
stable surfaces are relatively smooth and
typically grass-covered, with sporadic trees
and cacti. In a rainy year, these surfaces
also sprout a variety of wildflowers and
other similarly induced plants.

On this hike, the east-to-west-trending
trails follow the hilltops and are relatively
flat, although there is always a gentle
gradient toward the city. Trails trending
north–south cut across the outwash plain

and therefore cross the arroyos, creating a
hiking environment with more topography
and diversity. Most of the arroyo channels
have steep sides, while the valley bottoms
are filled with riparian brush and trees.

This route is a slightly longer "short"
hike (almost 4 miles), but because the
trails are wide-open, packed-dirt, and easy
to walk, it is a fast one. If desired, the
course can easily be reduced in distance
by removing the western loop section or
by cutting one leg short. If a shorter hike
is desired, one consideration is the number of other trail users in the area: fewer
people use the far western trails, while
the area around the Nature Trail tends
to be filled with picnickers and other day
hikers. Another section that could easily
be cut out is the southern loop, Trail 365
and Trail 366, which is more popular
with bike riders.

■ **THE HIKE**

Park at EGPA–Cottonwood Springs parking area.

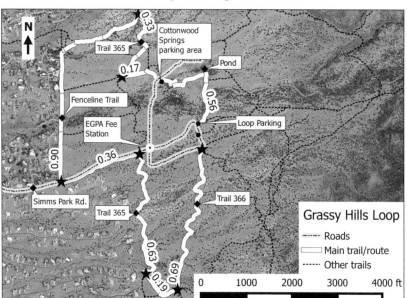

Start on Trail 230A, following it to the left (west), away from the mountains. After 0.2 mile, Trail 230A intersects Trail 365.

Turn right and follow Trail 365 for about 0.3 mile, which includes crossing an arroyo valley (the southern branch of the Domingo Baca Arroyo) and beginning to climb up onto the Domingo Baca outwash fan.

Turn left at the first unnamed trail to the left (west). Follow this along the grassy slope toward the housing area.

Turn left (south), cross back over the Domingo Baca Arroyo, and follow the property boundary trail south until you reach Simms Park Road (0.9 mile).

Cross the road and turn left to follow the roadside trail back to Trail 365 (0.36 mile).

Turn right onto Trail 365 and follow it south until you reach Trail 366 (0.8 mile).

Turn left onto Trail 366 and follow it north to EGPA loop road (0.7 mile).

Continue north along the eastern edge of the loop road and join up with the Nature Trail that continues north. At the wetland/pond/wildlife viewing area, turn left and head back to the Cottonwood Springs parking area (0.56 mile).

IF YOU LIKED THIS HIKE, try HIKE 28: Elena Gallegos Inner Trail Loop, which is a little more of the same terrain. Or try HIKE 31: Academy Camp Loop or HIKE 36: Mountain Base–Academy Camp Loop from Embudito Trailhead, two hikes that explore more of the classic foothills, but in a different area.

FOR THOSE USING GPS DATA
(DATUM: WGS 84)
Intersection of Trail 230A and Trail 356:
    –106.475853, 35.165937
Intersection of Trail 365 with small trail that follows the Domingo Baca Arroyo to the west:
    –106.474698, 35.169609
Intersection of Fence Trail with Simms Park Road: –106.480257, 35.159747
Intersection of Simms Park Road and Trail 365:
    –106.474466, 35.161441
Intersection of Trail 365 with Trail 366:
    –106.471502, 35.15356
End of Trail 366: –106.469808, 35.161796

Pino Arroyo Watershed

The Pino Arroyo Watershed is one of the larger watersheds in the area, and because it has a lot of catchment area, it also has a variety of flood-control structures along its length. A clearly visible earthen dam and reservoir area are located on the northwest side of Tramway Boulevard and Academy Road. Unfortunately, although several user-created trails crisscross all around the reservoir area, there are also Private Property signs and fences, clearly indicating that at least part of this area is non-public. As with the John B. Robert dam and recreation area on Bear Arroyo, just south of here, it would be nice if this reservoir area was public land, but sadly, it is not at this time. Maybe in the not-too-distant future, Open Space will either acquire the private lands in this area or obtain a recreational easement, but until that time, local hikers need to adhere to private property laws and stay out.

Fortunately, though, there is a small piece of Open Space land within this part of the Pino Arroyo and nearby. This little sliver of public property is located on the east side of Tramway Boulevard, upstream from the dam. Open Space owns a square chunk of land within the floodplain area and a long, slim section along Simms Park Road, which is paralleled by a trail for its whole length. Because there are no designated parking areas along Simms Park Road, access to this area must be from a distance: hikers can either walk there on the Tramway Trail (a paved trail along Tramway Boulevard) or via the roadside trail from the Elena Gallegos Picnic Area.

PINO ARROYO LOOP

Difficulty	2	
Distance	2.3 mi (3.7 km) loop	
Hiking Time	45–90 minutes	
Elevation	300 ft. gain (91 m)	Peak elevation: 6,760 ft. (2,060 m) at Wilderness boundary/Pino Trail; Low elevation: 6,460 ft. (1,969 m) at parking
Trail Condition	Good	Open Space–owned and -maintained
Trail Users	Hikers, bikers, and horses	
Best Time	Spring through summer	
Parking Lot	Elena Gallegos loop	
Fees	$1 weekdays, $2 weekends	

SPECIAL INFORMATION: This area can be crowded with picnickers, bikes passing through, nature trail walkers, and Pino Trail hikers. Holidays are the busiest days, with the fewest crowds on weekdays.

THIS IS A FUN and popular set of easy trails that forms a loop route around a small section of the Pino Arroyo Valley within the Elena Gallegos Picnic Area (EGPA), including both the Nature Trail and the lower section of the extremely popular Pino Trail. The Pino Trail and the whole surrounding area have an exquisite natural beauty that people understandably flock to. This, coupled with the easy access and picnicking opportunities, means the crowds are substantial during the weekends and especially on holidays.

Four features call to hikers to explore this loop: the Pino Arroyo Valley, the Nature Trail with the pond, and the two large trails, the Pino Trail and Trail 341. Hikers are invariably drawn to the arroyo crossings, where many stop for at least a moment to take in the beautiful surroundings of the channel. The Pino Arroyo Valley, in particular, has a well-formed riparian forest, filled with a variety of trees and shrubs. This vegetation covers the banks and often creates islands

ALTERNATE ROUTE: EXTENDED LOOP (RETURN ON TRAIL 305A)

Difficulty: 2
Distance: 2.96 miles round-trip.
Hiking Time: 1–2 hours round-trip
Elevation: 300 ft. gain; peak elevation: 6,750 ft.
  (same as for main route)
Longer loop uses Trails 342 and 305A.

in the valley bottom, the sandy channel splitting to go around the trees. This unique environment is a draw for trail users of every experience level and background, and subsequently leads to groups of people sitting and chatting in the shady channel. The Pino Trail, the other major draw on this loop, is wide open and offers the best views of the mountains, the grassy foothills, and, in the distance, the City of Albuquerque. Fewer people hike Trail 341; with the trees and hills blocking its openness, this trail offers a retreat from the nearby crowds along with a completely different environment to explore.

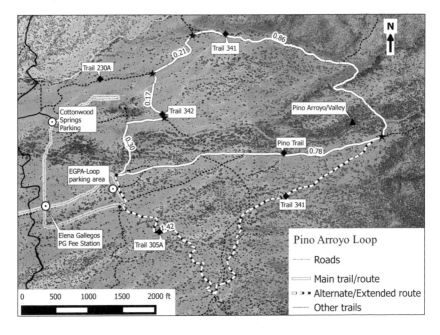

The whole area around the Pino Trail is usually crowded with casual and serious hikers, picnicking groups, and bike riders. Given the wonderful picnic grounds at EGPA, school field trips, company picnics, family gatherings, and all kinds of large-group activities occur every day of the week and they all use this trail and the surrounding area. Two crowd-avoidance strategies help here: hike the trail early or late in the day to avoid the midday peak of casual hikers/picnickers, and visit but don't linger along the popular lower section of the Pino Trail. Once you've moved along, the crowds will fade fast.

FOR THOSE SEEKING another attraction at the start of their hike or just after, consider a quick visit to *The Five Stones of Elena Gallegos*, a lovely side trip containing both local history information and naturally inspired art. This set of large stones with carvings by artist Billie Walters forms a linear sculpture near the Pino Trail within the Elena Gallegos Picnic Area. It honors the life of Philip B. Tollefsrud, a local conservationist who was proactive in preserving Albuquerque's open areas for public use.

■ THE HIKE

Park anywhere along the eastern edge of the loop road within the EGPA.

From the northeast corner of the EGPA loop road, the Nature Trail leads due north toward the pond area. Just before the pond, the Nature Trail turns right (east) and then ends at the Trail 342 junction (about 0.3 mile from the parking area).

Turn left onto Trail 342 and follow less than 0.25 mile to the end, at the junction with Trails 230A/230.

Turn right (east) onto Trail 230. Follow this about 0.25 mile to the Trail 341 junction.

Turn right (east) onto Trail 341 and follow until it reaches the Pino Trail (0.86 mile). This trail begins by following along

The Five Stones of Elena Gallegos

One of the special qualities of New Mexico culture is how art is integrated into daily life. Keeping in sync with this cultural heritage, in 1978 the City of Albuquerque introduced and approved a "1% for Art Ordinance" to promote art programs that increase public awareness of fine arts and cultural properties. The Capital Program includes funds for art equal to 1 percent of their projects' total construction cost. Thanks to this active program, beautiful and imaginative works of art now exist throughout the city, including several pieces in the foothills. One such display is *The Five Stones of Elena Gallegos*, created by Billie Walters in 1982–1983. This memorial recognizes the late Philip B. Tollefsrud's contributions as a local conservationist and his efforts to develop official Open Space throughout the city. Tollefsrud was instrumental in preserving the land associated with the former Elena Gallegos Land Grant.

The Five Stones of Elena Gallegos is located on the north side of the Pino Trail, near the parking lots. Five large native-granite stones set roughly in line on the desert floor are connected via a dirt path. Each stone has an abstract design on its face, with metal adornments. The first stone has cut into its face a circle containing thirty-eight copper pins, representing the thirty-eight years of Philip Tollefsrud's life. The other stones' emblems symbolize the city, the mountain, the river, and the tram.

a ridgeline, then drops into the wide
arroyo valley/floodplain. From there, it
rises up and over a small hill before dropping into the Pino Arroyo Valley. After the
valley area, Trail 341 intersects the Pino
Trail.

Turn right (west) onto the Pino Trail
to return to the parking area (0.8 mile).
The extended route (1.4 miles to parking
lot) continues straight on Trail 341, which
changes seamlessly into Trail 342 before
meeting up with Trail 305A. Turn right
onto trail 305A to return to the parking
area.

IF YOU LIKED THIS HIKE, try **HIKE 24: Grassy
Hills Loop**, which explores more of the EGPA,

or **HIKE 36: Mountain Base–Academy Camp
Loop from Embudito Trailhead**, which also
mixes trails at the base of the mountains with
grassy hills but offers more remoteness than
the EGPA.

FOR THOSE USING GPS DATA
(DATUM: WGS 84)
Junction of Trail 230A and Trail 342:
    –106.467724, 35.166048
Intersection of Trail 342 and Trail 230A:
    –106.468322, 35.168191
Junction with Trail 341: –106.466343, 35.170015
Intersection of Trail 341 with the Pino Trail:
    –106.456854, 35.165121

BEAR ARROYO LOOP FROM ELENA GALLEGOS PICNIC AREA

Difficulty	2	
Distance	2.9 mi (4.7 km) loop	
Hiking Time	45–90 minutes	
Elevation	180 ft. gain (55 m)	Peak elevation: 6,500 ft. (1,981 m) along Trail 305, W portion (Wilderness); Low elevation: 6,320 ft. (1,926 m) along Trail 365
Trail Condition	Excellent–Good	Open Space–, USFS-, and Wilderness-owned; Maintained
Trail Users	Hikers, bikers, and horses	No bikes on Trail 305 (W)
Best Time	Spring through fall	
Parking Lot	Elena Gallegos Picnic Area	
Fees	$1 weekdays, $2 weekends	

SPECIAL INFORMATION: Trail 305 (W) crosses a small corner of private property at the gravel road. Please be particularly courteous and respectful to help keep this trail open for future public use.

WHILE USING TWO very popular foothill trails, Trail 365 and Trail 305A, this route also utilizes two lesser-used trails, Trail 305(W) and Trail 366. The first two are well-traveled, larger trails that cross the rolling foothills with gentle curves and well-marked intersections. By contrast, Trail 305(W) is in the designated Wilderness Area and has more of a rugged feel to it. It is not only smaller, with tighter curves as it weaves its way through piñon trees, but it also has a secluded feel. Trail 366 is similar to Trail 305A, crossing through grassy, rolling foothills. Although off the beaten path, both Trail 305(W) and Trail 366 are in good condition.

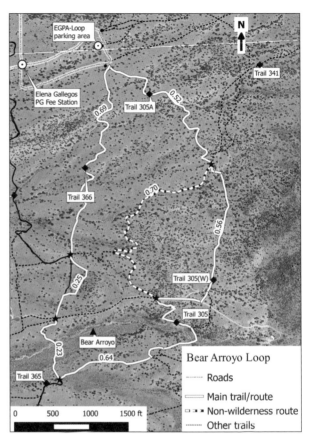

This loop starts in the EGPA but crosses into USFS lands and even a small patch of private land, a corner of the Albuquerque Academy Camp. As with all foothills trails, these wide-open routes offer fantastic views of the mountains, the grassy foothills, and, in the distance, the City of Albuquerque. Seeing wildlife is relatively common the farther one travels from the most popular locations, such as EGPA. Deer, coyotes, rabbits, ravens, hawks, roadrunners, and other creatures live in this area, especially liking the close proximity of the steep mountains to the gently sloping

ALTERNATE BIKE ROUTE

Difficulty: 2. Non-Wilderness route that avoids Trail 305(W)

Distance: 3.05 miles round-trip

Hiking Time: 45 minutes–1.5 hours

Elevation: 180 ft. gain; peak elevation: 6,500 ft. (same as for main route)

Wilderness Means No Bikes

The Wilderness Act of 1964 (Public Law 88-577) established the National Wilderness Preservation System (NWPS) and mandated that the National Park Service, US Forest Service, and US Fish and Wildlife Service review all federal lands under their jurisdiction for consideration for a wilderness designation. The Sandia Mountain Wilderness Area became part of the NWPS by an act of Congress in 1978. After a land trade with the City of Albuquerque in 1984, the Sandia Wilderness area expanded to its current size, a total of 37,877 acres.

The NWPS protects federally managed wilderness areas, with the goal of maintaining the land in its natural condition. The 1964 act defines wilderness as "an area where the earth and community of life are untrammeled by man, where man himself is a visitor who does not remain" and "an area of undeveloped Federal land retaining its primeval character and influence, without permanent improvements or human habitation, which is protected and managed so as to preserve its natural conditions." As such, Wilderness areas are subject to specific management restrictions and recreation is limited to non-motorized activities such as backpacking, hunting, fishing, and horseback riding. Although cars, dirt bikes, and mountain bikes are now prohibited by this designation, old road scars are scattered throughout the lower mountains and foothills, providing a lasting reminder of when vehicles ventured into these mountains. Nature is gradually reclaiming sections of these roads, but the process is slow. Throughout the country, there are currently 762 designated wilderness areas, totaling 108,916,684 acres, or about 4.5 percent of the area of the United States.

foothills. The best opportunity to see them is early in the day, and the most likely place along the mountain edges.

■ **THE HIKE**

Park near the southeast corner of the loop road within the EGPA.

Trail 305A and Trail 366 begin from the same location in this southeast corner. Stay left and take Trail 305A. This veers south-southeast, while Trail 366 goes south-southwest toward Trail 365 on the western side of the EGPA. Continue on Trail 305A for 0.50 mile until it reaches the Wilderness Boundary (marked by a fence).

From Trail 305A, continue straight. Cross through the USFS fence opening and into the Wilderness area. Turn right (south) to follow Trail 305(W) along the base of the mountains for about 0.4 mile, until the trail meets the gravel road, private access for the Albuquerque Camp. Turn right (west) onto the gravel road and walk about 0.2 mile to where Trail 305 crosses it.

Turn left (south) onto Trail 305. The trail descends into a deep but narrow valley (the main Bear Arroyo), then ascends up and around a hill before descending again into a wider, vegetated valley bottom. From here, Trail 305 starts another long ascent. As it curves out and around the nose of this grassy hill (about 0.3 mile from the road), an unmarked ridgeline trail intersects it. Turn right (west) onto this unmarked trail and follow it along this hill's ridgeline and eventually back down into the valley bottom (0.3 mile).

Once back in the arroyo valley, this trail intersects Trail 365. Turn right (north) onto Trail 365 and follow it a short distance (0.23 mile) back to the gravel road.

Continue north on Trail 365 another 0.25 mile until it reaches the Trail 365/366/305A intersection. Veer right onto Trail 366 and follow it 0.7 mile back to EGPA.

IF YOU LIKED THIS HIKE, try **HIKE 29: North Levee/Trail 305 Loop,** which passes through the same area, or **HIKE 20: Northern Elena Gallegos Boundary Loop from Sandia Peak Tram,** which has similar topography and remoteness.

FOR THOSE USING GPS DATA
(DATUM: WGS 84)
Intersection of Trail 341, Trail 305, and Trail 305W: –106.4652, 35.157506
Trail 305A at the private Academy Camp road: –106.467689, 35.151715
Trail 365 intersection with the small ridgeline trail: –106.472043, 35.148179
Trail 365 at the private Academy Camp road: –106.472212, 35.150822
Intersection of Trail 365 with Trail 366: –106.471502, 35.15356

ELENA GALLEGOS OUTER TRAIL LOOP

Difficulty	3	
Distance	5.7 mi (9.2 km) loop	
Hiking Time	1.5–3 hours	
Elevation	440 ft. gain (134 m)	Peak elevation: 6,760 ft. (2,060 m) at Wilderness boundary/Pino Trail; Low elevation: 6,320 ft. (1926 m) along Trail 365
Trail Condition	Excellent–Good	Open Space- and USFS-owned and -maintained
Trail Users	Hikers, bikers, and horses	No bikes on Trail 305 (W)
Best Time	Spring through fall	
Parking Lot	Elena Gallegos Picnic Area–Cottonwood Springs	
Fees	$1 weekdays, $2 weekends	

IF YOU WANT A longer hike or one that visits all the landscapes of the Elena Gallegos Picnic Area (EGPA), this one is for you. This perimeter hike follows the trail along the outer edge of the EGPA while utilizing several trails within it, as well as Trail 365 just outside the Open Space boundary to close the loop on the western edge. This hike captures all the various landscapes and their ecosystems included in the previous four hikes: it explores the outwash fan in the north, weaves along the grassy hills in the south and middle, cuts through the popular Pino Trail area, and skirts the mountain's

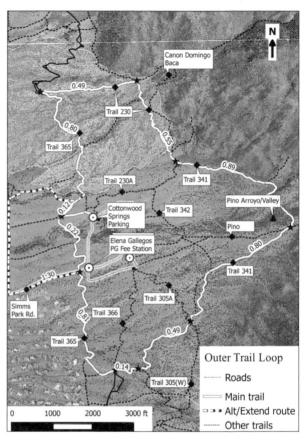

toes to the west, all the while climbing the small hills and crossing arroyo channels throughout the park.

All of the trails along this route are in good to excellent shape, creating a route that is not only easy to follow, but technically easy to walk. In fact, they are in such good condition that many of these trails are also popular with trail runners. Cyclists also like them, but with so many great trails around this area, the number of riders is small.

■ THE HIKE

Park in the EGPA–Cottonwood Springs parking area.

Take Trail 230A left (west) from the parking lot to meet up with Trail 365 (0.17 mile).

Turn right (north) onto Trail 365 and follow about 0.9 mile to Trail 230.

Turn right (east) onto Trail 230 and follow about 0.5 mile.

At the Trail 230/Domingo Baca Trail junction, turn right (south), staying on Trail 230 for another 0.5 mile to the Trail 341 junction.

Turn left (east) onto Trail 341 and follow to the Pino Trail junction, 0.9 mile.

Continue straight on Trail 341, which seamlessly turns into Trail 342, for another 0.8 mile, to the Trail 305A intersection.

Veer right onto Trail 305A and follow about 0.5 mile to the Trail 305 junction.

Turn right at the Trail 305A/305 intersection, staying on Trail 305A for a short 0.14 mile.

Continue straight onto Trail 365 at the Trail 365/305A/366 junction and follow it 0.8 mile as it turns north to lead back to EGPA–Simms Park Road.

Cross the road and follow Trail 365 to the Trail 230A junction, 0.3 mile.

Turn right (east) onto Trail 230A and follow it 0.2 mile back to the parking area.

ALTERNATE ROUTE: EXTENDED LOOP INCLUDING WESTERN FENCE LINE TRAIL

Difficulty: 3

Distance: 6.7 miles round-trip

Hiking Time: 2–4 hours for loop

Elevation: 440 ft. gain; peak elevation: 6,760 ft. (same as for main route)

The longer loop leaves Trail 365 early to turn west and travel along the western fence line.

IF YOU LIKE THIS HIKE, try **HIKE 28: Elena Gallegos Inner Trail Loop** or any of the other hikes that leave from EGPA. If the longer hike through the foothills is the attraction, try **HIKE 18: Trail 365–Sandia Peak Tram to Embudito Trailhead**, **HIKE 41: Trail 365–Comanche Road to I-40**, or **HIKE 42: Trail 401–Piedra Lisa Canyon to Hilldale Mound**.

FOR THOSE USING GPS DATA (DATUM: WGS 84)

Intersection of Trail 230A and Trail 356: –106.475853, 35.165937

Intersection of Trail 365 and Trail 230: –106.47761, 35.175877

Intersection of Trail 230 and Domingo Baca Trail: –106.466863, 35.171032

Intersection of Trail 230A and Trail 341: –106.468331, 35.168226

Intersection of Trail 341 with the Pino Trail: –106.456854, 35.165121

Intersection of Trail 341, Trail 305, and Trail 305W: –106.4652, 35.157506

Intersection of Trail 365 with Trail 366: –106.471502, 35.15356

History of the Elena Gallegos Picnic Area

This well-known land was first issued to Captain Diego Montoya by Spain in the late 1600s as part of a seventy-thousand-acre land grant. In about 1716, Montoya passed away and the property came into the ownership of Elena Gallegos, for whom the grant was later named. It's not clear why this transfer took place, but most likely, he sold or gave it to her. Some historians suggest that they were in love. Although distant relatives, they reportedly shared a large residence in Bernalillo, New Mexico, currently known as La Hacienda de la Luna but originally called the Montoya-Gallegos House.

After Elena died in 1731, the grant passed to her son, Antonio Gurulé. Thirty years later, after his death, the land was distributed to his many heirs. A large portion of the eastern area (foothills and mountain areas) was preserved as rangeland shared by the heirs. By the late 1800s, more than three hundred families were living on and working the granted lands.

In 1932, Albert G. Simms, a former US Congressman, purchased a large portion of the Grant and continued the tradition of working the land as a ranch. Upon his death in 1964, the majority of the Simms lands passed on to his heir, while about twelve thousand acres was bequeathed to the Albuquerque Academy. In 1982, the City of Albuquerque made a complex purchase of part of this property. These are the lands we use today in the Elena Gallegos Picnic Area and Albert G. Simms Park.

ELENA GALLEGOS INNER TRAIL LOOP

Difficulty	2	
Distance	3.4 mi (5.5 km) loop	
Hiking Time	1–2 hours	
Elevation	240 ft. gain (74 m)	Peak elevation: 6,560 ft. (2,000 m) at Trail 342/341 junction; Low elevation: 6,320 ft. (1,926 m) along Trail 365
Trail Condition	Excellent–Good	Open Space– and USFS-owned and -maintained
Trail Users	Hikers, bikers, and horses	
Best Time	Spring through fall	
Parking Lot	Elena Gallegos Picnic Area–Cottonwood Springs	
Fees	$1 weekdays, $2 weekends	

THE INNER TRAILS of the Elena Gallegos Picnic Area (EGPA) are popular for picnic area users, field trip groups, hikers, bikers, and trail runners. Their fame resides in the vast, open grassy-hill landscape so often associated with the Sandia Foothills area. The gently rolling terrain is easy to walk, with wide, hard-packed sandy trail surfaces, all the while never being too far from the park's amenities. In wet seasons, the grass blankets the landscape in various shades of green, while in the dry seasons, it turns a pale yellow that almost glows, even on the cloudiest days. Although these trails are cut through large swaths of grass, hikers will find that as they explore the delicate clumps of ground cover, they are weaving around trees, cacti, and yuccas, a beautiful example of the Upper Sonoran life zone.

This set of trails has the fewest steep hills and least elevation change, making this a popular area for those seeking an easier hike. However, don't be confused and think it will be flat. This area is the heart of the outwash plain, which slopes gently from the base of the mountains in the east toward the city in the west. Although you may not notice the long and consistent slight uphill grade, by the end of the hike, your legs will likely be aware of it.

A wonderful side trip is to visit Cottonwood Springs Trail, located

in the center of this loop. This paved trail has a variety of visitor-friendly features such as shade and a bench, but most important, it leads to a pond and blind that often has ducks and other wetland animals enjoying the water.

■ **THE HIKE**

Park in the EGPA–Cottonwood Springs parking area.

Take Trail 230A right (east) from the parking lot to meet up with Trail 342 (0.4 mile).

Turn right (south) onto Trail 342. You will pass the Pino Trail at 0.3 mile and reach the intersection with Trail 341 after another 0.25 mile.

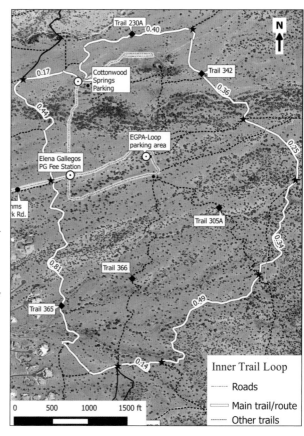

Continue on Trail 342 by turning right at the Trail 341/342 intersection and follow it for another 0.3 mile to the Trail 342/305A/305(W) intersection.

Continue straight onto Trail 305A. Follow this trail until it intersects with/ends at Trail 365 (0.6 mile).

Turn right onto Trail 365 and follow it back to Trail 230A. Trail 365 crosses Simms Park Road at 0.8 mile, then continues another 0.4 mile to reach Trail 230A.

Turn right onto Trail 230A and follow it 0.17 mile back to the parking area.

IF YOU LIKE THIS HIKE, try **HIKE 24: Grassy Hills Loop**. Or try **HIKE 27: Elena Gallegos**

Outer Trail Loop for a longer loop that covers more of the picnic area or **HIKE 31: Academy Camp Loop** for another area full of grassy hills.

FOR THOSE USING GPS DATA
(DATUM: WGS 84)
Junction of Trail 230A and Trail 342: –106.467724, 35.166048
Intersection of Trail 341, Trail 305, and Trail 305W: –106.4652, 35.157506
Intersection of Trail 365 and Trail 366: –106.471502, 35.15356
Intersection of Trail 230A and Trail 356: –106.475853, 35.165937

Cottonwood Springs Trail–ADA Trail

Trails that can accommodate visitors with physical disabilities are rare in the Sandia Mountains or its foothills; however, the Cottonwood Springs Trail on the north boundary of the Elena Gallegos Picnic Area fits the bill. This trail was constructed for hikers of all ages and skill levels, with specific designs to accommodate visitors in wheelchairs, meeting Americans with Disabilities Act (ADA) standards. Parking and toilets are available at the Cottonwood Springs parking area, next to the Kiwanis Reservation Area. Along with the trail, this large reservation area is also wheelchair-accessible.

Beyond the relaxed nature of the wide, paved Cottonwood Springs Trail, two popular features along the route attract hikers and visitors from around the park: a series of shaded rest stops with original artwork by Margy O'Brien (an esteemed local nature artist), and

a pond surrounded by cattails, willows, and a variety of other wetland species. A beautiful wildlife blind allows hikers and other visitors to peek at the pond through small openings in the hope of spotting some of the more common wildlife that frequent this rare water source. Spending a leisurely hour observing the artwork, exploring the surrounding landscape, and watching the wild residents of the pond is delightful for people of all ages and hiking abilities.

NORTH LEVEE/TRAIL 305 LOOP

Difficulty	3	
Distance	2.96 mi (4.8 km) loop	
Hiking Time	45–90 minutes	
Elevation	260 ft. gain (78 m)	Peak elevation: 6,440 ft. (1,962 m) at Trail 305/gravel road; Low elevation: 6,180 ft. (1,884 m) at Michial Emery Trailhead parking
Trail Condition	Excellent–Good	Privately and USFS-owned and -maintained
Trail Users	Hikers, bikers, and horses	
Best Time	Spring through fall	
Parking Lot	Michial Emery Trailhead	
Fees	None	

SPECIAL INFORMATION: The Michial Emery Trailhead parking lot is located on private land and is owned and maintained by the High Desert Homeowners Association. The first section of the Michial Emery Trail is also on private land.

THIS LOOP ROUTE starts at the Michial Emery Trailhead in the classic foothills landscape. It heads north toward the Elena Gallegos Picnic Area (EGPA), where it turns east and returns to the Bear Arroyo. Once back in the Bear Arroyo Watershed, the route crosses through several deep arroyos, providing a completely new landscape to experience. As hikers climb up and down over the tall hills, gaining a feeling of solitude is easy, even though civilization is not far away. Especially along Trail 305, the landscape feels wild, with the tallest hills on the route, open space, and a variety of bird-songs that aren't drowned out by traffic noise.

The landscape near the parking area is gently rolling hills covered in a relatively thick mat of grasses interspersed with all the common desert species of cacti, yuccas, and the occasional tree and bush. As the route gains elevation, more trees and bushes dot the hills, while the landscape character shifts slightly as the arroyo

ALTERNATE/EXTENDED ROUTE TO ELENA GALLEGOS PICNIC AREA LOOP ROAD

Difficulty: 3
Distance: 4.4-mile loop
Hiking Time: 1–2 hours
*Elevation:*320 ft. gain; peak elevation: 6,500 ft., along Trail 305(W)
No bikes allowed on Trail 305(W). Use Trail 305A as non-Wilderness alternate.

channels become more deeply cut into the outwash plain, creating a landscape that is less gentle, with taller and steeper hills. This increase in relief characterizes the trails closer to the mountains, making them just a little bit more strenuous to hike and providing vastly different fauna to watch for. A noticeable effect of the taller hills and deeper channels is a nearly complete reduction in city noise and fewer views of other trail users.

The Michial Emery Trail, the levee trail, and Trail 365 are popular routes that can be accessed from either the

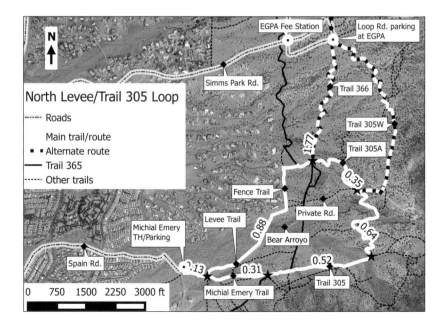

North Levee/Trail 305 Loop

----- Roads
Main trail/route
■ ■ Alternate route
—— Trail 365
----- Other trails

N

EGPA Fee Station
Loop Rd. parking at EGPA
Simms Park Rd.
Trail 366
Trail 305W
Trail 305A
1.77
0.35
Fence Trail
Private Rd.
Levee Trail
0.88
Bear Arroyo
0.64
Michial Emery TH/Parking
Spain Rd.
0.13
0.31
0.52
Trail 305
Michial Emery Trail

0   750   1500 2250 3000 ft

Michial Emery or the Embudito Trailhead parking area. These and a lot of other, unnamed trails crisscross the gently rolling, grass-covered hills. Although not entirely desolate, the trails in the higher elevations are lesser-used and have more space available for people to spread out. On weekdays, this area has an almost desolate feel to it, in stark contrast to the much busier weekends. Early-morning hikes on any day may lead to views of deer as they browse the upper watershed area or coyotes engaging in their favorite activity: hunting rabbits.

■ **THE HIKE**

Park in the Michial Emery Trailhead parking area.

Start on the Michial Emery Trail, turning left (east) out of the parking area and hiking 0.13 mile toward the mountains.

Cross into the USFS land at the fence. Immediately turn left and head up the hill and walk along the "levee" that leads

to the northeast. Staying to the left, turn north and cross the gravel road to follow the private/USFS boundary line, marked with a fence. Continue along the fence line a short distance, then turn right onto the first major trail that heads east. Follow this until you reach the Trail 365/366/305A junction (0.88 mile).

Continue straight onto Trail 305A. Staying to the right, veer onto Trail 305 and proceed up the hill (veering to the south) and across the gravel road (0.35 mile).

Continue on Trail 305 for about 0.64 mile, crossing several deep arroyo channels.

Staying on Trail 305, turn right (west) as the trail nears the base of the mountains. Continue west about 1 mile back to the parking area. Trail 305 seamlessly turns into Trail 365. After a short distance on Trail 365, veer right onto the Michial Emery Trail to continue west. (Trail 365 veers to the south at this intersection.) Stay on the Michial Emery Trail until you reach the parking area.

Outwash Plains: It's All About the Sediment

The massive size of the foothills' outwash plain could only have been made possible by a lot of mountain sediment. As the Sandia Mountains began to form ten to fifteen million years ago, they were tilted, crushed, and fractured as enormous sections of basement rock rubbed against each other, shifted, and simply broke apart. Eventually watersheds formed. As stream channels developed, they began carrying immense amounts of sediment out of the mountains. Along these paths, the streams sorted the rock debris, carrying the largest rocks just beyond the edge of the mountains while transporting the smallest (sand grains) all the way to the Rio Grande. Over time, the large piles of debris at the edge of the mountains became connected as they filled the area between the mountain

front and the river, forming the outwash plain that we see today.

In the hiking area, the outwash plain is at its steepest, ranging from 6 to 10 percent in grade. As the plain extends through the city to the Rio Grande, the sediment composing the plain decreases in size, corresponding with the grade, which lessens to 3 to 6 percent near the river. The ephemeral streams, also known as arroyos, continually rearranged the sediments, cutting into the plain, forming deep channels and/or floodplains. Due to the inexhaustible supply of sediment and the steep slope of the plain, flows in these high-energy arroyos are dangerous. This is obvious because the water usually looks like flowing chocolate: thick, brown, and turbulent.

IF YOU LIKE THIS HIKE, try **HIKE 24: Grassy Hills Loop** or **HIKE 31: Academy Camp Loop** for grassy landscapes. If the Michial Emery Trailhead parking area is full, hikers can access much of the same terrain from the EGPA with **HIKE 26: Bear Arroyo Loop from Elena Gallegos Picnic Area.**

FOR THOSE USING GPS DATA
(DATUM: WGS 84)
Michial Emery Trail at the private/public
boundary: −106.480411, 35.145693

Intersection of Trail 365 with Trail 305A:
−106.471487, 35.153629
Trail 305 as it crosses the private Academy
Camp Road: −106.467681, 35.151708
Trail 305 corner: −106.466373, 35.147209
Intersection of Trail 365 and Michial Emery Trail:
−106.475193, 35.145828

MOUNTAIN BASE LOOP FROM MICHIAL EMERY TRAILHEAD

Difficulty	3	
Distance	2.01 mi (3.2 km) loop	
Hiking Time	45–90 minutes	
Elevation	300 ft. gain (91 m)	Peak elevation: 6,480 ft. (1,975 m) at farthest point; Low elevation: 6,180 ft .(1,884 m) at Michial Emery trailhead parking
Trail Condition	Good	Privately and USFS-owned. Most trails unmaintained
Trail Users	Hikers, bikers, and horses	Bikes and horses are rare along the trails at the base of the mountains
Best Time	Late spring through fall	
Parking Lot	Michial Emery Trailhead	
Fees	None	

SPECIAL INFORMATION: The Michial Emery Trailhead parking lot is located on private land and owned and maintained by the High Desert Homeowners Association. The first section of the Michial Emery Trail is also on private land.

THIS OFF-THE-BEATEN-PATH loop is relatively short and follows one of the most distinct features in this area: a small trail along the base of the mountains. The mountain base trail is narrow and unmarked and may take a little bit of exploring to find, as sediment coming out the mountains sometimes covers it up. But, once found, it climbs a little way up the mountainside while heading east toward the back of the foothills area and the Bear Arroyo Watershed. Although views along the trail are continually either up at the Sandia Mountains or down at the city, depending on the direction hiked, it is really the view to the north—of the Elena Gallegos Picnic Area and the whole northern outwash plain—that makes this route special. This fantastic vista highlights the gentle slope of the plain as it extends from the base of the Sandia Mountains until it is covered with houses in the west. From this vantage point, hikers can also see the larger trails such as Trail 365 and Trail 305 as they cross up and over the small hills and valleys.

This trail is much narrower than the well-worn Trail 365 or 305, and it is far less used. Its channel crossings, steep, rocky sections with abrupt dips, and deeply shaded sections that stay icy throughout the winter make it less appealing to both bike riders and trail runners and keep the crowds low overall.

Either hiking direction works well for this loop. If hiking the mountain base trail first, return along the well-graded Trail 305 for a quick and easy return to the parking area. Or hikers can make this an out-and-back by using only the mountain trail in both directions. Nearby trails make this loop easy to cut short or to extend. The option described above adds length to the hike primarily by extending the hike along the base of the mountains; it leads to the back edge of the foothills area, near the privately owned Bear Canyon mouth.

■ THE HIKE

Park in the Michial Emery Trailhead parking area.

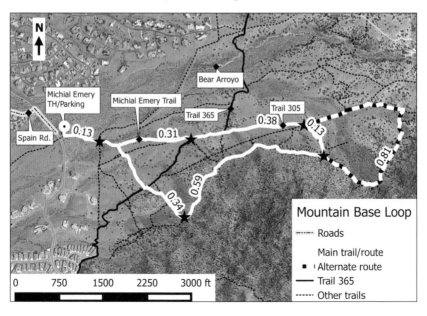

Start on the Michial Emery Trail, turning left (east) out of the parking area and hiking toward the mountains (0.13 mile). Cross into the USFS land and continue on the Michial Emery Trail for a short distance. After crossing the arroyo, this trail gradually climbs a small hill to its right (south). Turn right (south) onto the first trail (unmarked) to climb up to the ridge of this small hill. Continue to follow it toward the mountains to the south. This trail will cross Trail 365 and pick up on the other side (about 0.34 mile).

As the unmarked trail approaches the mountains, it can become intermittent because of rocks and sand washing down from the slopes. Look up to find the trail that runs 30 to 40 feet above the base of the mountains. Turn left (east) onto the mountain trail and follow for about 0.6 mile to where it ends at a larger, well-worn but unnamed trail.

Turn left (north) and follow this unnamed trail a short distance downhill to Trail 305.

Turn left (west) onto Trail 305, which seamlessly turns into Trail 365 before veering onto the Michial Emery Trail and returning to the parking area (about 1 mile).

ALTERNATE/EXTENDED MOUNTAIN BASE ROUTE

Difficulty: 3
Distance: 2.8-mile loop
Hiking Time: 1–2 hours
Elevation: 380 ft. gain; peak elevation: 6,560 ft.
  at farthest point
This alternate route extends the amount of trail hiking along the base of the mountains before looping back to Trail 305.

IF YOU LIKE THIS HIKE, try **HIKE 25: Pino Arroyo Loop** or **HIKE 23: Domingo Baca Outwash Fan–North EGPA Loop**, which both hike through similar topography.

FOR THOSE USING GPS DATA
(DATUM: WGS 84)
Intersection of Trail 365 and the small trail
  that leads up to the base of the mountains:
    −106.478757, 35.143089

Northern Aspects and Frozen Ground

In the wintertime, snowfall on the foothill trails (and throughout the city) generally melts within a few hours, even when the air temperatures are hovering around freezing. This is due to the warming effects of the sun, which heats up the ground during the day and keeps most of the soil from freezing. During long-lasting cold spells, the ground will freeze everywhere, but once the daytime temperatures rise, the sunnier slopes quickly thaw.

Slope aspect, however, plays a major role in determining duration and extent of frozen soils in the foothills. The north-facing slopes are particularly susceptible to freezing and staying frozen for the entire winter. The boundary between a frozen, icy slope and an unfrozen, sometimes muddy one can be just a couple of feet, as a trail turns sharply on a curving hill. The north-facing mountain base trail is one of these cold slopes that stays frozen throughout the winter and into spring. Because it and other slopes with a northern aspect don't warm up until the nighttime temperatures are consistently above freezing, the best time to hike them is late spring, after the ground has thawed and the soils have had a chance to dry out a bit.

ACADEMY CAMP LOOP

Difficulty	2	
Distance	2.6 mi (4.2 km) loop	
Hiking Time	45–90 minutes	
Elevation	300 ft. gain (91 m)	Peak elevation: 6,480 ft. (1,975 m) at farthest point; Low elevation: 6,180 ft. (1,884 m) at Michial Emery Trailhead parking
Trail Condition	Excellent–Good	Privately- and USFS-owned; Maintained
Trail Users	Hikers, bikers, and horses	
Best Time	Fall through spring	
Parking Lots	Michial Emery Trailhead	
Fees	None	

SPECIAL INFORMATION: The Michial Emery Trailhead parking lot is on private land owned and maintained by the High Desert Homeowners Association. The first section of the Michial Emery Trail is also on private land.

IN TIGHT COMPETITION with **hike 24: Grassy Hills Loop**, this route explores one of the best examples of classic foothills by following a long string of small ridges filled with native grama grasses. This route heads due east, directly toward the back of the foothills area where Bear Canyon exits the mountains at the Albuquerque Academy mountain camp. Here, at the farthest portion of the loop, the trail climbs up a short, grassy hill that overlooks the gravel road leading to the camp buildings and the privately owned canyon mouth. From this vantage point, the primary trail feature is the elongated, east–west trending ridgeline that leads almost uninterrupted all the way back to the parking area. A series of small hills compose this ridgeline trail, created as a series of east–west flowing arroyos cut into the outwash plain sediments. Because the surface wasn't extensively eroded, it is relatively smooth, and typically covered in grass with sporadically growing trees and cacti.

The outward-going or uphill route follows well-worn trails with good signs: from the Michial Emery Trail to Trail 365 to Trail 305. From Trail 305, a small, unnamed trail veers off to continue leading to the east and up to the camp/road overlook hill. The return route follows the grassy ridgeline back to the parking area. This enjoyable trail runs almost the entire length of these grassy hills; it is small and has no name, but is in good condition.

■ THE HIKE

Park in the Michial Emery Trailhead parking area.

Start on the Michial Emery Trail, turning left (east) out of the parking area toward the mountains (0.13 mile).

Cross into the USFS land and continue straight on the Michial Emery Trail for another 0.3 mile until it ends at Trail 365.

Turn left (east) onto Trail 365 and continue east. At about 0.4 mile, Trail 365

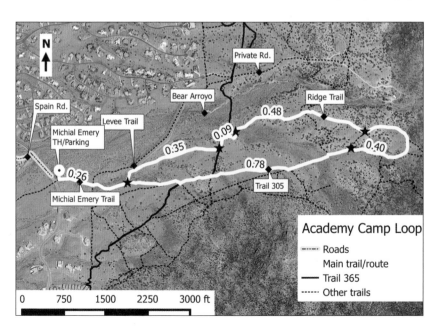

turns north, while Trail 305 is straight ahead, continuing to lead to the east.

Continue straight onto Trail 305. After a short distance (0.3 mile), veer left to stay on the trail, which descends a steep hill into a wide arroyo valley.

At the far edge of the arroyo valley (0.2 mile), veer to the right (east) and ascend on a small unnamed trail. (Note: Trail 305 continues to the left and also ascends out of the arroyo valley.)

Stay on the unnamed trail. When it reaches the top of the hill, it continues to the right toward the base of the mountains, then loops around to the left, never climbing into the mountains (0.4 mile).

After looping back toward the west, the trail overlooks a gravel road and some private buildings (the Academy Camp) on the right. Continue west, staying on top of the hill. Veer right on a small unnamed trail that continues to follow the nose of the ridgeline to the right (about 0.25 mile).

As this small trail crosses Trail 305, it descends onto a lower area of the hill, still following the ridgeline. Continue until it descends into the arroyo valley and joins up with Trail 365 (about 0.45 mile).

Turn left onto Trail 365 and follow for a short distance (0.1 mile) as it climbs back up a small hill.

Grama Grass

Many hikers come to the wide-open foothills to walk the plains and see the grasses blowing in the wind. Three of the many common grama grasses native to the foothills area are blue grama, black grama, and sideoats grama. These delicate grasses are high-value feed for cattle, which is likely why this area was initially used as rangeland. Today, they provide food for a variety of wildlife, such as deer, rodents, and birds including grouse and quail. All three of these grasses grow with their seed heads extending up from a mass of leaves that stay relatively close to the ground. Growing collectively and side by side throughout the foothills, they are easiest to identify using their seed heads.

Blue grama is likely the most easily identified native foothills grass, as it has a distinctive curled seed head when mature. This grass typically grows in clumps less than half a foot tall with a purplish seed stalk that fades to a white-yellow color and curls, looking like a bushy tail. These curled seed heads have become an iconic symbol in this area, and are pictured on the High Desert Residential

Owners Association signs. Black grama is similar in appearance to the blue variety, with two exceptions: its seed head does not curl, and the plant grows into a ring over the years as the middle of the clump dies back and runners send up new shoots. Sideoats grama grows the tallest of the three, one to two feet above the ground, with the main plant looking similar to the other grama grasses, just a little taller and bushier. However, its seeds are distinctive from the other grasses: they are attached individually and to only one side of the stem, the source of the plant's name.

Turn right onto the smaller hilltop trail and continue to hike west toward the parking lot (0.35 mile). This trail gradually descends back into the arroyo valley, then turns left and joins up with the Michial Emery Trail.

Turn right onto the Michial Emery Trail and follow it back to the parking lot.

IF YOU LIKE THIS HIKE, try **HIKE 24: Grassy Hills Loop** or **HIKE 28: Elena Gallegos Inner Trail Loop**, both of which explore grassy lands just to the north in the EGPA.

FOR THOSE USING GPS DATA
(DATUM: WGS 84)
Intersection with alternate trail for small loop
  option: –106.46502, 35.147564
Ridgeline trail near Academy Camp:
  –106.464194, 35.148354
Intersection of Ridgeline trail with Trail 365:
  –106.471926, 35.148252
Restart of Ridgeline trail from Trail 365:
  –106.472887, 35.147469
Intersection of the Michial Emery Trail with the
  small Ridgeline Trail: –106.478282, 35.145782

BEAR CANYON OVERLOOK

BEAR CANYON OVERLOOK

Difficulty	4	Relatively steep, rocky mountain climb to overlook area. Some route-finding.
Distance	3.8 mi (6.1 km) round-trip	
Hiking Time	1.5–3 hours	
Elevation	820 ft. gain (250 m)	Peak elevation: 7,000 ft. (2,134 m) at overlook; Low elevation: 6,180 ft. (1,884 m) at Michial Emery Trailhead parking lot
Trail Condition	Good–fair on overlook climb	Privately and USFS-owned; Unmaintained
Trail Users	Hikers and horses	
Best Time	Late spring through fall	
Parking Lot	Michial Emery Trailhead	
Fees	None	

SPECIAL INFORMATION: The Michial Emery Trailhead parking lot is on private land owned and maintained by the High Desert Homeowners Association. The first section of the Michial Emery Trail is also on private land.

THE BEAR CANYON OVERLOOK route
is an often-solitary hike that ascends a
small mountain trail to the overlook for
Bear Arroyo to the west and the headwaters of Bear Canyon to the east. The
trail is small, a bit rocky, fairly steep, but
luckily the overlook is only about half
a mile along it. The views during the
climb and at the overlook are spectacular, and are very much worth the effort
of climbing up. A pile of large boulders marks the overlook spot, which is
located just beyond a small saddle along
the ridgeline. This overlook has unobstructed views of the foothills area and
into the upper Bear Canyon Watershed
with the larger Sandia Mountains in the
background.

After a short break at the overlook
location, the return route is the same as
the incoming route. Two trails near the
overlook can be a lure for hikers who
want to do a little more exploring. Hikers
might continue up the ridge, heading in
a southerly direction from the overlook

on a smaller trail that ascends to the
southern ridgeline (the North Embudito
Watershed ridge). Or they could leave the
ridge at the little saddle, heading east near
the overlook to explore upper Bear Canyon. Neither of these routes is covered in
this guide; both require some amount of
route-finding skill and should be taken
seriously. Bringing extra water, some
food, and the traditional mountain hiking
equipment described in the Introduction
will make for a more pleasant exploratory
hike.

■ **THE HIKE**

Park in the Michial Emery Trailhead parking area.

Start on the Michial Emery Trail,
turning left (east) out of the parking area
toward the mountains (0.13 mile).

Cross into the USFS land and continue straight on the Michial Emery Trail
for another 0.3 mile until it ends at Trail
365.

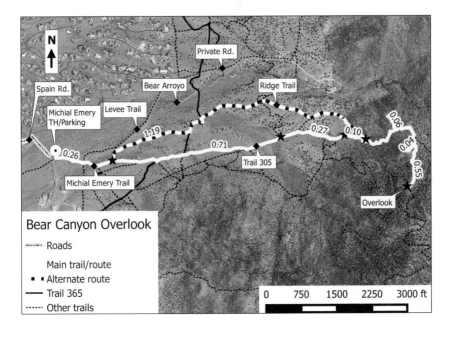

Bear Canyon Overlook

----- Roads
　　　Main trail/route
■ ■ Alternate route
——— Trail 365
----- Other trails

Turn left (east) onto Trail 365 and continue east. At about 0.4 mile, Trail 365 turns north while Trail 305 is straight ahead, continuing to lead to the east.

Continue straight onto Trail 305. After a short distance (0.3 mile), veer left and descend a steep hill into a wide arroyo valley to stay on Trail 305.

At the far edge of the arroyo valley (0.2 mile), veer to the right (east) and ascend on a small unnamed trail. (Note: Trail 305 continues to the left and also ascends out of the arroyo valley.)

Continue right on the unnamed trail to the top of the grassy hill and continue to head east. (This is the Academy Camp trail.) As the trail approaches the base of the mountains, look for one of two side trails that veers to the right/toward the mountains. The first trail veers right, just before the Academy Camp trail starts to turn to the left. If you miss it, stay on the Academy Camp trail a little farther; after it crosses a small channel/arroyo, look for the next trail that turns right. These two trails join after a short distance.

After a short distance, the route begins to climb steeply up the mountain toward the overlook. Two "false overlooks" can lead hikers astray; it may require some

backtracking and route-finding to reach the higher overlook area. About halfway to the overlook area, the trail reaches a small bench and then follows the ridgeline to a small saddle. Just beyond is the pile of boulders/overlook area (0.5 mile on the main trail). Return to the parking area along the same route.

IF YOU LIKE THIS HIKE, try either **HIKE 37: Embudito Canyon Overlook Loop** or **HIKE 22: Pino Trail to the Dead Trees**. Both these hikes climb up the lower mountains to wonderful overlooks and views of the mountains, but from the south and north of this one. Another relatively easy small-trail mountain hike is **hike 44: Candelaria Bench Loop**.

FOR THOSE USING GPS DATA
(DATUM: WGS 84)
Intersection of the Michial Emery Trail with the small Ridgeline Trail: –106.478282, 35.145782
Location where the small Academy Camp trail veers off from Trail 305: –106.466316, 35.14724
Location where the small trail leading to the overlook veers east off of the Academy Camp Trail: –106.461797, 35.14739
Overlook area: –106.457275, 35.144519

Connecting to Embudito Canyon/Trail

If you look carefully at the Bear Canyon Overlook, a very small trail continues to climb up through the trees and up the ridgeline to the south. This may best be described as a deer trail and is a little hard to follow. But it continues up this ridgeline leading into the dense piñon–ponderosa pine forest. Eventually, as it continues in a southerly direction, it will lead hikers to **HIKE 39: Embudito North Ridge Trail Loop**. Although this sounds easy, the ridgeline is fairly steep, and finding the correct route at the top can take a little effort. But the reward is worth it: this small side trail creates a beautiful loop option, joining Bear Arroyo with the larger Embudito Watershed.

A word of warning: although this route doesn't go too high or too far back into the mountains, it does present a fair chance to get lost. The Embudito North Ridge has a surprising number of trails, some in good shape, some not, but their presence alone increases the risk of taking an erroneous turn. As such, this extension is recommended only for hikers with some trail-finding experience, a map of the area, good map-reading skills, and extra endurance. Anyone who pursues it should have extra time and be prepared for mountain conditions, with a GPS and the remaining Ten Essentials outlined in the Introduction.

33 MIDDLE BEAR ARROYO LOOPS FROM MICHIAL EMERY TRAILHEAD

MIDDLE BEAR ARROYO LOOPS FROM MICHIAL EMERY TRAILHEAD

Difficulty	1	
Distance	3 mi (4.8 km) loop	
Hiking Time	45–90 minutes	
Elevation	280 ft. loss (85 m) from Trail 365 to Tramway	Peak elevation: 6,240 ft. (1,902 m) at Embudito Trailhead; Low elevation: 5,960 ft. (1,817 m) at Tramway Bridge
Trail Condition	Good	Privately, Open Space–, and USFS-owned; Some unmaintained
Trail Users	Hikers, bikers, and horses	
Best Time	Fall through spring	
Parking Lots	Michial Emery Trailhead	
Fees	None	

SPECIAL INFORMATION: A large portion of this hike is on private property sandwiched between different housing units of the High Desert Homeowners Association.

THE BEAR ARROYO area is a surprisingly interesting place to hike and explore, and is a wonderful example of how private and governmental interests have worked together to keep this natural corridor open for public and wildlife use. The Bear Arroyo floodplain is a fully connected wildlife corridor from the mouth of the canyon at the edge of the steep mountains to the John B. Robert Dam near Juan Tabo Boulevard. It is mostly contained within public lands, but passes through the privately owned High Desert residential neighborhood near the Michial Emery Trailhead before turning back into public lands for the remaining downstream distance to the dam. With such good connection to the mountains, many wild animals visit this corridor, even though houses surround it. This little bit of untamed land within the city is a blessing to animals and birds and showcases how thoughtful urban expansion can coexist successfully with our adaptable wild neighbors.

This area has the normal array of desert grasses, cacti, yuccas, and a few trees, but because it is also an active arroyo system with a large, undeveloped floodplain, it also has a dense and wide

ALTERNATE/SHORTER ROUTE: CUTOFF TRAIL VIA THE POND TRAIL

Difficulty: 1
Distance: 1.8-mile loop trip, same difficulty
Hiking Time: 30–60 minutes
Elevation: 120 ft. gain; lowest point is 6,120 ft. near pond

ALTERNATE PARKING

Embudito Trailhead parking lot (6,240 ft. elevation)

growth of desert bushes, especially along the two arroyos that join in this open space. The long lines of chamisa and Apache plume plants draw a surprising number of wild creatures—deer, coyotes, a variety of rodents—but more impressive is the extremely large number of birds. Roadrunners are numerous here. Cactus wrens have recently moved in. The area is home to many other more common birds, such as hawks, ravens, quail, hummingbirds, robins, juncos, towhees, and too large an array of songbirds to name individually. Occasionally, most often in summer when the land is parched, small black bears roam this corridor searching for water and something to eat. The long historical occurrence of bears here is undoubtedly the source of its name.

Given this area's high usage, it is important to remember hiking safety, especially in inclement weather. With so many trail and road options, there is no good excuse to risk crossing a flowing arroyo; instead, wait out the flood or simply go around it using another trail. Flood waters flow fast and are particularly dangerous. Even shallow flows with one foot of water can sweep hikers off their feet.

Bull snake

■ THE HIKE

Park in the Michial Emery Trailhead parking area and turn left (east) onto the trail toward the mountains (0.13 mile).

Cross into the USFS land and turn right (south) onto the trail that follows the fence line (0.27 mile).

Continue south on Trail 365 after the fence trail joins Trail 365 (0.5 mile).

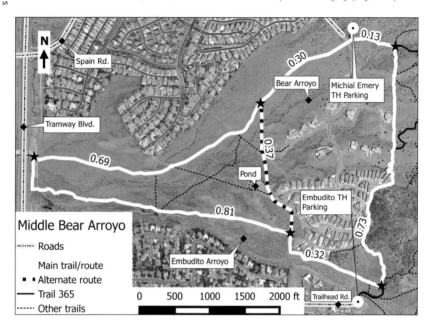

Michial Emery

The Michial Emery Trailhead is dedicated to and named after the man who played a principal part in developing the arroyo and Open Space system throughout the High Desert residential area. Mike was an engineer with the Bohannan Huston engineering firm when the project to develop the High Desert property got under way. As an avid outdoorsman, he preferred development that maintained the original character of the environment. He was especially interested in the Bear Arroyo Watershed, and was largely responsible for the innovative way the arroyo system throughout High Desert was designed. He sought input from the City of Albuquerque and the Albuquerque Metropolitan Arroyo Flood Control Authority (AMAFCA). The

resulting plan left many wild acres for native plants and animals to coexist within the community. Mike was a steward of this precious land and carefully nurtured its responsible development. His efforts helped the High Desert residential area realize a shared vision of sustainable development.

Today the High Desert Residential Owners Association owns and is responsible for maintaining the open spaces within the community, including the arroyos and the trailhead parking area. The Michial Emery Trailhead is located off High Desert Place NE. Take Spain Road to High Desert Place and turn right (south). The Trailhead parking lot is located on the left, just before the bridge.

After the housing unit but before the Embudito Trailhead parking lot, turn right (west) onto a small unmarked trail that leads into the Bear Arroyo Open Space area.

Continue on this west-facing trail until it reaches Tramway Boulevard (about 1 mile). At about 0.3 mile, it makes a hard right to follow the housing unit, then a hard left to follow the ridgeline to the west along the south side of the Open Space area. If the left turn is missed, the trail leads to the pond area.

Before crossing Tramway Boulevard, turn right (north) and follow either the paved trail next to the road or the small trail next to the arroyo toward the bridge. The shade under the bridge is always a nice break on this hike.

Turn right (east) onto the large unmarked trail on the northern edge of the Open Space and follow it back to the Michial Emery Trailhead parking area (about 1 mile). This large trail follows the north side of the Open Space area.

IF YOU LIKE THIS HIKE, try **HIKE 34: Lower Bear Arroyo Loops from John B. Robert Dam,** which explores the lower portion of this arroyo valley. For the upper watershed areas, try either **HIKE 29: North Levee/Trail 305 Loop** or **HIKE 26: Bear Arroyo Loop from Elena Gallegos Picnic Area,** which both take in the eastern area of this arroyo valley.

FOR THOSE USING GPS DATA (DATUM: WGS 84)
Michial Emery Trail at the private/public boundary and fence trail:
   –106.480411, 35.145693
Small unnamed trail that leads south into the Bear Arroyo area from Trail 365 near Embudito Trailhead: –106.497474, 35.141255
Southern ridgeline trail that leads straight toward Tramway Blvd.:
   –106.480858, 35.136615
Tramway Bridge over Bear Arroyo:
   –106.485209, 35.138548

LOWER BEAR ARROYO LOOPS FROM JOHN B. ROBERT DAM

Difficulty	1	
Distance	2.5 mi (4 km) loop	
Hiking Time	45–90 minutes	
Elevation	220 ft. gain (67 m) from dam to Tramway	Peak elevation: 5,960 ft. (1,817 m) at Tramway Bridge; Low elevation: 5,740 ft. (1,750 m) at dam
Trail Condition	Good	Privately, Open Space–, and AMAF-CA-owned; Unmaintained
Trail Users	Hikers, bikers, and horses	
Best Time	Fall through spring	
Parking Lot	John B. Robert Dam along Juan Tabo Blvd.	AMAFCA-owned
Fees	None	

THE CHARACTER OF THIS HIKE is closely related to **HIKE 33: Middle Bear Arroyo Loops from Michial Emery Trailhead**, with two important differences: the open space is narrower in this area and the riparian habitat is less complex and poorly retained compared to the high-quality habitat upstream of Tramway Boulevard. These differences result in less wildlife. Having said that, there are still animals here and this little bit of open space is easy to access and has a truly wild oasis feel. As with the open space uphill/upstream from Tramway Boulevard, residences are packed along the edge and densely line the hillside. Wide, well-used, packed sand trails abound in this area, with two main trails following the northern and southern edges of the open space. Regardless of these differences, this beloved area is popular with hikers and bikers, who are usually present at all times of the day, every day of the week.

As described in the previous entry,

avoid hiking in the arroyo when it is flowing. As little as one foot of water can sweep a hiker downstream. Also, this area contains the reservoir for the dam, which is designed to store flood waters temporarily. During large storm events, the water delivered by the arroyo may partially fill the area behind dam; avoid this reservoir when the ground is wet or muddy.

∎ THE HIKE

Park in front of the John B. Robert Dam along Juan Tabo Boulevard, or on a side street.

Walk up the well-used maintenance access road on the left (north) side of the dam. Do not walk up the face of the dam.

Once at the top of the access road, continue straight, descending along this road toward the arroyo bottom/reservoir area, and continue following it east to Tramway Boulevard (1.1 miles). Even if not planning to continue up into the Bear Arroyo

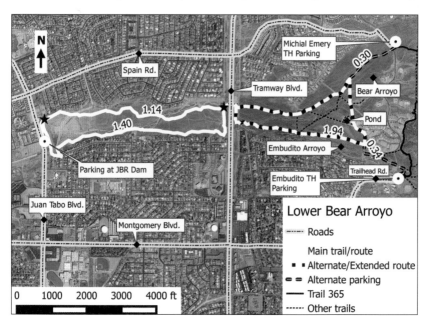

Lower Bear Arroyo

----- Roads

    Main trail/route

■ ■ Alternate/Extended route

● ● Alternate parking

—— Trail 365

----- Other trails

Open Space, the shade under the bridge is always a nice break on this hike.

Turn right just before the bridge and follow a small unmarked trail for a short distance south. This trail then turns back to the west at the southern edge of the floodplain. Follow it back to the south side of the dam (about 1.4 miles from Tramway Boulevard). Cross the dam and return to the parking area via the maintenance access road.

IF YOU LIKE THIS HIKE, try **HIKE 33: Middle Bear Arroyo Loops from Michial Emery Trailhead** to explore the portion of this arroyo valley just upstream from Tramway. Or try either **HIKE 29: North Levee/Trail 305 Loop** or **HIKE 26: Bear Arroyo Loop from Elena Gallegos Picnic Area**, which both pass through the upper section of the arroyo valley.

FOR THOSE USING GPS DATA
(DATUM: WGS 84)
Trail at John B. Robert Dam: –106.51573, 35.14007
Tramway Bridge over Bear Arroyo: –106.485209, 35.138548

ALTERNATE/LONGER ROUTE:
POND TRAIL LOOP

Difficulty: 1
Distance: Additional 2 miles to main loop
Hiking Time: Additional 30–60 minutes
Elevation: 380 ft. gain; highest point is 6,120 ft. near pond

ALTERNATE PARKING

Embudito Trailhead parking lot (6,240 ft. elevation)
Michial Emery Trailhead parking lot (6,180 ft. elevation)

John B. Robert Dam

The John B. Robert Dam is owned and operated by the Albuquerque Metropolitan Arroyo Flood Control Authority (AMAFCA). Designed and constructed in the 1970s, it is named after AMAFCA's first executive engineer, John B. Robert. The most notable feature of this dam is its emergency spillway or downstream face. This popular *Breaking Bad* landmark is covered in distinctive energy-dissipating baffles, concrete blocks that stick out of the dam face; when in use, they slow the speed of the flowing water. This dam is capable of fully detaining the rains from a 1 percent (one-hundred-year) storm; however, a storm greater than that could activate the emergency spillway, causing some downstream flooding. Normally this is a dry dam, which simply means that no water is stored behind it; instead, it is released immediately, but in a controlled manner. (Per New Mexico state regulations, all storm water must be released to the Rio Grande within ninety-six hours after a storm.) When the upstream watershed delivers runoff water to the reservoir area, it is routed through the dam via pipes to the downstream channel that eventually flows to the Rio Grande.

AMAFCA was formed in 1963, with specific responsibility for reducing existing and future flooding problems in the greater Albuquerque area. Although it is not part of their primary mission, AMAFCA works closely with other agencies in making land such as this reservoir area available for recreation. Hiking trails have been either built or publicly created along many of AMAFCA's engineered arroyo channels and other reservoirs located throughout the city. Even though this dam only holds water once in a great while, a permanent reservoir area is required. When dry, the land within the reservoir is perfect for hiking and biking. When wet, stay out.

TRAIL 365–LEVEE LOOP FROM EMBUDITO TRAILHEAD

Difficulty	2	
Distance	3 mi (4.8 km) loop	
Hiking Time	45–90 minutes	
Elevation	120 ft. gain (37 m)	Peak elevation: 6,360 ft. (1,939 m) at Trail 365/gravel road; Low elevation: 6,240 ft. (1,902 m) at Embudito Trailhead
Trail Condition	Good	Privately and Open Space–owned and -maintained
Trail Users	Hikers, bikers, and horses	
Best Time	Fall through spring	
Parking Lot	Embudito Trailhead	Parking lot is Open Space–maintained
Fees	None	

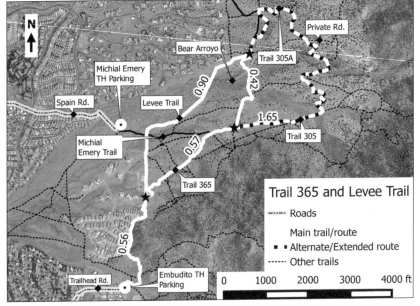

Trail 365 and Levee Trail

---- Roads

Main trail/route

■ ■ Alternate/Extended route

----- Other trails

0 1000 2000 3000 4000 ft

ALTHOUGH THIS LOLLIPOP-STYLE loop trail starts at the Embudito Trailhead, it utilizes a relatively large portion of Trail 365 while combining the South Fence and Levee Trails, two popular small trails that neighbor High Desert and the Michial Emery Trailhead parking area. This route travels through the classic foothills landscape that characterizes the Bear Arroyo Watershed: gently rolling hills covered in a relatively thick mat of grass. Along Trail 365, the route drops into the inner floodplain area of Bear Arroyo, which is full of classic desert plants such as chamisa and Apache plume. These bushes grow densely in the bottom of the arroyo, enough to fill the valley bottom and choke the trails.

Given the close proximity of the two large parking areas, these trails are popular, but with many trail options and plenty of space available, people naturally spread out and traffic jams or lines along the trails are rare. This short loop can easily

ALTERNATE/LONGER ROUTE:
TRAIL 305 ADDITION

Difficulty: 2
Distance: 4.25-mile loop
Hiking Time: 1.25–2 hours
Elevation: 200 ft. gain; highest point is 6,440 ft.
   at Trail 305/gravel road

be extended by adding Trail 305, which expands it to the east. This eastern leg of the larger loop is a less-used area of the foothills; with its steeper hills and deeper channels, hikers will feel a little bit of solitude even on busy days.

■ THE HIKE

Park at Embudito Trailhead parking area and start on Trail 365 at the north end.

Follow Trail 365 about 1.1 miles to the Trail 365/305 junction.

Turn left to continue on Trail 365. This section of trail descends into the Bear

Arroyo floodplain, then ascends to a private gravel road (about 0.4 mile).

Before crossing the road, make a hard left onto the unmarked levee trail, which leads back to the south. After crossing the Michial Emery Trail, it follows the fence line trail and ends at Trail 365, just before the latter enters the confined housing section (0.9 mile).

Continue south on Trail 365 and follow it about 0.5 mile back to the parking area.

IF YOU LIKE THIS HIKE, try **HIKE 29: North Levee/Trail 305 Loop** to explore more of this landscape or **HIKE 26: Bear Arroyo Loop from Elena Gallegos Picnic Area**, which hikes through similar topography.

FOR THOSE USING GPS DATA
(DATUM: WGS 84)
Intersection of Trail 365 with Trail 305A:
 −106.471487, 35.153629
Trail 365 at the private Academy Camp road:
 −106.472212, 35.150822

Apache Plume and Chamisa/Rabbitbrush

Two of our favorite shrubs thrive throughout Albuquerque and are especially common in the foothills: Apache plume and chamisa. Hikers will often find these drought-tolerant bushes growing right next to each other, especially in valley bottoms. Upon closer inspection, they will also notice that Apache plume flourishes on steep, rocky hillsides, while chamisa (also known as rabbitbrush) seems to grow thickest along the edges of and within arroyos. Luckily, these shrubs are easy to distinguish, and both truly thrive in the high-desert environment.

Apache plume, a true Southwest native, has little green leaves on stiff, woody branches, as this bush belongs to the rose family. Its habitat is valley bottoms and dry rocky slopes in piñon-juniper woodlands, up to 8,000 feet elevation. Its white blossoms in the spring are followed by small, seemingly delicate purplish-pink feathery seed heads. This shrub requires sandy, extremely well-drained soil to live: it cannot tolerate wet feet.

Chamisa, a bush with bold wintergreen-colored branches and bright-yellow blooms in late summer, belongs to the sunflower family. These bushes grow in thick clusters, with long, flexible branches that extend out of the ground. Like Apache plume, this native plant is found throughout the western United States, but chamisa also extends as far north as southwestern Canada. It is a hardy shrub that seems to like disturbed sandy soils such as those found along active arroyos.

MOUNTAIN BASE–ACADEMY CAMP LOOP FROM EMBUDITO TRAILHEAD

Difficulty	3	
Distance	4.2 mi (6.75 km) loop	
Hiking Time	1.25–2.5 hours	
Elevation	240 ft. gain (73 m)	Peak elevation: 6,480 ft. (1,975 m) at farthest point; Low elevation: 6,240 ft. (1,902 m) at Embudito Trailhead
Trail Condition	Excellent to good	USFS- and Open Space–owned; Most maintained
Trail Users	Hikers, bikers, and horses	
Best Time	Late spring through fall	
Parking Lot	Embudito Trailhead	Parking lot is Open Space–maintained
Fees	None	

THIS SLIGHTLY LONGER hike combines the trail along the base of the mountains from **HIKE 30: Mountain Base Loop from Michial Emery Trailhead** with the grassy ridgeline descent from **HIKE 31: Academy Camp Loop**, all the while leaving from the Embudito Trailhead parking area. The beauty of this hike is that it traverses lesser-used trails in both the lower mountains and the classic foothills area. Although a relatively easy hike, the trail in the lower-mountain area has some short rocky sections and a few steeper ups and downs and, of course, it is small. This section of the route has fantastic views to the north of the outwash plain and the southern lands of the Elena Gallegos Picnic Area. The hike leads to the back of the foothills area, where a few Albuquerque Academy Camp buildings can be seen at the mouth of Bear Canyon. This outer region is one of the least-used areas and hikers have a higher likelihood of seeing wildlife.

Along the entire route, hikers have views of the mountains, the city, and the northern foothills, making this a hike that feels open and remote. As is common in this area, the foothills landscape is characterized by gently rolling hills covered in a relatively thick mat of grasses interspersed with all the common desert species of cacti, yuccas, and the occasional tree and bush. The trees and bushes are just a little taller and bushier along the mountain base trail, with rockier soils and fewer grasses than in the traditional foothills area. Beyond hiking, these trails seem to be especially popular with trail runners and less popular with bike riders.

∎ **THE HIKE**

Park at the Embudito Trailhead parking area.

Follow Trail 365 through the tight housing area, through the steep-sided channel, and up the curvy hill where the trail goes through several large switchbacks. At about 0.75 mile the trail straightens and then crosses an unnamed

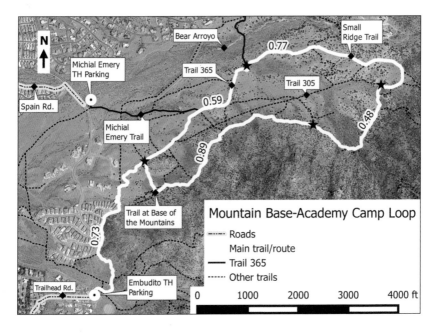

Mountain Base-Academy Camp Loop

---- Roads
      Main trail/route
──── Trail 365
----- Other trails

0   1000   2000   3000   4000 ft

Albert G. Simms and the City's Open Space

Albert G. Simms lived almost all of his adult life in Albuquerque, where he dedicated his later years to collecting lands that were then or formerly part of the Elena Gallegos Land Grant. After moving to Albuquerque in 1915, Simms practiced law and worked as a banker. He then moved into politics, but his career ended in 1931 when he was not reelected to the US House of Representatives. Together with his wife, Ruth Hanna McCormick Simms, he returned to Albuquerque and purchased a large section of the Elena Gallegos Land Grant from Ambrosio and Juan Cristobal Armijo. After assembling additional lands, the couple's property extended from the present-day ranch (Los Poblanos Farm) to the crest of the Sandia Mountains. Albert and Ruth Simms had strong feelings about the value of education and the arts and were instrumental in founding and supporting several schools, including the Albuquerque Academy. The strength of their belief was most obvious when the Academy received a bequest of approximately twelve thousand acres of the foothills upon Albert's death in 1964.

Eventually, a large portion of these bequeathed lands became the Elena Gallegos Picnic Area/Albert G. Simms Park, now owned and managed by the city. The process for the purchase of these lands from the Academy was long and drawn-out, spanning about a decade and ending in 1982. Although the purchase had many moving parts, politics stalled it for years. Ultimately it was also politics that forced the deal to move forward. The city held on to the picnic area section of the property, but in a not-so-obvious move, made a complicated series of exchanges that transferred another large portion of land to USFS ownership, greatly expanding the agency's continuous Cibola National Forest acreage. (Later, most of these lands were incorporated into the Sandia Mountain Wilderness Area.) In return, the USFS transferred title to a variety of other properties in and around Albuquerque to the city. The city sold these and a small portion of the former Academy lands to augment its original purchase and to fund the newly formed City of Albuquerque Open Space Division. So when you're out hiking in the Elena Gallegos Picnic Area or even overlooking this vast, array of wild land, say a special thank you to all those people who persevered through the difficult and sometimes thorny purchase process to secure these public lands for our use.

and unmarked intersection, the first trail junction after the switchback.

Turn right (south) and start hiking the small unnamed trail that climbs up to the base of the mountains. This is prone to being buried with sediment, so a little route-finding may be needed to find the trail that parallels the mountain base.

Turn left (east) onto the trail that runs east-to-west along the base of the mountains. Follow it east for about 0.7 mile, always staying on the trail.

When this small trail ends, it intersects with a larger one. Turn right, to continue following the base of the mountains.

Continuing to choose trails on the right will lead hikers to the Academy Camp overlook area, about 0.5 mile.

From the Academy Camp overlook area, the hilltop trail curves to the left and turns back to the west.

Once the trail loops back toward the west, the gravel road will be on the right. Continue in this direction and stay on top of the hill. Veer right on a small unnamed trail that continues to follow the nose of the ridgeline to the right (about 0.25 mile).

As this small trail crosses Trail 305, it descends onto a lower area of the hill, but still follows the ridgeline. Continue until it descends into the arroyo valley and joins up with Trail 365 (about 0.5 mile).

Turn left onto Trail 365 and follow it for 1.3 miles back to the parking area.

IF YOU LIKE THIS HIKE, try either **HIKE 25: Pino Arroyo Loop** or **HIKE 23: Domingo Baca Outwash Fan–North EGPA Loop**, which pass through similar topography.

FOR THOSE USING GPS DATA
(DATUM: WGS 84)

Intersection of Trail 365 and the small trail that leads up to the base of the mountains:
–106.478757, 35.143089

Intersection of the ridgeline trail with Trail 365:
–106.471926, 35.148252

EMBUDITO CANYON OVERLOOK LOOP

Difficulty	4	
Distance	2.8 mi (4.5 km) loop	
Hiking Time	2–4 hours	
Elevation	760 ft. gain (232 m)	Peak elevation: 7,000 ft. (2,134 m) at Old/New Trail junction; Low elevation: 6,240 ft. (1,902 m) at Embudito trailhead
Trail Condition	Good	USFS-owned; Current trail maintained; old trail not maintained
Trail Users	Hikers and horses	
Best Time	Spring and fall	
Parking Lot	Embudito Trailhead	Parking lot is Open Space–maintained
Fees	None	

SPECIAL INFORMATION: Snow and ice often cover the trail in the winter season. Check with USFS for trail conditions during this season.

THE EMBUDITO TRAIL is one of the more popular USFS trails in the Sandia Mountains. It climbs up to the Sandia Crest via the tight, rocky, steep Embudito Canyon. Although not as popular as the La Luz Trail, on occasional spring days, visitors might not believe that statement: this entire canyon fills with hikers exploring all the available routes, confirming that this trail is rarely a private experience. It seems to be popular for two reasons: the parking is easy and close to the city and the trail is unique, such that it climbs up a tight canyon at mid-slope for most of its journey. The mid-slope feature creates a different experience, because hikers see more of the canyon walls and mountains and occasionally into the valley bottom.

Scaling up and over rock outcrops and boulder steps, this trail climbs steadily to the crest, creating a strenuous hike even for well-conditioned hikers. Given that this trail is halfway up the side of the canyon wall, shade is rare until the tree line, which is about 2.5 miles from the parking area. As is the case with all of the truly mountainous trails, if the crest is your destination, preparation for mountain conditions is a must, year-round. Refer to the *Sandia Mountain Hiking Guide* by Mike Coltrin for more specific hiking information about the upper Embudito Trail.

There is an obvious shorter hiking option: the Embudito Canyon Overlook Loop, the main trail described in this guide. (The full Embudito Trail to the crest is described as an optional hike.) The overlook loop option utilizes an old Embudito Trail segment that dips to the canyon bottom about 1.2 miles from the parking area before climbing steeply up the north canyon wall to meet up with

EMBUDITO TRAIL TO CREST TRAIL OPTION

Difficulty: 5
Distance: Additional 4.3 miles one-way from the overlook to the Crest Trail (about 11 miles round-trip from parking to crest)
Hiking Time: Additional 2–4 hours one-way from the overlook
Elevation: 3,080 ft. gain; highest point is 9,320 ft. at the Crest Trail junction

the current Embudito Trail. The easiest way to access the old trail section is to dip to the canyon bottom on the way out, before climbing up to the overlook area. However, finding either end of old trails can be difficult, as the new route is so obvious and connects so smoothly that the old segment is simply overlooked by most travelers in either direction. Hikers seeking the loop option may need a little extra time to find the old trail section.

The overlook area is a great spot for a sunny picnic, with a relatively large and flat area overlooking the canyon and nearby mountains. If shade is desired, the valley bottom along the old trail segment will be more desirable, with its relatively thick riparian forest and ephemeral springs that may (or may not) be flowing. The overlook area can be blazing hot during the summer and is not a good destination on hot, sunny afternoons, as the tight canyon heats up fast and takes the whole night to cool off.

Although this trail is predominantly on the hillside, it follows the arroyo channel near the parking area. Remember never to cross a flowing arroyo. Flood flows rarely last more than an hour, and *everyone* has that much time when safety is involved. If hiking this route during a large thunderstorm, it is recommended to stay on the high-elevation trail segments until it is safe to cross the valley bottom.

■ THE HIKE

Park at the Embudito Trailhead parking area.

Follow Trail 365 for 0.1 mile to the Embudito Arroyo and turn upstream (east) to follow the sandy arroyo bottom. At about 0.2 mile from the parking area, the official trail turns left (north) and leaves the sandy arroyo route.

The Embudito Trail gradually climbs up along the north valley wall and follows the canyon for much of the distance to the Crest Trail.

At almost 1 mile from the parking area, the old trail segment veers off to the right and descends steeply to the canyon bottom. It is easy to overlook, as the old trail drops over a boulder at this junction

and is not obvious unless it is specifically being looked for. The new/main Embudito Trail continues to climb from this junction. If you are seeking the old trail, you have gone too far on the main trail if it passes tightly between a tree and boulder. (See photo below.)

Descend on the old trail to the valley bottom. Hike a short distance up the canyon bottom. The old trail turns left (north) and begins a steep ascent with numerous tall boulder steps, ending at the main Embudito Trail, about 0.34 mile.

Turn left (west) onto the Embudito Trail and begin descending. After about 0.2 mile, the trail dips steeply into a well-defined channel, then climbs steeply to a small ridge. The trail veers to the right at the top of this ridge and the overlook area is to the left.

From the overlook area, the trail

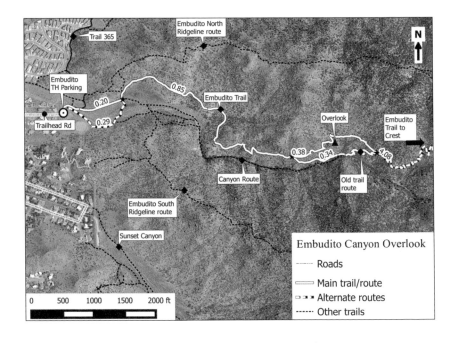

continues to descend back to the parking area, about 1.2 miles.

IF YOU LIKE THIS LARGE-TRAIL MOUNTAIN HIKE, try HIKE 22: Pino Trail to the Dead Trees. For a small-trail mountain hike of similar endurance that is nearby, try HIKE 32: Bear Canyon Overlook. Try HIKE 44: Candelaria Bench Loop, for a small-trail hike into the lower mountains to the south of the Embudito Trail.

FOR THOSE USING GPS DATA
(DATUM: WGS 84)
Intersection of Trail 365 and the Embudito Trail:
   −106.478749, 35.136659
First intersection of the current and old trail
   segments of the Embudito Trail:
   −106.469665, 35.133665
Second intersection of the current and old trail
   segments of the Embudito Trail:
   −106.465064, 35.133849
Overlook area: −106.467372, 35.134382

Canyon Heat . . . Avoid Summer Afternoons

Embudito Canyon and many other deep, narrow canyons in the Sandia Mountains become superheated on sunny summer afternoons, significantly hotter than the areas outside the canyons. Although this occurs on every sunny day regardless of season, during the summer it can easily become a safety hazard for hikers who are unprepared for the extra heat. The physics of this effect are similar to those of echoes: the sun's rays get "trapped" in the canyon and they bounce back and forth between the steep, rocky walls, rather than bouncing out. Because wall height is important, the deeper canyons experience more of this process, so they become hotter than the shallow canyons. As the waves stay in the canyon, they heat the rocks, soil, and the entire terrain, making it feel a lot like an oven, with heat radiating from all the surfaces. This extra heat can make a hike on a sunny summer afternoon so intense that you think your skin is melting. Consequently, summer hikes in these environments should be completed by 11:00 a.m. to avoid the worst of the heat in the afternoons.

On the positive side, experienced hikers can use this canyon effect to their advantage. For example, in the spring and fall, when air temperatures in Albuquerque are just a little chilly, a hike up one of these deep canyons on a sunny day can lead to an extremely pleasant afternoon with short-sleeve temperatures. Also, these relatively warmer canyons tend to retain less snow in the winter, translating into great spring hiking opportunities.

EMBUDITO CANYON ROUTE/LOOP

Difficulty	3	
Distance	2.2 mi (3.5 km) loop	Uses Embudito Trail for return.
Hiking Time	1–2.5 hours	
Elevation	520 ft. gain (158 m)	Peak elevation: 6,760 ft. (2,060 m) at old Embudito Trail; Low elevation: 6,240 ft. (1,902 m) at Embudito Trailhead
Trail Condition	Fair, but brushy	USFS-owned; Canyon route unmaintained
Trail Users	Hikers	
Best Time	Spring through fall	
Parking Lot	Embudito Trailhead	Parking lot is Open Space–maintaine
Fees	None	

SPECIAL INFORMATION: Poison ivy is often found around the active springs.

LIKE THE EMBUDITO TRAIL, the Embudito Canyon is one of the more popular areas to hike in the Sandia Mountains, with other hikers in the area on all days of the week, but especially on weekends and holidays. The canyon route is especially popular for several reasons: active springs (in spring and early summer), lush riparian vegetation including deciduous trees, and easy bouldering opportunities. The springs and the trees are a delightful escape from the hot, dry desert landscape for just about every hiker and animal that has ever explored this area. A water trough is located at the regularly flowing spring at the mouth of the canyon; however, it is often buried under sand. Several other springs up the canyon flow during the springtime unless the winter was especially dry. All springs are likely to be dry in the summertime unless it has been an exceptionally wet season.

Just like all the other wet canyon bottoms in the Sandia Mountains, Embudito's is usually filled with thick vegetation containing a wide variety of invasive and native species. Grapevines, apple trees, and other planted species attest to the longstanding interest in this canyon. Although poison ivy is not the hiker's favorite by any means, this canyon also has an abundant supply, so take care when venturing up this little strip of paradise.

On this route, the mouth of Embudito Canyon is by far the chief attraction, and people spend hours hanging out in this small area. Given that this one place has it all—a spring, trees, and smooth rock steps—it's no wonder that scads of recreationists descend upon this spot. After a short stop and water break at this wonderful canyon entrance, the route continues straight up the canyon bottom for about a mile. One of the more fun aspects of

this canyon is its bedrock steps: the first set is near the mouth of the canyon. With most of the sharp edges worn away by hundreds of years of water flowing over the rock, these steps create an ideal opportunity for some easy bouldering, attracting people of all ages. Embudito is also a great introduction to canyon hiking for beginners and children, as there are no large waterfalls, and the return route has a trail option.

Canyons are particularly dangerous places to be during any rain event and should be avoided at those times. Storms in the mountains can create a flash flood that travels through this hiking area without warning, even when no rain has fallen in the valley bottom. And because this canyon is deep, it may be difficult to see that mountain storms are taking place. With steep walls and often-sheer rock faces, climbing out during a flood would be extremely difficult. Be smart and avoid this entire hike if mountain thunderstorms have been forecast or you see a rainstorm/thunderstorm on the way.

▪ THE HIKE

Park at the Embudito Trailhead parking area.

Follow Trail 365 a short distance (0.1 mile) to the Embudito Arroyo and turn upstream (east) to follow the sandy arroyo bottom.

Follow the channel upstream to the mouth of the canyon (0.5 mile from parking). Here, the valley walls tighten to form the canyon section, and typically, this is the location of a regularly flowing spring. Several bedrock steps immediately upstream from the mouth are extremely popular snack stops for families with children.

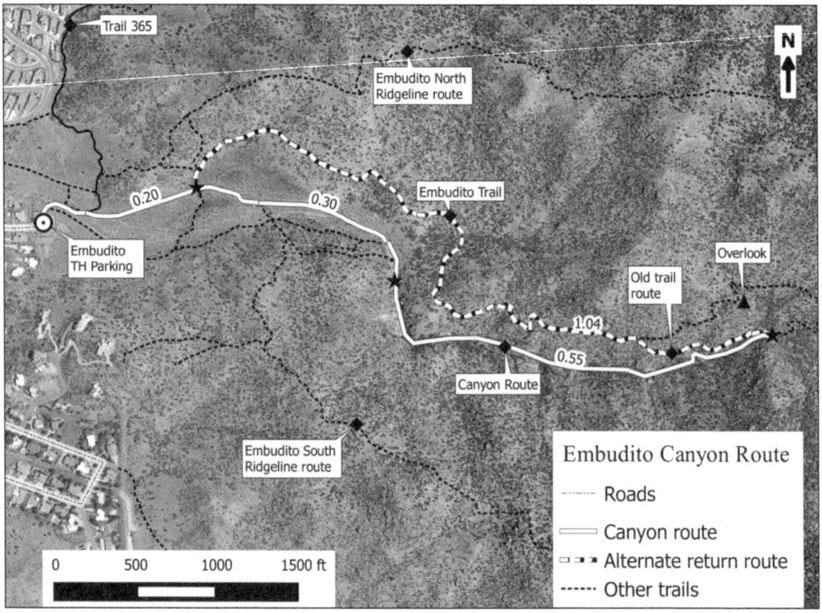
Trail 365
N
Embudito North Ridgeline route
Embudito Trail
0.20
0.30
Embudito TH Parking
Overlook
Old trail route
1.04
0.55
Canyon Route
Embudito South Ridgeline route
Embudito Canyon Route
Roads
Canyon route
Alternate return route
Other trails
0
500
1000
1500 ft

Poison Ivy and Urushiol

Luckily for hikers, only one of the three most common poisonous-to-touch plants, western poison ivy, grows in this part of New Mexico. Unluckily, however, most of the population, about 75 percent, is sensitive to it. It takes most people only one encounter to establish this sensitivity through rashes and blisters. A toxic oil called urushiol (you-ROO-shee-all), is found on the leaves, stems, veins, and roots of poison ivy, as well as in the sap, flowers, and berries. Urushiol is produced by plants in the cashew family (anacardi-aceae), which includes poison ivy, poison oak, poison sumac, and also mango, cashew, and karee trees. Repeated contact with the plants can increase a person's sensitivity to all members of the anacardiaceae family with each subsequent exposure. Urushiol can be inhaled, ingested, or absorbed through the skin; responses vary depending on the route of exposure.

Europeans discovered poison ivy when they first came to the Americas and, unfortu-nately, decided to take it back with them as an ornamental plant. Despite its rather irri-tating personality, poison ivy continues to be used as a decoration in Europe today.

Continue to follow the canyon upstream for another 0.5 mile. At this location, the old Embudito Trail dips down to the canyon bottom and follows it for a couple of hundred feet. Here, the valley walls are slightly set back, creating a nice canopy opening where a small stand of cottonwood trees provide a patch of shade, while desert species (mostly brush) encroach on both sides of the canyon bottom. Upstream from this location, the canyon becomes very tight and the going gets much tougher; the canyon walls narrow and dense vegetation creates a far darker environment.

For the return trip, two options exist: simply turn around and retrace the route along the canyon or return along the Embudito Trail. For the trail route, and to complete the loop, leave the channel bottom in this opening and take the old trail segment to the current Embudito Trail. This old trail climbs up out of the valley bottom by winding its way along the northern hill slope until it intersects with the current trail. From here, follow the well-maintained trail back to the arroyo near Trail 365 and the parking area.

IF YOU LIKED THIS HIKE, try **HIKE 21: Cañon Domingo Baca Trail**, a longer hike to a canyon route with springs, or **HIKE 7: Waterfall Canyon via Piedra Lisa Trail**, which is a slightly more difficult canyon hike.

FOR THOSE USING GPS DATA
(DATUM: WGS 84)
Intersection of Trail 365 and the Embudito Trail:
    −106.478749, 35.136659
First Spring in Embudito Canyon:
    −106.474632, 35.134808
Intersection of Embudito Canyon and the old segment of the Embudito Trail:
    −106.46674, 35.133736

EMBUDITO NORTH RIDGE TRAIL LOOP

Difficulty	5	Due to steepness, rocky trails, and route-finding.
Distance	3.9 mi (6.3 km) loop trip	Uses Embudito Trail for return.
Hiking Time	2–4 hours	
Elevation	1,400 ft. gain (427 m)	Peak elevation: 7,640 ft. (2,329 m) near where ridge trail meets Embudito Trail; Low elevation: 6,240 ft. (1,902 m) at Embudito Trailhead
Trail Condition	Fair	USFS-owned; Ridge route unmaintained
Trail Users	Hikers	
Best Time	Spring through fall	
Parking Lot	Embudito Trailhead	Parking lot is Open Space–maintained
Fees	None	

SPECIAL INFORMATION: Snow and ice often cover the trail in the winter season. Given the remoteness of this trail, it should not be hiked in inclement weather or when trails are icy.

ALTHOUGH THIS LOOP ROUTE is located between two very popular hiking areas, it is a small, remote trail with few users. The trail leads hikers into a dense mountain forest before looping back to the Embudito Trail. It climbs up into an out-of-the-way area of the middle mountains, along the watershed divide between Bear Canyon and Embudito Canyon. Several lesser-known and primarily unmapped trails crisscross in a high-mountain bench area through a dense forest with small hills and house-sized boulders that litter the landscape. Old fire circles within this area attest to a time when camping in these woods was a popular pastime. As found on other nearby hikes, recently dead piñon trees create a "ring" along the lower elevations of the mountain forest at about 7,600 feet. A recent study performed by the USFS indicates that this tree mortality was likely caused by a combination of drought and insects.

If you have the stamina and an adventurous nature, this is a splendid trail and area to explore. Because the route is steep, with several loose rocky sections and high boulder steps, it is not a "beginner" trail. A bit of route-finding may be needed in the forested area, as there are several hiking options. Hikers may need extra time and a sense of adventure to find the correct trail to complete this loop on the larger, better-graded and -maintained Embudito Trail. Especially in the mountain forest and bench areas, this route has quite a remote feeling to it: a sense of isolation due to the lack of other nearby hikers. Although the whole route is never more than a few miles from the car, hikers should be prepared for mountain conditions and bring along extra water during warm weather.

■ THE HIKE

Park at Embudito Trailhead parking area.

Follow Trail 365 for 0.1 mile to Embudito Arroyo and turn upstream (east) to follow the sandy arroyo bottom. Turn left

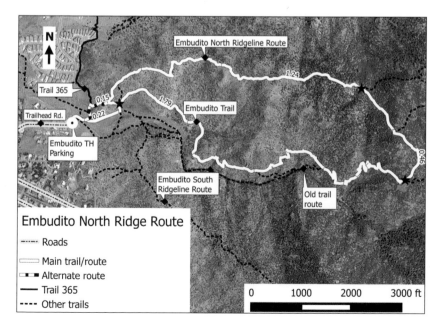

Embudito North Ridge Route

---- Roads
⊏⊐ Main trail/route
⊏■■ Alternate route
— Trail 365
---- Other trails

Camping in the Woods

Throughout the foothills, camping is not allowed on private land or lands managed by the City of Albuquerque's Open Space Division; however, camping via backpacking is permitted within the Sandia Mountains Wilderness Area. In the wilderness area, there are no formal campgrounds and water is scarce, but if you're willing to carry your bed and a lot of extra gear and water up the mountains, then you can stay the night.

A many-day camping trip requires a water source; however, for a single night, the items you need to take can be surprisingly few. Consider the following: a small tent or bivy sack, sleeping bag, sleeping pad, small trowel (for burying your own scat), headlamp/flashlight, warmer clothes for evening and morning, ready-to-eat or just-add-water food for dinner and breakfast, and extra water. This list augments the survival items that you should carry whenever you venture into the mountains: map/compass/GPS, sun protection, first aid supplies, fire-starter, and knife. If staying multiple days, you will likely need to treat water that you find along the trail, so having some iodine or a water filter is a must. (See extra information in HIKE 5: **Hidden Falls Canyon Route**.)

---

onto the Embudito Trail and leave the arroyo at about 0.2 mile from the parking area.

Once on the Embudito Trail, look to the left for a relatively well-worn, but rocky trail that ascends to the top of the northern hill. Follow this steep trail to the ridgeline and then along it, continuing to head up into the Sandia Mountains. This trail drops off the ridgeline onto the north side of the ridge, then follows the ridgeline for 1.25 miles to an unnamed trail junction, where a small unmarked trail veers off to the right.

Going right and following this smaller trail, always staying right and on the better trail, for almost 0.5 mile will lead to the Embudito Trail. (Several small trails in this area can lead a hiker astray. It may take a few tries to reach the Embudito Trail, but luckily, this area's dense forest provides copious amounts of shade while you explore.)

Once at the Embudito Trail, turn right (west) onto the larger trail and follow it back to the parking area, about 2 miles.

IF YOU LIKE THIS HIKE, try **HIKE 32: Bear Canyon Overlook** or **HIKE 44: Candelaria Bench Loop**, which are easier lower-mountain hikes. Or, for another small-trail mountain hike that is slightly more difficult, try **HIKE 40: Embudito South Ridge Trail to Boulder Cave**.

FOR THOSE USING GPS DATA
(DATUM: WGS 84)
Intersection of Embudito Trail and small
  trail that leads to the North Ridge Trail:
  −106.478797, 35.137063
Intersection of North Ridge Trail with small cut-
  off trail that veers off the ridgeline and leads
  to the Embudito Trail: −106.462673, 35.138104
Intersection of small cutoff trail and Embudito
  Trail: −106.459646, 35.133317

EMBUDITO SOUTH RIDGE TRAIL TO BOULDER CAVE

Difficulty	5	Due to steep sections and poor trail condition.
Distance	3.4 mi (3.6 km) loop	
Hiking Time	2–4 hours	
Elevation	1,760 ft. gain (536 m)	Peak elevation: 8,000 ft. (2,438 m) near boulder cave; Low elevation: 6,240 ft. (1,902 m) at Embudito Trailhead
Trail Condition	Fair with poor sections	USFS-owned; Unmaintained
Trail Users	Hikers	
Best Time	Spring through fall	
Parking Lot	Embudito Trailhead	Parking lot is Open Space–maintained
Fees	None	

SPECIAL INFORMATION: Snow and ice can cover the trail in the winter season, especially in the wooded area. Given the remoteness of this trail, it should not be hiked in inclement weather or when trails are icy.

Embudito Trail

0.28

0.32

Embudito
TH Parking

Old trail
route

Overlook

Canyon Route

Embudito South
Ridgeline route

Sunset Canyon

1.92

Boulder
Cave

Embudito South Ridge Route

---- Roads

===== Main trail/route

▫ ▪ ▪ Alternate route

------ Other trails

0   1000   2000   3000 ft

N
↑

THIS IS ONE OF THOSE HIKES that is tough but leads to places that few people venture: a beautiful mountain forest, mountain benches where the deer like to hang out, and the upper Embudito Watershed. Best of all, the described route ends at a very large boulder cave surrounded by large trees. This hike has a truly isolated feel to it, as few people make it past the first steep ascent. Attaining the peak and finding the cave has a refreshing and satisfying feel to it. The "trail" is quite small and rocky for most of the route, and it only gets narrower the further in you go. However, it does become less rocky once it enters into the piñon forest near the peak and continues into the upper Embudito Watershed/ mountains. For experienced hikers with some route-finding skills, this unnamed trail is a wonderful, secluded hike with some strenuous exercise. The path is steep, in poor condition for a notable

amount of the distance, and sometimes requires a bit of route-finding. It is definitely off the beaten path, with a high level of remoteness.

As is normal in this part of the Sandia Mountains, the tree line starts at about 7,600 ft., but seems to be creeping higher as the lower piñon trees die. Although not unique in the Sandia Mountains, it is quite noticeable on this hike, as the trail winds it way through the dead trees before reaching the high point on the hike. The typical desert fauna seems to be encroaching into the forest here: cacti and yucca species are growing seemingly well within the coniferous forest.

Given the state of the trail, steep climbing, and lack of shade, persevering all the way to the mountain forests and the cave is a challenge but well worth it. The cave is located at the furthest point on this route: it is created by several house-sized boulders that are clustered together.

Mountain Benches and Mule Deer

As part of the Rio Grande Rift Valley, the western Sandia Mountains are a series of faulted and downthrown ("step-faulted") sections of the mountains. These blocks have formed a series of "benches" or "steps" along the lower mountains, settling to form fairly flat or slightly eastward-tilted tops. Several of the small trails that climb up the steep mountain slopes cross over these steps: three great bench examples can be found at Embudito South Ridge, Candelaria Bench, and along the Tijeras Canyon–Four Hills Overlook Loop, which is home to a whole series of them.

Although mule deer reside throughout the foothills and Sandia Mountains, they seem to really like these bench areas. Their preference is probably attraction to a combination of features such as a greater variety of habitats and plants available or more space.

But maybe the most important feature is the relative solitude that the benches offer. Few hikers visit these areas. The bench tops tend to be covered in a thick mat of grass, while the surrounding steep hillsides have more woody bushes and trees, two features that likely attract deer. Although their legs look spindly, deer are natural-born mountain hikers and runners; when spooked, these skittish animals will simply run off the bench onto a nearby steep hillside full of boulders, small cliffs, and cacti, where few predators are willing to follow. Also, deer are browsers, meaning that they feed primarily on the nutritious leaves, stems, and buds of woody plants, which grow readily on these steep hillsides. Weeds, other forbs, and grasses, which are more prevalent on the benches, can also be important food items, especially when they have a productive growth season.

Although not a true underground cave, this place is dry during a storm and has a cooler air temperature, even on a hot summer day.

■ THE HIKE

Park at the Embudito Trailhead parking area.

Follow the Embudito Trail into the arroyo and continue upstream for a short distance (about 0.25 mile from the parking lot).

Turn right (south) onto the small unmarked trail that heads straight up the south valley hill slope. There are several trails in this area, so the "correct" one can be hard to find. The best one starts up a small ridgeline/hill at the bottom near the arroyo channel. But more importantly, the correct trail goes straight up, while mostly avoiding the steep drainages scattered along the hillside. This trail does not contour much, nor does it have any switchbacks. All trails leading up this hillside are rocky and narrow, but luckily, the hill is relatively short, about 0.1 mile. The correct trail gets to the top of the hill where a small grassy bench is located.

Once up this first hill, turn left to follow the larger ridgeline to the east and into the mountains. The trail follows but is rarely on the actual ridgeline; instead, it is just to the north and slightly further downhill. Although not quite as steep as the first hillside, this trail still has sections that are rocky, steep, gravelly or slippery slopes, or boulder steps that require all four limbs. Follow this trail into the mountain forest, pass the peak/high bench area, and then descend a short distance from the peak to the cave, about 1.4 miles from Embudito Arroyo.

Return route is on the same trail.

IF YOU LIKE THIS HIKE, try **HIKE 32: Bear Canyon Overlook** or **HIKE 44: Candelaria Bench Loop**, which are easier lower-mountain hikes. Or, for another nearby mountain hike with similar difficulty, try **HIKE 39: Embudito North Ridge Trail Loop**.

FOR THOSE USING GPS DATA
(DATUM: WGS 84)
Beginning of South Ridge Trail as it leaves the
    Embudito Canyon Trail: –106.47746, 35.13632
Approximate location of Boulder Cave:
    –106.46352, 35.12381

3

SOUTH

CENTRAL

TRAILS

THE SOUTHERN TRAILS area prominently displays the Upper Sonoran life zone, typically described as our high-desert landscape. Cacti, yuccas, and a few trees and bushes scattered about results in a drier feel to the air and less shade but better views. Even when climbing into the mountains, which seem to be even steeper in this area, reaching the tree line is usually beyond a "short" hike. If trees and lush vegetation are what you seek, you will find small but dense patches growing in many of the canyons. The foothills vegetation, unlike that in the north, shifts noticeably toward the more

drought-tolerant plants commonly found throughout the greater Albuquerque area and Upper Sonoran life zone. This landscape sports all the same features as the other hiking areas, with canyons, dry waterfalls, high-mountain grassy benches, and steep slopes surrounding rolling foothills. But unlike the other areas, numerous steep-sided mounds here beg to be explored.

These mounds are a unique feature of the Southern Trails area, found prominently south of the Embudito Trail. Two of them are officially named: Hilldale Mound and the perfectly shaped cone called U-Mound, both near the end of Copper Avenue and the Open Space parking area. The other mounds discussed in this guide are not officially named, but are easy to identify based on either their location or a specific local characteristic; for example, Powerline Mound has power lines that go up and over the mound.

As you begin to recognize these distinctive features, you will see mounds of all different sizes and shapes scattered throughout this area. Some of the smaller ones are made up of large boulders piled together, creating the perfect structure for rock-climbing and bouldering. At first glance, one might mistakenly think the larger mounds are small volcanic vents or cones. Although that is a good guess, they are not: they are pinnacle-shaped hills, filled with the granitic rock commonly found throughout the lower mountains. The mounds are spectacular sights, and can be seen for miles in and around the foothills area. Many hikers like simply to look at these special features and are content to walk the perimeter trails around them, while others have that

uncontrollable desire to climb them. More often than not, a well-worn trail leads to the summit of each mound.

The hiking system in the Southern Trails area is more complex than those in either the Northern or Central Trail areas. The main reason is that there are simply more trails here, especially the unnamed variety. (This area has had human neighbors, and a lot of them, for longer than the other two areas.) The lower mountains are also more extensive, with a network of trails that, in combination with the foothills trails, create a variety of unique foothill/mountain loop options. The residential communities bordering the Southern Trails area developed several years earlier than those to the north; the former were well-developed by the mid-1960s, while development around Spain Road is still ongoing following a peak in the early 2000s. These early southern communities gave a local population easy access to the foothills and they created a vast trail system. The two large north–south trending trails that provide the most extensive

interconnection throughout this hiking area are the southern portion of Trail 365 and Trail 401. Several other named and maintained routes lead from parking areas to these two large trails, such as Trail 365A at Embudo Trailhead or Trail 400 at the Copper Avenue parking area, both of which also lead to Trail 365. With the exception of the Embudo Trail and the Horse Bypass Trail, the routes leading into the mountains are unnamed and unmaintained. A dense network of small trails in both the mountains and foothills produce a vast array of options that allow for loop hikes from just about everywhere.

Like all the trails in the foothills and lower Sandia Mountains, the southern routes have amazing city views. However, the larger southern Sandia Mountains, such as South Peak, can typically not be seen from the southern foothills, as the lower mountains block the view. If seeing the crest or the high mountains

is paramount on your hike, focus on the trails that either climb up and over the lower mountains (e.g., **HIKE 46: Piedra Lisa Ridge Overlook Loop**) or pass through the lower mountains (such as at hike 51: Embudo Trail Loop to Upper Watershed/Headwall, which leads to a laid-back upper watershed area that has a direct line of sight to the crest).

This area's mountain benches—which formed as a series of fault blocks dropped away from the great mountains—are more easily accessed than those in the north because they are closer to the foothills. Several small unnamed trails crisscross them, creating a wonderful playground for hikers with a little endurance and a desire for exploring. These small trails are not necessarily in good condition, especially the steep ones that climb up the edges of the mountain slope, requiring hikers to climb over rocks, walk up slippery bedrock outcrops, and cross steep inclines filled with loose stones.

Some are better likened to deer trails. Luckily they all interconnect, creating a multitude of loop options for adventurous hikers who are seeking a somewhat more strenuous route. The best-defined trails are described in this guide, but with all of the bench hikes, always budget some extra time, just in case it takes longer than anticipated or you want to explore a little.

In comparison to the rest of the terrain described in this guide, the southernmost area next to I-40 is distinctly different. First, the land south of Hilldale Mound tilts and drains south into the large Tijeras Valley rather than to the west like the rest of the foothills area. Second, it feels almost like a bowl, as mounds surround it on three sides and the steep lower Sandia Mountains bound it on its eastern side. Maybe the most important aspect is that its grand views are not of the city, but rather the Four Hills area and the Manzano Mountains. If you haven't visited this small and somewhat secret area before, now might be a good time to explore it.

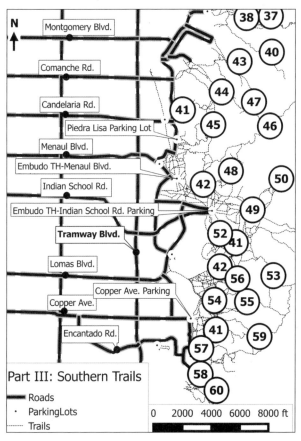

Part III: Southern Trails

▬ Roads
· ParkingLots
⋯⋯ Trails

0   2000 4000 6000 8000 ft

BEST TIME TO VISIT

This area is best seen in fall through spring, but the hiking is good year-round, especially along the foothill trails. Summer afternoons can be quite hot in this area given the lack of shade, so morning hikes are recommended at midyear. The mountainous trails here have all the same problems as the ones described elsewhere in this guide; however, snow and ice is less likely to stick for long, as the sun readily melts it.

SPECIAL INFORMATION FOR THIS AREA

This hot and dry area requires hikers to bring a bit of extra drinking water, especially if heading up into the lower mountains in the summer. Even in the wettest years, surface water is extremely scarce. The only exception is the spring located at the mouth of Embudo Canyon, but even this dries up earlier than the springs to the north.

Even though this area is dry, wildlife is plentiful. Deer, coyotes, birds, snakes, and a variety of rodents roam this area regularly. Less common are larger species such as bears, bobcats, and cougars.

Know your abilities and stay safe, especially on the mountainous trails. Although the routes described are short, typically less than four miles, the hills are usually steep and rocky and often in poor condition. Anyone can trip and fall.

DIRECTIONS TO THE AREA

This general area is located east of Tramway Boulevard, between Comanche Road and I-40. Four primary parking areas are available: from north to south, the Piedra Lisa Canyon, Embudo Trailhead–Menaul Boulevard, Embudo Trailhead–Indian School Road, and Copper Ave. parking lots. All parking lots have specific directions from Tramway Boulevard in appendix A.

TRAIL 365—COMANCHE ROAD TO I-40

Difficulty	3	
Distance	6.24 mi (10 km) one-way	
Hiking Time	2–4 hours one-way	
Elevation	600 ft. gain (183 m)	Peak elevation: 6,400 ft. (1,950 m) near Embudo Trail
		Low elevation: 5,800 ft. (1,768 m) near I-40
Trail Condition	Excellent	Open Space– and USFS-owned and -maintained
Trail Users	Hikers, bikers, horses	
Best Time	Year-round	
Parking	On-street at Comanche Rd. access point or Camino de la Sierra near I-40 access point	
Fees	None	

THIS LOWER SEGMENT OF
Trail 365 is also a premier
foothills trail in the southern
area, and it is extremely popular for hiking and bike riding.
This trail primarily follows the
eastern edge of the foothills
landscape at the base of the
mountains, which forms a
diverse landscape to navigate,
while providing a more mountainous feel for both hikers
and bikers. As in the Central
Trail area, Trail 365 is a wide
and well-maintained track
that seamlessly snakes its way
through both USFS and City
of Albuquerque Open Space
lands. This trail connects the
end of Comanche Road with
the routes that run along I-40
and everything in between.

Trail 365 travels across an
interesting landscape where
an alternating pattern repeats

One-Way Hiking Distances and Estimated Completion Times

	Piedra Lisa parking lot	Embudo Trail-head–Menaul Blvd. lot	Embudo Trailhead–Indian School Rd.	Copper Ave. lot near Trail 400	Camino de la Sierra near I-4 access point
Comanche Rd. access point	0.8 mi. (15–45 minutes)	1.5 mi. (30–60 minutes)	3.2 mi. (1–1.5 hours)	4.95 mi. (1.75–4 hours)	6.24 mi. (2.5–5 hours)
Piedra Lisa parking lot	—	0.72 mi. (15–45 minutes)	2.34 mi. (45–90 minutes)	4.14 mi. (1.5–3 hours)	5.43 mi. (2–4 hours)
Embudo Trailhead–Menaul Blvd. lot	—	—	1.86 mi. (45–75 minutes)	3.62 mi. (1–2 hours)	4.91 mi. (1.75–3.5 hou
Embudo Trailhead–Indian School Rd.	—	—	—	2.26 mi. (45–90 minutes)	3.82 mi. (1–2 hours)
Copper Ave. lot near Trail 400	—	—	—	—	1.83 mi. (45– minutes)

itself as it parallels the lower mountains and passes between them and the back sides of many mounds. This pattern starts at the Piedra Lisa Canyon/Watershed parking area: the trail crosses through traditional foothills topography, then large, rolling hills with relatively steep ups and downs, before dropping back into the relatively flattish foothills landscape. This pattern repeats several times as the trail travels south toward I-40. These foothills/large-hill units fashion a more complex trail than those found along Trail 365 in the Central Trails section, providing more of a wilderness feel.

packed soil, sand, and rocks, with only a couple of steep or rocky-step sections.

Difficulty: 2

Distance: 0.8 mile one-way

Hiking Time: 20–40 minutes

Elevation: 40 ft. gain; highest point is 6,000 ft. at Piedra Lisa Canyon/Watershed parking

2. Piedra Lisa Watershed Parking Lot to Trail near the Embudo Trailhead–Menaul Blvd. Parking Lot

Another short section of Trail 365 is located between these two popular parking lots. It is characterized primarily as traditional foothills, with small hills and relatively flat sections of trail.

PARKING OPTIONS

Piedra Lisa Watershed
  Parking Lot (6,000 ft.
  elevation)
Embudo Trailhead–Menaul
  Blvd. Parking Lot (5,960
  ft. elevation)
Embudo Trailhead–Indian
  School Road Parking Lot
  (6,200 ft. elevation)
Copper Ave. Parking Lot
  (5,920 ft. elevation)

SPECIFIC TRAIL DESCRIPTIONS

1. Comanche Road to the Piedra Lisa Watershed Parking Lot

This is a tightly confined section of Trail 365 that skirts the edge of public land and the base of the lower Sandia Mountains. This section is part of the city's Open Space land and is well-maintained. The trail is characterized by

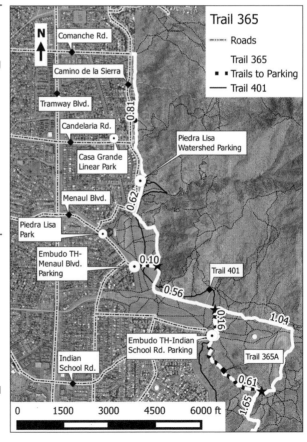

Trail 365

----- Roads

Trail 365
■ ■ Trails to Parking
—— Trail 401

N

Comanche Rd.

Camino de la Sierra

Tramway Blvd.

Candelaria Rd.

Casa Grande
Linear Park

Menaul Blvd.

Piedra Lisa
Park

Embudo TH–
Menaul Blvd.
Parking

Indian
School Rd.

Embudo TH–Indian
School Rd. Parking

Piedra Lisa
Watershed Parking

Trail 401

Trail 365A

0.18

0.62

0.10

0.56

0.10

1.04

0.61

1.65

0   1500   3000   4500   6000 ft

Difficulty: 1

Distance: 0.6 mile one-way

Hiking Time: 15–30
minutes

Elevation: 40 ft. loss;
highest point is 6,000 ft.
at Piedra Lisa Canyon/
Watershed parking

**3. Trail near Embudo
Trailhead–Menaul Blvd.
Parking Lot to Trail 365A
(South Side of Embudo
Trailhead–Indian School
Road Parking Lot)**

In this segment, the real
foothills/large-hill pattern
emerges. As Trail 365
leaves the Menaul Bou-
levard area, it crosses a
traditional foothills landscape. Once it turns east,
toward the Embudo Trail, it
follows the power lines and
rolls through moderately
tall hills, a combination of
the foothills landscape and
arroyo fans. It then drops
into the Embudo Valley just upstream from the
dam, crosses the valley, and heads up into the
large-hill landscape along the base of the mountains. The trail through these hills is in good to
great shape as it passes behind the Embudo
mounds and meets up with Trail 365A.

Difficulty: 2

Distance: 1.6 miles one-way

Hiking Time: 30–60 minutes

Elevation: 480 ft. gain; highest point is 6,440 ft.
at the Trail 365/365A intersection

**4. Trail 365A (South Side of Embudo Trailhead–
Indian School Parking Lot) to Trail 400 near
Copper Ave.**

From the trail junction with Trail 365A, this

route drops steeply as it reaches and passes
Trail 285. From this junction, the trail follows
the eastern edge of the foothills; the steep hills
abate for a while before the trail climbs up the
back side of U-Mound to the Trail 400 junction.
Trail 400 leads to the Copper Ave. parking area.

Difficulty: 2

Distance: 1.65 miles one-way

Hiking Time: 30–60 minutes

Elevation: 360 ft. loss; highest point is 6,440 ft.
at the Trail 365/365A intersection

5. Trail 400 to Camino de la Sierra near I-40

From Trail 400, Trail 365 continues to hug the
base of the lower Sandia Mountains as it drops
down into a traditional foothills landscape with

Yucca Facts

- The yucca is a celebrated symbol of sturdiness, life, and beauty in the Southwest.
- In 1927, the state legislature agreed with the schoolchildren who had nominated it and named the yucca New Mexico's official state flower.
- The genus Yucca includes some fifty species of perennials, shrubs, and trees in the family Agavaceae.
- Yuccas can reproduce vegetatively, meaning without seed or sexual reproduction.
- The plants' seeds must be physically pollenated, usually by the Yucca moth, which transfers the pollen from the stamens of one to the stigma of another, and at the same time lays a single egg in the flower. The developing larva eats some of the seeds, but leaves most of them untouched.
- Yuccas are native to the hot, dry parts of North America, Central America, and the West Indies.
- The fragrance of yucca flowers is most pronounced at night.
- The leaves of the yucca plant are usually stiff and spearlike, often with marginal threads.
- Most parts of the Yucca plant—the fruits, seeds, flowers, flowering stems, and, more rarely, roots—are edible.
- Native Americans used the yucca's fibers to make sandals, cordage, baskets, and other everyday items.

rolling hills and small mounds. But this easier landscape is short-lived, as the trail climbs up to pass behind Hilldale Mound. From this saddle, Trail 365 descends approximately 280 ft. to reach the last small section of foothills landscape north of I-40.

Difficulty: 3
Distance: 1.6 miles one-way
Hiking Time: 30–60 minutes
Elevation: 420 ft. loss; highest point is 6,080 ft. at the Trail 365/400 intersection

IF YOU LIKED THIS TRAIL, try **HIKE 18: Trail 365–Sandia Peak Tram** to Embudito Trailhead or **HIKE 42: Trail 401–Piedra Lisa Canyon** to Hilldale Mound.

FOR THOSE USING GPS DATA (DATUM: WGS 84)
Trail 365 at the Piedra Lisa Canyon/Watershed parking lot: –106.488067, 35.112237
Trail 365 near the Embudo Trailhead–Menaul Blvd. parking lot: –106.486466, 35.104983
Trail 365 as it crosses Trail 401, near the Embudo Trailhead–Indian School Road parking lot: –106.480145, 35.101223
Trail 365 at Trail 365A, near the Embudo Trailhead–Indian School Road parking lot: –106.474881, 35.094242
Trail 365 at Trail 400, near the Copper Ave. parking lot: –106.479753, 35.07891
Trail 365 near Powerline Mound: –106.483454, 35.068121

TRAIL 401–PIEDRA LISA CANYON TO HILLDALE MOUND

TRAIL 401–PIEDRA LISA CANYON TO HILLDALE MOUND

Difficulty	2	
Distance	3.5 mi (5.6 km) one-way	
Hiking Time	1.5–3 hours one-way	
Elevation	420 ft. loss (127 m)	Peak elevation: 6,400 ft. (1,950 m) near Embudo Trail; Low elevation: 5,980 ft. (1,823 m) at end of trail
Trail Condition	Excellent	Open Space–owned and -maintained
Trail Users	Hikers, bikers, horses	
Best Time	Year-round	
Parking	Piedra Lisa Copper Ave.	
Fees		

SPECIAL INFORMATION: This is a primary foothills trail that can be accessed in several locations, creating opportunities for shorter round-trips.

TRAIL 401 COVERS a similar area of the foothills as does Trail 365, but it is west of the latter, which is closer to the residential properties. This trail climbs up and around mounds while crossing over sections of foothills that have the more classic Central Trails character of gently rolling grass-covered hills. However similar, the charm of these southern foothills is their distinctive integration of the mounds with the grassy plains, creating a special 3-D experience. Although several small arroyos cut through the fan sediments in the Southern Trails section, there are fewer of them, and they are smaller than elsewhere. The smaller size means that they cut less into the plain sediments and do not form deep channel valleys. Because the plain is less dissected, the vegetation is more uniform in nature, such that lines of trees or swaths of grassy ridgelines are absent. These differences result in Trail 401 crossing a more uniform landscape with more unobstructed views of the city and the mountains.

This trail brushes all the major southern parking lots on its path from Piedra Lisa Canyon to Hilldale Mound, creating an easily accessed trail. It is wide, well-maintained packed sand and seamlessly snakes its way around the various mounds. With less elevation, this is a popular trail for both hikers and bike riders.

PARKING OPTIONS

Piedra Lisa Canyon/Watershed Parking Lot (6,000 ft. elevation)

Embudo Trailhead–Menaul Blvd. Parking Lot (5,960 ft. elevation)

Embudo Trailhead–Indian School Road Parking Lot (6,200 ft. elevation)

Copper Ave. Parking Lot (5,920 ft. elevation)

SPECIFIC TRAIL DESCRIPTIONS

1. Piedra Lisa Canyon/Watershed to Embudo Trailhead–Menaul Blvd. Parking Lot

Starting near the Piedra Lisa Canyon and its falls, this short and easy trail section (0.6 mile long) is located between two popular parking lots and is primarily characterized as traditional foothills: relatively flat countryside. To get to the start of the trail, hike toward Piedra Lisa Canyon about 0.2 mile from the parking area, where signs mark the beginning of Trail 401.

Difficulty: 1

Distance: 0.78 mile one-way (includes short trail to the start of Trail 401 near the falls)

Hiking Time: 20–40 minutes

Elevation: 120 ft. loss; highest point is 6,080 ft. at the start of Trail 401, near the falls

2. Embudo Trailhead–Menaul Blvd. Parking Lot to Embudo Trailhead–Indian School Road Parking Lot

Trail 401 crosses next to both of these parking lots, but not straight between them; instead, it wanders up to the mouth of a small canyon, where a far-off picnic table/shelter sits. The trail turns south near the table, crossing Trail 365 on its way to the Embudo Trailhead–Indian School Road parking area.

Difficulty: 1

Bear Grass

Bear grass is not actually a grass. It is currently considered part of the lily family. (Interestingly, this designation is somewhat controversial and has alternated between the agave lily and the asparagus families.) Bear grass grows from a large underground root stem, forming a big bushel/bunch of leaves on the surface. The main difference between this plant and a yucca is in the flowers: a stalk at the center of the plant bears hundreds of tiny greenish, pink, purple, or white flowers, which turn into papery seed capsules after pollination. It seems to like hillsides such as the mounds or boulder-covered hills in the foothills and lower mountains. Bear grass has been an important plant for desert people for thousands of years: the leaves can be used for weaving (mats, cordage, thatch, basketry), the roots are used for medicinal purposes, and the fruit, seeds, flowers, and stalks are edible either cooked or raw.

During the spring, look inside bear grass leaves to see if there are any Sandia hairstreak butterflies or caterpillars hanging around. The Sandia hairstreak butterfly was first discovered in Albuquerque in 1959 at La Cueva Canyon. It is relatively rare and has a short life cycle, but can be found easily in the foothills, living in the native bear grass. The butterfly is gold and green in color, while its caterpillar is pink, lavender and white. In 2003, the state legislature adopted the Sandia hairstreak as the official New Mexico state butterfly.

ONE-WAY HIKING DISTANCES AND ESTIMATED COMPLETION TIMES

	Piedra Lisa parking lot (start of trail)	Embudo Trailhead– Menaul Blvd. lot	Embudo Trailhead– Indian School Rd. lot	Copper Ave. lot	Hilldale Mound (end of trail)
Piedra Lisa lot	—	0.6 mi. (15–45 minutes)	1.4 mi. (45–90 minutes)	3.1 mi. (1.5–3 hours)	3.5 mi. (1.5–3 hours)
Embudo Trailhead– Menaul Blvd. lot	—	—	0.8 mi. (45–75 minutes)	2.5 mi. (1–2 hours)	2.9 mi. (1–2 hours)
Embudo Trailhead– Indian School Rd. lot	—	—	—	1.7 mi. (45–90 minutes)	2.1 mi. (45–90 minutes)
Copper Ave. lot	—	—	—	—	0.4 mi. (15–45 minutes)

Distance: 0.84 mile one-way (includes short trail to the start of Trail 401 near the falls)

Hiking Time: 20–40 minutes

Elevation: 200 ft. gain; highest point is about 6,160 ft. near trail leading to Narrow Falls

3. Embudo Trailhead–Indian School Road Parking Area to Copper Ave. Parking Lot

This part of the trail climbs partway up the mound just to the south of the Embudo Trailhead–Indian School Road parking area, but then veers to the right to head around the mound. After a short distance, Trail 401 leads to the mountain side of Embudo Mound. After edging around the mound, the trail descends into a relatively open valley area as it approaches U-Mound and the Copper Ave. parking area.

Difficulty: 2

Distance: 1.7 miles one-way

Hiking Time: 30 minutes–1.25 hours

Elevation: 280 ft. loss; highest point is 6,200 ft. at Embudo Trailhead–Indian School Road

4. Copper Ave. Parking Lot to Hilldale Mound (End of Trail)

This is the shortest and least hilly of the Trail 401 segments. Here, Trail 401 continues south from the Copper Ave. parking area through a relatively open plain as it heads up toward the end of the trail at Hilldale Mound, a distance of 0.4 mile.

Difficulty: 1

Distance: 0.4 mile one-way

Hiking Time: 10–20 minutes

Elevation: 120 ft. gain; highest point is 6,040 ft. at end of trail

IF YOU LIKED THIS TRAIL, try **HIKE 18: Trail 365–Sandia Peak Tram to Embudito Trailhead** or **HIKE 41: Trail 365–Comanche Road to I-40.**

FOR THOSE USING GPS DATA

(DATUM: WGS 84)

Trail 401 at Embudo Trailhead–Menaul Blvd. parking lot: –106.48776, 35.105033

Trail 401 at Embudo Trailhead–Indian School Road parking lot: –106.47984, 35.098985

Trail 401 at Copper Ave. parking lot: –106.48289, 35.079409

SUNSET CANYON ROUTE

Difficulty	2	
Distance	1.2 mi (1.9 km) round-trip	
Hiking Time	45–90 minutes	
Elevation	360 ft. gain (110 m)	Peak elevation: 6,680 ft. (2,036 m) where the canyon tightens; Low elevation: 6,320 ft. (1,926 m) at flood control structure
Trail Condition	Fair	USFS-owned; Unmaintained with deep sand and brush
Trail Users	Hikers	
Best Time	Spring and summer	
Parking	On-street near Sunset Canyon Pl. access point	
Fees	None	

SPECIAL INFORMATION: Parking is limited, with lots of "no parking" signs near the trailhead. Please be respectful of regulations and the landowners in this area.

THIS CANYON IS ONE of the more easily seen watersheds from within Albuquerque, and looks like a wonderful place, even from a distance. With its wide valley that extends halfway up the greater Sandia Mountains, it's hard not to notice from Tramway Boulevard. Sunset Canyon is known for its late sunrises, its quiet nature and spectacular scenery, and, of course, the wildlife that use this intact and healthy arroyo habitat. This little mountain watershed has wide, set-back valley walls. The valley bottom is filled with a dense growth of riparian vegetation similar to that found in Bear Canyon; chamisa and Apache plume dominate. Although it's a little scratchy at times, it is a truly beautiful canyon to spend a morning exploring.

At first glance, one might think that this hike and its landscape should be listed with the Central Trails area, as it looks so similar to Bear Canyon. But even a quick visit shows that it fits in nicely with the Southern Trail area, as the northernmost mounds line the bottom of the southern canyon wall and it is disconnected from trails to the north. The north valley walls of this canyon are quite steep. Even deer trails are hard to follow on this hillside, which means that this canyon is isolated from the Central Trails area. Instead, a small, rocky trail climbs up the less-steep south valley wall and between the two mounds and eventually connects this canyon to Trail 365 at the Comanche Road access point. Due to its low connectedness to other area trails, difficulty in finding the trailhead, and limited street parking, few non-local visitors seem to explore this area. Given these conditions, especially the limited parking, visitors should remember to be considerate of those who live near the trailhead and abide by all parking regulations and posted signs.

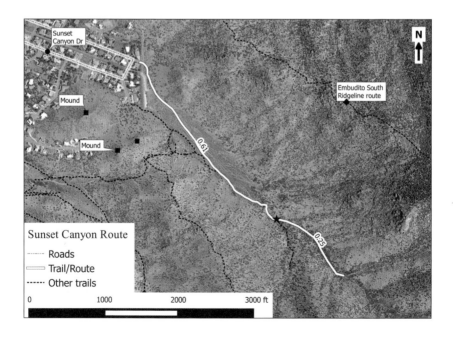

Sunset Canyon Route

------ Roads
====== Trail/Route
------ Other trails

0   1000   2000   3000 ft

Per canyon safety, the valley bottom should be avoided during inclement weather. Pay particular attention to storms brewing over the mountains, and be smart and avoid this hike if a rainstorm/thunderstorm is on the way.

■ THE HIKE

Park near the Sunset Canyon access point and walk up the dirt maintenance access road into the lower valley.

From this initial access point, a well-established trail follows the left (north) side of the valley for a short distance before dropping into the arroyo channel.

Follow the channel/valley as far upstream as desired. The channel splits about 0.6 mile upstream.

Return along the same route.

IF YOU LIKED THIS HIKE, try **HIKE 38: Embudito Canyon Route/Loop** to hike in a larger

canyon or **HIKE 50: Hanging Rock Canyon Loop** for a similar valley but a little longer hike with a loop option.

FOR THOSE USING GPS DATA
(DATUM: WGS 84)
Edge of the public lands in Sunset Canyon:
  –106.48035, 35.13102
Sunset Canyon where the two channels
  branch: –106.47431, 35.12424

Sunset Canyon Faults and Fans

One of the most interesting aspects of Sunset Canyon is its wide valley with setback walls forming a beautiful V-shaped valley. Unlike other canyons in the Sandia Mountains, Sunset Canyon follows a large fault system that extends from the foothills to the crest. As this northwest–southeast trending fault formed, likely during numerous rock-crushing events, the Sunset Canyon Watershed simultaneously formed within the faulted landscape. There, the valley stream carried tons and tons of crushed rock downstream out of the mountains, essentially excavating the fault zone. Once the broken rock was removed, it left behind a wide valley lined with relatively unfaulted, coherent Sandia granite.

Downhill from the mountain front, all this crushed rock formed an extremely large and steep outwash fan. Today, this area is fully developed with residential homes, making the surface topography somewhat difficult to see. While driving up to the trailhead for this hike or others from the Embudito Trailhead, observant drivers will notice that the roads cutting through the Glenwood Hills neighborhood climb up steep hills that slope up to the mouth of Sunset Canyon. Large, rounded granite boulders carried from the fault zone are scattered throughout this neighborhood, and are often used as yard ornaments, combined with cement to make retaining walls, or haphazardly strewn along property lines.

CANDELARIA BENCH LOOP

Difficulty	4	
Distance	2.3 mi (3.7 km) loop	
Hiking Time	1–2.5 hours	
Elevation	760 ft. gain (231 m)	Peak elevation: 6,720 ft. (2,048 m) along fence/ USFS boundary; Low elevation: 5,960 ft. (1,817 m) at parking
Trail Condition	Fair with poor sections	Open Space– and USFS-owned; Unmaintained
Trail Users	Hikers and horses	Bikes along the base of the mountains
Best Time	Spring through fall	
Parking	On-street near Comanche Rd. access point	
Fees	None	

SPECIAL INFORMATION: Parking is on-street along Camino de la Sierra or a side street. Please be respectful of the landowners in this area and any designated no-parking areas.

THIS SHORT ROUTE into the lower Sandia Mountains is a wonderful quick hike for experienced hikers simply seeking the mountains or a great introduction to small-trail mountain hiking for less-experienced hikers. Although it is rare to see more than a couple of people on these mountainous trails, the routes obviously get regular use and are surprisingly visible, which reduces the need for a lot of route-finding. The relatively easy mountain hiking, coupled with the outstanding city and mountain views, makes this a favorite mountain bench hike. With so few hikers and a good vegetation complex, deer (and their fawns) frequent these hills. Additionally, this loop can easily be extended all the way to Piedra Lisa Watershed, with the Falls Trail being used for the downhill descent.

This loop climbs up the first set of steep hillslopes to reach the lowest mountain bench area, located along an old fence line, presumably an old property boundary as it extends fairly regularly from this point to I-40. Although it is in poor condition and sections are missing, it provides a fixed landscape marker for hikers. These mountain bench areas have a general character that is wide-open, flat, or slightly tilted land covered in thick grasses, and the bench along this hike is no exception to this general description.

Unlike Trail 365, the mountain trails on this loop are small, unnamed, unmaintained tracks that typically lead straight up the steep lower mountainside and are kept open solely by foot (and hoof) traffic. Although this loop could be hiked in either direction, clockwise is recommended because the southern trail is better-graded for descending off the bench area; plus this direction allows extending the hike to the Piedra Lisa Falls Trail if desired. After the descent, hikers will enjoy the ease of walking the

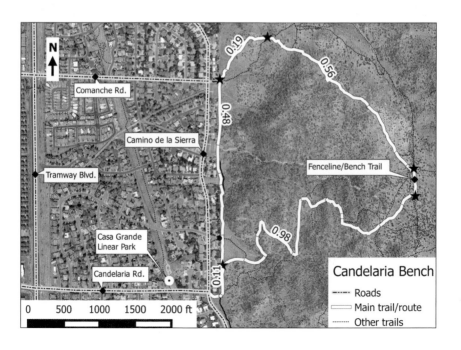

Cactus Wrens and Cane Cholla

Many birds use the cacti in the foothills for habitat, flitting about hunting bugs, but the cactus wren actually builds its home in cane cholla and other prickly desert plants such as yuccas. A few nesting pairs of this predominantly southern species now call the foothills home, and their interlaced grass nests, about the size of a football, are found at about head-height in the middle of large cholla plants. In fact, a nesting pair of wrens will often build more than one nest within their territory, giving them choices for shelter and roosting throughout the year. The cactus wren's call is often considered the voice of the desert: a loud, hoarse and throaty set of *cha-cha-cha* or *chug-chug-chug-chug*. This brown-and-white-speckled bird, about the size of a robin, easily blends with the desert, but it has a prominent white eyebrow and a white chin patch that distinguish it.

Cane cholla is probably the easiest cactus to identify in the foothills. Because it grows up to eight feet tall, it can be seen clearly from a distance. This common species develops a thick trunk with branches of cane that gives it a tree-like quality. The canes are gray-brown to green in color and covered in strong, sharp spines. Its (usually) purple or magenta flowers emerge in late spring, after which the cholla develops edible fruits that turn yellow to yellow-green as they ripen through the winter months.

well-maintained Trail 365 as it parallels the Camino de la Sierra. This segment of Trail 365 is less visited by hikers. A major point of interest is the extensive "Cholla Forest" located between the Candelaria Road and Comanche Road access points. Walking through this dense grouping of sharp-spined plants, good foot placement and balance feel even more important than on the steep slopes of the mountains.

■ THE HIKE

Park along the street near the Comanche Road access point.

Follow the main trail to the left (north) from the access point/fence. This trail immediately begins to climb up a grassy hill just north of the entrance fence. It passes through a saddle near the top of the hill (about 0.25 mile).

At this saddle, look up the larger mountainous hill to the right and find the small trail that curves to the southeast and heads uphill. Follow it to the top of the slope, about 0.4 mile. Continue on the ridgeline to the upper fence line trail that marks the Open Space/USFS property boundary, another 0.2 mile.

At the fence, turn right (south) and follow for a short distance, about

0.1 mile. As this trail descends into a small drainage, another trail veers to the right, leading into the heart of the grassy bench area.

Follow this trail toward the southwest as it passes between the two small peaks at the edge of the bench and to Trail 365 at the base of the mountains, about 1 mile.

Turn right and follow Trail 365 back to the Comanche Road access point, about 0.5 mile.

IF YOU LIKED THIS HIKE, try **HIKE 32: Bear Canyon Overlook** for a similarly difficult small-trail mountain hike or **HIKE 45: Piedra Lisa Falls and Bench Loop** for a longer and slightly harder small-trail mountain hike.

FOR THOSE USING GPS DATA (DATUM: WGS 84)

Intersection of small trail that climbs up to the Bench area: –106.487017, 35.124951

Intersection of Bench trail with small trail that connects to Trail 365: –106.480042, 35.119206

Intersection of Trail 365 with small trail that connects with the Bench trail: –106.48893, 35.116558

PIEDRA LISA FALLS AND BENCH LOOP

Difficulty	4	
Distance	2.5 mi (4 km) loop	
Hiking Time	1–2.5 hours	
Elevation	880 ft. gain (268 m)	Peak elevation: 6,880 ft. (2,097 m) along fence/ USFS boundary; Low elevation: 6,000 ft. (1,829 m) at parking
Trail Condition	Fair with poor sections	Open Space– and USFS-owned; Sections unmaintained
Trail Users	Hikers and horses	Bikes along the base of the mountains
Best Time	Spring through fall	
Parking Lot	Piedra Lisa	Parking lot is Open Space–owned and -maintained
Fees	None	

SPECIAL INFORMATION: The waterfall area/trail is very popular and can get congested on busy days. For smaller crowds, visit this area on a weekday or plan on the loop, which is less-used.

THIS RELATIVELY SHORT HIKE starts by ascending up the Piedra Lisa Watershed and the falls (a.k.a. Whitewash), a dry waterfall that can be seen easily from Tramway Boulevard and elsewhere within the area. In fact, this white-colored outcrop of Sandia granite actually glows in the setting sun. It is a major attraction with a well-tended Open Space parking area and a well-marked trail that leads to the top of the falls. The loop hike continues past the falls, going up the canyon and then leaving it behind to explore the mountain bench area to the north.

As with the previous hike, this is a great route for experienced hikers who want a short, quick trek that takes them into the lower mountains. It is also a great introduction to hiking small-trail mountain tracks for those with less experience. While the falls area can get extremely busy, rivaling the very popular USFS trails just north of here, hiking a short distance upstream in the canyon even on the busiest days leaves most of the congestion behind. And for hikers who are committed enough to climb out of the canyon to complete the loop, the route gets eerily quiet in the bench area after all the waterfall commotion.

The mountainous trails are narrow and tend to be rocky but obviously get regular use. They are surprisingly visible, hence the need for a lot of route-finding is reduced. This relatively easy mountain route, coupled with the waterfall and outstanding city/mountain views, makes this a great hike.

Both the trail up to the falls and the canyon above the waterfall should be avoided during inclement weather, as this area is dangerously prone to flash floods. Because this is a small watershed, a flash flood could descend before a storm has even ended, and exiting the steep falls area may not be a quick enough option for avoiding it. The bedrock in this canyon, especially the large bedrock steps, have been worn smooth over time and can instantly become slippery when wet. Pay particular attention to storms brewing over the mountains, and be smart and postpone this hike if rain is on the way.

■ **THE HIKE**

Park at the Piedra Lisa Canyon/Watershed parking lot.

Follow the main Falls Trail to the top of the waterfall. Although this is a steep climb, it is only a short distance, about 0.4 mile.

From the top of the waterfall, head upstream, following the canyon as it goes through an S-shaped set of turns. The first turn is a large arc toward the north; then there is a smaller arc to the south. The trail then turns back toward the north. Before the apex of this turn, about 0.2 mile from the falls, look toward the slope to the north for the small upward-leading trail.

Turn left (north) and hike uphill on this small trail out of the channel area. Continue in a northerly direction until reaching the bench area. With so many small trails in this area, remember not to turn east toward the larger Sandia Mountains. This bench is best described as flattish, but it has notable rolling hills and the trail travels across small drainage channels. Continue north until a relatively good trail turns off to the left (west) at a fairly deep channel crossing. To its left is a grassy bench area between two hills that resemble small mounds (0.6 mile from canyon bottom).

Turn left and follow this small trail toward the southwest for almost 1 mile as it passes between the two small peaks at

The Many Faces of Sandia Granite

Sandia granite, the rock that makes up most of the Sandia Mountains, formed about 1.5 billion years ago in the Precambrian geologic period as a large magma chamber trapped below the earth's surface. As the magma cooled slowly, crystals formed. As the crystals became somewhat organized, the rock needed less space and shrank, forming cracks; pockets of still-molten magma slipped into the voids, where it cooled and created crisscrossing veins of quartz, orthoclase, and mica within the more common granitic rock. These large, dominant, and interconnected minerals formed the Sandia granite, which is known for its large crystals, most notably pink orthoclase, also called potassium feldspar. As the mountains were uplifted and fractured, some of the other non-orthoclase minerals were altered into a green mineral called epidote, thus creating boulders filled with large pink crystals intermixed with green.

Exploring the canyons and the various falls is a great way to see many of the joints within the Sandia granite. The steep mountain trails, such as La Luz, Pino, or Embudo, are great places to inspect the large boulders where the pink-colored crystals are easiest to find.

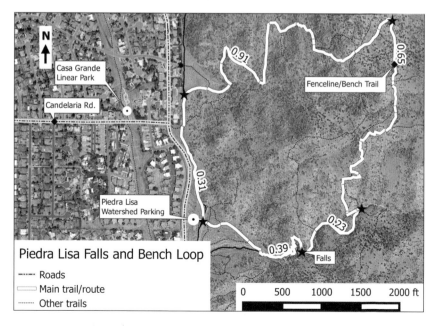

N

Casa Grande Linear Park

Candelaria Rd.

0.91

0.65

Fenceline/Bench Trail

Piedra Lisa Watershed Parking

0.31

0.23

0.39

Falls

Piedra Lisa Falls and Bench Loop

----- Roads
⬜ Main trail/route
········ Other trails

0   500   1000   1500   2000 ft

the edge of the bench, begins to quickly descend the hillside, and reaches the base of the steep mountain face at the Trail 365 junction.

Turn left (south) onto Trail 365 and follow it back to the Piedra Lisa Canyon/ Watershed parking area, about 0.3 mile.

IF YOU LIKED THIS LOOP coupling a falls with mountain hiking, try **HIKE 55: Old Man Canyon Loop** for another falls loop, but one where the hiker climbs the falls. If the small-trail mountain hike component is the most desired attribute, try **HIKE 44: Candelaria Bench Loop** for a similarly difficult hike or **HIKE 59: Tijeras**

Canyon–Four Hills Overlook Loop for a longer and slightly harder route.

FOR THOSE USING GPS DATA
(DATUM: WGS 84)
Small trail that leads uphill to the Bench
    Trail from the Piedra Lisa Canyon area:
    –106.48122, 35.11279
Intersection of the Bench Trail with the
    small trail that connects with Trail 365:
    –106.480042, 35.119206
Intersection of Trail 365 with the small trail
    that connects with the Bench trail:
    –106.48893, 35.116558

PIEDRA LISA RIDGE OVERLOOK LOOP

Difficulty	5	Steep, rocky, and long.
Distance	4.18 mi (6.7 km) loop	Overlook at about 1.65 mi from parking
Hiking Time	3–4 hours	
Elevation	1,960 ft. gain (597 m)	Peak elevation: 7,920 ft. (2,414 m) at overlook; Low elevation: 5,960 ft. (1,817 m) at parking
Trail Condition	Fair, with poor sections	Open Space– and USFS-owned; Unmaintained
Trail Users	Hikers and horses	Bikes along the base of the mountains
Best Time	Spring and fall	
Parking Lot	Menaul Blvd.	Parking lot is Open Space–owned and -maintained
Fees	None	

SPECIAL INFORMATION: Snow and ice often cover the trail in the winter season. Given the remoteness of this trail, it should not be hiked in inclement weather or when trails are icy.

ONE OF THE MORE interesting places along this and the next hike is the Piedra Lisa–Embudo Watershed divide/ridgeline. Here, the ridgeline of a steep hill is wide-open, with very few trees, boulders or hillsides to walk next to, which results in a strong feeling of exposure. Hikers will feel as if they are in the middle of nowhere, even though there are constant views of the city and the taller mountains. Given the steep and rocky trails that lead to this ridgeline, only the hardiest of hikers travel this route, leading to relative solitude as well.

With initially stunning views of the falls (a.k.a. Whitewash), this route follows the Piedra Lisa south ridge before crossing into Embudo Watershed, which leads to fantastic views of the southern Sandia watersheds. From here, the route follows the Embudo Watershed almost due east, directly up and into the larger Sandia Mountains. A gorgeous overlook area at the edge of the tree line provides opportunities for great shade and views into

Three Gun Springs Watershed/Tres Pistolas. This unique watershed to the south and east of the overlook area is full of less-steep terrain and trees. Beyond it, hikers can also see Tijeras Canyon, the Four Hills area, the Manzanita Mountains, and all the way to the Manzano Mountains on clear days.

A word of warning: this unnamed trail is a steep climb, especially on the last uphill before the overlook. It continues past the overlook and is one of the few trails that eventually reaches the Sandia Crest. A short distance uphill from the overlook area, another small trail from Sunset Canyon joins it as it continues to climb and join with the Embudito Trail near the Embudito–Three Guns Spring Trail junction. This route is not for the faint of heart. It goes mostly straight up everything: straight up the hill, up and over bedrock outcrops, straight up slippery slopes covered in pea gravel, and, of course, up and over all the various boulder steps. Without a doubt, this is a very

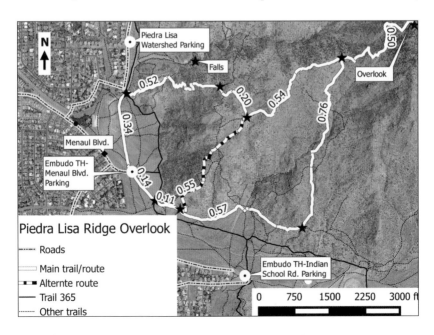

Piedra Lisa Ridge Overlook

- ---- Roads
- ---- Main trail/route
- ▪-▪ Alternte route
- —— Trail 365
- ······ Other trails

difficult hike, and one best suited to experienced hikers with some route-finding skills, endurance, and extra time for the slow going.

Like many of these small mountainous trails, in a short but strenuous distance, this one takes hikers up and into the lower mountains and the forested hillslopes, where the landscape feels remote and few people venture. As on most of the routes along the benches, deer are the most commonly seen wildlife; they seem to particularly like the steep, rocky slopes intermixed with the grassy bench areas. This is a quiet hike where the focus is on the views, the trail, and wiping the sweat off your brow.

Two important trail notes. First, the initial hill-climb is recommended over the other options because the longer trail with something like a switchback is slightly less steep. Second, the trail recommended for the major downhill route is the best option: again, it has some switchback-like features, making it steep, but not quite as difficult as the other two. For those hikers who would rather walk further to minimize the difficult trails, use the recommended downhill route in both directions.

■ THE HIKE

Park at the Embudo Trailhead–Menaul Boulevard parking lot.

Hike Trail 401 to where it intersects with Trail 365. Find a small trail that turns right and begins to climb up the steep hill to the east of Trail 365, 0.34 mile from the parking area. Several trails and paths ascend this hill, all leading to the correct place, the ridgeline, which continues to climb toward the larger mountains. A

Tres Pistolas Open Space Area and the Three Gun Spring Trail (USFS Trail 194)

The Three Gun Spring Watershed is an interesting valley in the southern Sandia Mountains that is a bit hard to find and somewhat reminiscent of upper Embudo Canyon. Although not located within Albuquerque, Three Gun Spring Trail begins in city-managed Open Space lands before it passes into USFS lands and ultimately into Wilderness Area. As with many of the large USFS trails in the Sandia Mountains, this trail was once an old road that drove straight up the watershed; when the road disappears at the back of the valley, the trail begins a steep climb up to the watershed divide and the Embudo Trail Junction (about 2.5 miles from the parking lot). From here, hikers can continue for another 2–3 miles on the Three Gun Spring Trail to the Sandia Crest Trail via the Embudito Trail.

For those seeking shorter hiking options, there are numerous side trails in the main Three Gun Spring Valley with interesting features and places to visit. Near the parking lot, a set of small trails veer off the main trail leading toward the valley bottom and the large outwash fans that have formed along the western valley wall. At the Wilderness boundary, Hawk Watch Trail branches to the east, leading to an area where volunteers monitor migrating birds of prey. Just before the Three Gun Spring Trail starts its steep climb with switchbacks, a couple of small trails veer right to continue up the small creek that leads to Three Gun Spring.

The trailhead is tucked behind a residential area off NM 333/Rte. 66 in Carnuel, New Mexico. Take I-40 east, driving toward Tijeras, take the Carnuel Exit, and continue east on NM 333 for about 1.5 miles. Turn left (north) onto Monticello Drive and follow this small residential road to Alegre Drive, turn left, and then turn right at the Siempre Verde/Tres Pistolas Trail intersection. Follow this road to its end and a small parking lot.

slightly less steep trail option to reach the ridgeline is just to the south of the Trail 401/365 intersection, off of Trail 365: it can be difficult to find and may take a little bit of searching, but it begins its ascent a little further from the parking area and climbs up a small drainage/hollow. This trail is still steep, but it is a little less rocky and less exposed than the other ones that climb the face of the hill.

Follow the ridgeline trail as it climbs about 0.5 mile up the steep ridge that forms the southern watershed boundary for the Piedra Lisa Watershed.

This trail veers to the right (south) and joins with another, larger ridgeline trail (0.2 mile). The ridgeline is the divide between the Piedra Lisa and Embudo Watersheds. If on the shortest loop, turn right and descend on this trail to the parking area.

If continuing on to the overlook, turn left and continue uphill on the Piedra Lisa–Embudo Ridgeline Trail for another 0.5 mile. This trail climbs until it passes a small peak on the right, then descends

a very short distance into a saddle where there is a well-worn trail intersection and shady picnic spot. At this saddle, the right (south) trail is the recommended downhill route. If not going to the overlook, turn right to descend off the ridgeline and return to parking area.

For the overlook, continue up the

SHORTER LOOP OPTIONS

1. Shortest Loop
Difficulty: 4, due to steep, rocky trails
Distance: 1.86-mile loop
Hiking Time: 1–2 hours
Elevation: 800 ft. gain; peak elevation: 6,760 ft.
Parking: Embudo Trailhead–Menaul Boulevard parking lot

2. Loop without the Overlook Segment
Difficulty: 4, due to steep, rocky trails
Distance: 3.18-mile loop
Hiking Time: 1.5–2.5 hours
Elevation: 1,280 ft. gain; peak elevation: 7,240 ft.
Parking: Embudo Trailhead–Menaul Boulevard parking lot

ridgeline trail, which climbs steeply for about 0.5 mile.

After a short break at the overlook, turn around and return to the saddle area and veer onto the south-trending trail (0.5 mile).

Follow the trail about 0.76 mile down the steep hill, across the bench with rolling hills, and down the last steep hill, returning to the foothills trail.

Once back on the foothills trail, turn right (west) to head back to the parking area. The trail under the power lines is Trail 365 and is the fastest route, but the one that follows the base of the mountains (and turns seamlessly into Trail 401) is more scenic.

IF YOU WOULD LIKE AN EASIER small-trail mountain hike, try either HIKE 44: Candelaria Bench Loop or HIKE 59: Tijeras Canyon–Four Hills Overlook Loop. For similarly difficult small-trail mountain hikes, try HIKE 39: Embudito North Ridge Trail Loop or HIKE 40: Embudito South Ridge Trail to Boulder Cave. For a more difficult hike, try HIKE 47: Piedra Lisa–Sunset Canyon Loop.

FOR THOSE USING GPS DATA (DATUM: WGS 84)

Beginning of small trail that leads up the south ridge of Piedra Lisa Watershed: –106.488862, 35.109389

Intersection of several small trails along the south ridge of Piedra Lisa Watershed: –106.482191, 35.109863

Intersection of a moderate-sized trail at the Piedra Lisa–Embudo ridgeline, the larger trail leads up from the Embudo Trailhead–Menaul Blvd. parking lot (alternate route): –106.480225, 35.108139

Intersection of small trail at a saddle that leads downhill to near Trail 365: –106.47356, 35.111581

Start of the small saddle trail: –106.476198; 35.101941

Start of small trail from the Menaul Blvd. parking lot leading to the Piedra Lisa–Embudo ridgeline: –106.48496, 35.102916

Intersection of Trail 365 and Trail 401: –106.486779, 35.103377

Overlook: –106.468383, 35.113481

PIEDRA LISA–SUNSET CANYON LOOP

Difficulty	5	Steep, rocky, and long.
Distance	4.1 mi (6.6 km) loop	Overlook at about 1.65 mi from parking
Hiking Time	4–5 hours	
Elevation	2,130 ft. gain (649 m)	Peak elevation: 8,130 ft. (2,478 m) at furthest point on loop; Low elevation: 6,000 ft. (1,829 m) at parking
Trail Condition	Fair with poor sections	Open Space– and USFS-owned; Unmaintained
Trail Users	Hikers and horses	Bikes along the base of the mountains
Best Time	Spring and fall	
Parking Lot	Piedra Lisa	Parking lot is Open Space–owned and -maintained
Fees	None	

SPECIAL INFORMATION: Snow and ice often cover the trail in the winter season. Given the remoteness of this trail, it should not be hiked in inclement weather or when trails are icy.

THIS LOOP FOLLOWS around the Piedra Lisa Watershed, then continues north to descend along Sunset Canyon before returning along the base of the mountains. The fantastic views of the Piedra Lisa Falls at the beginning of this loop are soon forgotten as this small trail begins to climb up the Piedra Lisa–Embudo Watershed divide. The tree line is at the top of the watershed, and its shade is well-earned, as the climb to that point is a steep one with long rocky sections. The quick elevation gain leads to fantastic views in most directions, and an increasingly better vista of the lower watersheds as the headwater ridge is reached and followed to the north. Once beyond the tree line, this route veers to the left to follow the Piedra Lisa Watershed boundary and eventually leads to the Sunset Canyon Watershed. Hikers who miss the turn will likely realize it fairly quickly, as the route continues in an easterly direction, clearly leaving the Piedra Lisa Watershed and eventually meeting up with the Embudito Trail that leads to the crest.

As with the previous trail description, a word of warning: this unnamed route/loop has numerous steep climbs and the trails are a little smaller in the higher mountainous terrain. As with many of these small mountainous trails, don't let the short distance fool you. This is not a casual hike: the route goes mostly straight up, then turns north along small trails that, if followed correctly, lead back down to Trail 365 along a relatively not-too-bad trail/path. But if a hiker loses or misses the main trail or takes the wrong one down, this pleasure jaunt can quickly turn into a difficult, steep bushwhacking event that will be remembered for some time. The route is best suited for experienced hikers with good route-finding skills, endurance, and plenty of extra time. The difficult access, however, has a great payoff: it leads into a remote landscape with outstanding views and a forest setting seldom visited by other hikers.

■ THE HIKE

Park at the Piedra Lisa Canyon/Watershed parking lot.

Hike south on Trail 365 about 0.2 mile to where it crosses Trail 401 and brushes up against the base of the mountains.

Small Trail to the Crest

At the apex of **HIKE 47: Piedra Lisa–Sunset Canyon Loop**, the route in this guide directs hikers to turn left (if coming from the Menaul/Piedra Lisa area) onto the small trail that curves north along the headwaters of Sunset Canyon. However, expert hikers who have good trail-finding skills could choose to turn right and stay on the larger trail that continues to ascend. This small, unmaintained trail doesn't have an official name, but is used by a surprising number of local hikers who know the area well. Some of them call it the Menaul route, others the Whitewash Trail, and still others use one of a series of locally derived names. Regardless, this route continues in a mostly eastward direction and joins with the Embudito Trail before it finishes the climb up to the South Crest Trail (Trail 130). On the return, ambitious hikers could make a loop by returning to the foothills via the Embudito Trail (Trail 192), or head south on the Three Gun Spring Trail (Trail 194) to return via the Embudo Trail (Trail 193). Hikers considering this small trail should be prepared for mountain conditions by carrying a really good map of the area along with the rest of the Ten Essentials.

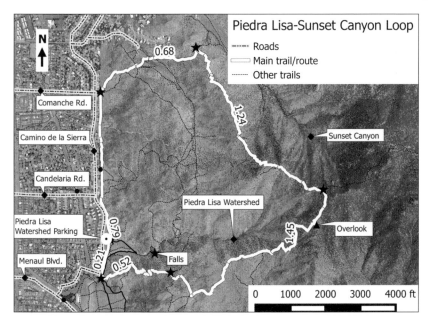

Piedra Lisa-Sunset Canyon Loop
- - - - Roads
▭ Main trail/route
.... Other trails

(This ridge is the southern watershed divide for Piedra Lisa Watershed.)

Once at the hill, veer left off Trail 365 onto a small, unnamed trail that leads upward. Several trails and paths ascend this steep hill, and all lead to the correct place: the ridgeline, which continues to climb up toward the larger mountains. Follow the ridgeline trail as it climbs up this first hill, about 0.5 mile.

After veering right (south) on this small ridgeline trail, it joins with a larger ridgeline trail. Turn left (east) as this new trail continues to climb up a second ridgeline (about 0.7 mile). This second ridgeline is the watershed divide between the Piedra Lisa and Embudo Watersheds. This trail continually climbs until it passes by a small peak on the right, then descends a very short distance into a saddle where there is a well-worn trail intersection and shady picnic spot. If desired, hikers can abort this longer loop and create a shorter loop back to the car by turning right at

this saddle and following the unnamed trail to the south to descend back to the foothills trail. (See previous hike for details.)

If continuing, stay on the main trail that climbs up the very steep hill to the overlook area about 0.5 mile east of the saddle/intersection.

Continuing past the overlook area, follow the ridgeline, which veers left (north) as it starts around the top of the Piedra Lisa headwaters area. In a short distance, the trail divides, with the main trail continuing to the right (east) and eventually meeting the Three Gun Spring Trail, and a smaller trail—the correct one—veering to the left (north). This junction is about 2 miles from the parking area.

Choose the smaller trail that veers left and curves left around the headwaters of the Piedra Lisa Watershed. After a short distance, views of Sunset Canyon Watershed emerge to the right (north) of the trail. The trail starts in the trees, but after several steep descents leaves them and the Piedra Lisa Watershed behind. Continue on this ridgeline trail, following the Sunset Canyon Watershed divide almost to the residential area, 1.24 miles. Several small trails turn left along this route, but all of them lead to extremely steep descents that entail a fair bit of bushwhacking and exploratory hiking (no trail). Do not turn off this trail too early unless prepared for a crazy steep descent.

The Sunset Canyon ridgeline trail ends at a "T" intersection behind a group of mounds, just uphill from a housing unit. The correct trail at this intersection is the left one, which leads away from Sunset Canyon and into another small watershed area.

Passing by the edge of residences and a flood-control structure, continue in a westerly direction, climbing up the small hill and then down the other side toward the edge of the public lands. After about 0.7 mile, this unnamed trail ends near the Comanche Road/Camino de la Sierra intersection and the beginning of Trail 365.

Turn left (south) and follow Trail 365 back to the Piedra Lisa parking area, about 0.8 mile.

FOR SIMILARLY DIFFICULT SMALL-TRAIL mountain hikes, try **HIKE 46: Piedra Lisa Ridge Overlook Loop**, **HIKE 39: Embudito North Ridge Trail Loop**, or **HIKE 40: Embudito South Ridge Trail to Boulder Cave**.

FOR THOSE USING GPS DATA
(DATUM: WGS 84)

Beginning of small trail that leads up the south ridge of the Piedra Lisa Watershed:
    −106.488862, 35.109389

Intersection of several small trails along the south ridge of the Piedra Lisa Watershed:
    −106.482191, 35.109863

Intersection at the top of the watershed, with the right (east) trail continuing to the crest and the left (north) trail to Sunset Watershed:
    −106.4678, 35.11629

Intersection of the Sunset Watershed ridgeline trail and a small trail that leads into Hidden Valley and then back to Trail 365:
    −106.48014, 35.126847

Comanche Road access point:
    −106.4892, 35.123369

Piedra Lisa parking lot: −106.48802, 35.112255

NARROW FALLS

Difficulty	3	
Distance	1 mi (1.6 km) round-trip	
Hiking Time	1 hour	
Elevation	360 ft. gain (110 m)	Peak elevation: 6,560 ft. (2,000 m) at furthest point on loop; Low elevation: 6,200 ft. (1,890 m) at parking
Trail Condition	Fair	Open Space– and USFS-owned; Unmaintained
Trail Users	Hikers	Horses and bikes along the base of the mountains
Best Time	Fall through spring	
Parking Lot	Embudo Trailhead	Parking lot is Open Space–owned and -maintained
Fees	None	

SPECIAL INFORMATION: The canyon has tall, smooth bedrock steps that can be slippery year-round.

THIS IS A WONDERFUL short hike to a spectacular dry waterfall, which is close to two parking lots, making it easy to reach and explore. The narrow canyon that leads to this series of surprisingly tall falls is hidden from the main foothill trails, so hikers need a little faith in following this route. In addition to the steep falls, the valley walls are tight and many are nearly vertical, making just about everyone feel a little bit claustrophobic while exploring the canyon on their way to the tallest waterfall. Once in the canyon, hikers will scramble up bedrock outcrops/steps that get increasingly taller as they approach the main falls. Notice that the color of the granite changes between the lower steps and the tallest falls. Small and sometimes not-so-small dikes (places where pockets of magma slipped into cracks, forming long lines of different-colored rocks) cut across the granite, and numerous faults can be seen in the canyon walls and along the alignment of the tallest waterfall.

Given that these beautiful falls are close to the roads, a major USFS trailhead (Embudo Trail), and a picnic area, this area is sometimes crowded. The longest stretch of trail is along Trail 401 from the Embudo Trailhead–Indian School Road parking lot, through Embudo Arroyo to the mouth of the canyon. While crossing Embudo Arroyo, be sure to stay on the main trail (Trail 401), which crosses over several sandy channels and is obscured by thick chamisa. For a slightly longer route, start your hike from the Embudo Trailhead–Menaul Boulevard parking lot. To explore the waterfall in solitude, try this trip midweek.

This hike can quickly become dangerous in a rainstorm due to the potential for flash floods. Although this is not a slot canyon, it is narrow and steep with smooth rocks that become instantly slippery when wet. The tall waterfall should not be scaled by inexperienced climbers, nor should it be climbed by anyone when it is wet. Because these canyon walls are very steep, finding an alternate route out

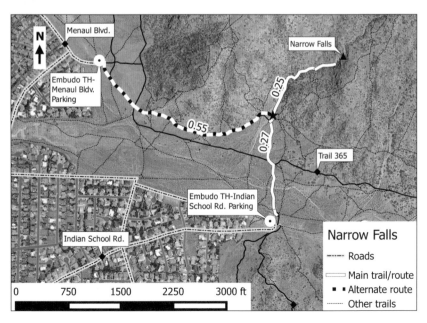

Jackrabbits versus Cottontails

Hikers exploring the foothills, especially those who bring their dogs, will quickly notice that two distinct rabbit species reside along these trails: black-tailed jackrabbits and desert cottontail rabbits. The jackrabbits seem to be more wary of hikers, as they more readily hop away from your trail, while the cottontails rely more on stealth and hide in place, often waiting until the last moment to bolt. Both of these species are an important food source for the predators that hunt them, including coyotes, bobcats, foxes, bears, cougars, and larger birds such as owls, hawks, and eagles.

The black-tailed jackrabbit, also known as the American desert hare, is the larger of the two, and is often seen when it stops and sits up on its long hind legs and tail. This hare builds its nest in a shallow hole under a bush or tree, called a "form." The cottontail is a little more versatile: it may dig a form or use an abandoned burrow or simply nest under a bush. Both rabbits occupy the mixed shrub–grassland terrains, and neither migrates or hibernates during the colder winter months.

Their diets are composed of various shrubs, small trees, grasses, and forbs, with cottontails eating 80 percent grass and also munching on cacti when times are tough. When the grass is gone, shrubs and tree bark make up the bulk of their fall and winter diets. They get most of their water from either the plants they eat or the dew that forms on them.

is also problematic. Pay particular attention to storms brewing over the mountains, and be smart and avoid this hike if rain is on the way.

▪ THE HIKE

Park at the Embudo Trailhead–Indian School Road parking lot.

Hike north on Trail 401 for about 0.25 mile, crossing the Embudo Arroyo and Trail 365 to where Trail 401 turns sharply to the left (west).

Rather than turning with Trail 401, follow the channel, heading straight up the valley/arroyo toward the canyon. After a few bedrock steps, the canyon leads to the tallest waterfall at about 0.25 mile from Trail 401.

Turn around and return on the same route.

FOR OTHER IMPRESSIVE FALLS found along hikes, try HIKE 5: Hidden Falls Canyon Route, HIKE 45: Piedra Lisa Falls and Bench Loop, or HIKE 55: Old Man Canyon Loop. A great introduction to scaling small waterfalls is HIKE 7: Waterfall Canyon via Piedra Lisa Trail in the Northern Trails section of this guide.

FOR THOSE USING GPS DATA
(DATUM: WGS 84)
Beginning of Narrow Falls Canyon Area:
 −106.48020, 35.10311
Base of Narrow Falls: −106.47728, 35.10508

EMBUDO DAM LOOP

Difficulty	2	Hills increase the exertion
Distance	1.8 mi (2.9 km) for inner loop	
Hiking Time	30–60 minutes	
Elevation	300 ft. gain (91 m)	Peak elevation: 6,500 ft. (1,981 m) near Trail 365/365A junction; Low elevation: 6,200 ft. (1,890 m) at parking
Trail Condition	Excellent	Open Space– and USFS-owned and -maintained
Trail Users	Hikers, bikers, horses	Bikes especially along the large named trails
Best Time	Fall through spring	
Parking Lot	Embudo Trailhead	Parking lot is Open Space–owned and -maintained
Fees	None	

SPECIAL INFORMATION: Add an extra mile to either loop option by parking at the Menaul parking area.

THIS SHORT LOOP shows off the character of the southern foothills area while completing a route around Embudo Dam. It starts by rolling up and down along the base of the mountains to the north of the Embudo Trail, then crosses the valley bottom to climb up the back of a mound before returning to the parking area. The trails for the main (inner) loop are large and well-maintained, with excellent signs and a wide walking area, making this a nice hike for a group. Rabbits and lizards are common sights throughout this hike, but especially in the reservoir area.

The larger Trail 365 and 365A are popular for both hiking and biking, so they can be very busy on weekends. If a more solitary experience is desired, the outer loop option is less busy, even though it still employs some sections of the larger named trails. Both routes loop about the dam and the mound and have great views.

Although the dam is the most noticeable feature along this route, the mound located immediately south of the parking area, with Trail 365A on its southern slopes, is the largest: in fact, it blocks views of the city for the southern half of the hike. Coupled with the slightly more rugged landscape, with longer and steeper hills than the area north of Embudo Trail, the trails along the southern route have a wilder feeling.

The shorter (main) hike is perfect for those who are new to the area, short on time, or need an introduction to hiking. The slightly longer outer loop is ideal for those who want to do a little bit of exploration by getting away from the large trails.

■ THE HIKE

Park at the Embudo Trailhead–Indian School Road parking lot.

Hike north on Trail 401 (0.16 mile).

Turn right (east) onto Trail 365, which passes by the Embudo Dam, then turns to pass behind and upstream of the dam (0.5 mile).

After a short distance, Trail 365 climbs

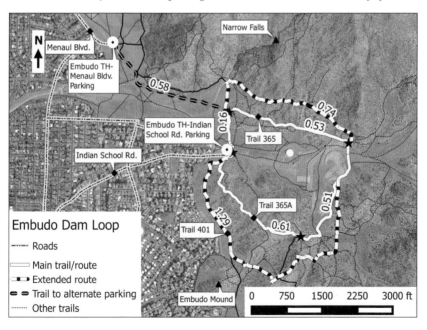

Embudo Dam Loop

---- Roads
▭▭ Main trail/route
■▬▶ Extended route
●　● Trail to alternate parking
----- Other trails

a notable hill and meets up with Trail 365A, on the mountainside of the mound (0.5 mile).

Turn right onto Trail 365A and follow it back to the parking area (0.6 mile).

IF YOU LIKED THIS HIKE, try the outer loop along this hike. Or, for hikes in similar landscapes, try (in rough order of difficulty) **HIKE 57: Hilldale Mound Loop**, **HIKE 56: Two Mound Loop**, **HIKE 28: Elena Gallegos Inner Trail Loop**, or **HIKE 29: North Levee/Trail 305 Loop**.

FOR THOSE USING GPS DATA
(DATUM: WGS 84)
Intersection of Trail 365 with Trail 401:
   –106.480145, 35.101223

Location of Trail 365 as it turns south to cross the reservoir area: –106.471589, 35.099592
Intersection of Trail 365 and Trail 365A:
   –106.474872, 35.09427

ALTERNATE/EXTENDED ROUTES

1. Outer Loop Route
Difficulty: 3
Distance: 2.4-mile loop
Hiking Time: 45 minutes–1.5 hours
Elevation: 380 ft. gain; peak elevation: 6,580 ft., uphill from Trail 365/365A junction; rolling foothills
Parking: Embudo Trailhead–Indian School Road

2. Add an Extra Mile
Park at the Embudo Trailhead–Menaul Boulevard parking area. Same difficulty.

Lizards

In the foothills, the lizards always seem to know you're coming before you get there. The only sign they give most hikers of their presence is rustling in the bottoms of bushes and in piles of leaves as they scurry away. However, if you are lucky and spend enough time out there, you will see a variety of lizards scuttling across the sand, rocks, and boulders. The most common lizards seen during the day are horned lizards (a.k.a. horny toads), skinks, and whiptails.

Whiptail lizards are the most common of the lizards that hikers see. They are easily identified by their slightly scaly skin, long pointy nose, and a series of pale-yellow stripes extending the length of their body, from their heads to their tails. These energetic and fast-moving animals scurry and dive for cover if approached. The New Mexico whiptail lizard was named the official state reptile in 2003. Interestingly, it is a crossbreed between a western whiptail, which lives in the desert, and the little striped whiptail, which favors grasslands. This all-female species reproduces by cloning: their eggs require no fertilization, and the offspring are exact genetic duplicates of the mother.

The variable skink, also called the many-lined skink, looks and acts a lot like the whiptail. This quick little lizard also has a series of yellow/pale lines that extend from near the animal's nose to the top end of its tail. But this species has very shiny and smooth skin, a generally beefier body, and a swollen-looking tail with mottled colors. Great Plains skinks also reside in this area, but are much less common. All these skinks are more likely to be found near water sources.

The Hernandez's short-horned lizard is the most likely horned lizard you may see in the foothills; however, because they tend to be quiet, you may simply pass right by without even noticing them. These cute short-tailed lizards are small and round-bodied, with rows of spines jutting out from the backs of their heads and along their sides. When these ordinarily calm creatures are startled, they freeze and flatten themselves against the ground, relying on their inherent camouflage to go unnoticed.

All of these lizards dine primarily on ants and other ground insects. Birds, other lizards, and snakes are their main predators.

HANGING ROCK CANYON LOOP

Difficulty	3	
Distance	2 mi (3.2 km) round-trip	
Hiking Time	30–60 minutes	
Elevation	560 ft. gain (170 m)	Peak elevation: 6,760 ft. (2,060 m) at hanging rock; Low elevation: 6,200 ft. (1,890 m) at parking
Trail Condition	Good	Open Space– and USFS-owned; Unmaintained
Trail Users	Hikers, bikers, horses	
Best Time	Fall through spring	
Parking Lot	Embudo Trailhead	Parking lot is Open Space–owned and -maintained
Fees	None	

WITH A SIMILAR FEEL as **HIKE 43**: **Sunset Canyon Route**, this small side valley to the larger Embudo Valley is a beauty. While in the lower mountains, it is a narrow, steep canyon, but it fans out into a wide, brushy valley/fan as it joins with Embudo Arroyo along the Embudo Trail. Like Sunset Canyon, it follows a large fault system and the resulting wide valley bottom has a well-established riparian corridor. Over time, this little canyon has obviously drawn many hikers and adventurers: two well-worn trails lead up the valley. Although not maintained, these routes have been stomped into the soil and are in good shape. In combination with the Embudo Trail, they create a nice valley loop option.

Just upstream from the fan, the valley narrows to form a canyon, the location of the hanging rock. As with many canyon routes, hikers can explore as far as desired, but the going gets rough up the canyon with steep bedrock-step sections,

ALTERNATE/EXTENDED ROUTE

Add an Extra Mile
Park at the Embudo Trailhead–Menaul Boulevard parking area. Same difficulty.

loose rock, and boulders and trees that block the channel. There is no obvious ridgeline or other trail that crosses the valley to make a larger loop option in the upper canyon area. Therefore, the return route in the canyon is the same as the one upstream. This side canyon, as well as others nearby, has a nice riparian corridor filled with trees and bushes that can be a mecca for smaller animals and birds. The most common creatures found in these areas are birds, whether a small hummingbird or something larger like an owl or hawk; regardless of species, it is easy to feel the healthy vibe of this habitat.

As with all canyons, this hike should be avoided during rainy weather. Beyond

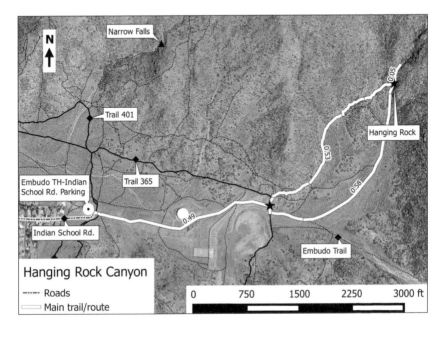

Great Horned Owls

Exploring small, quiet places such as Hanging Rock Canyon can yield unexpected surprises, such as a great horned owl perched in a tree. The great horned owl, one of the most common and widespread owls in North America, has been nicknamed the "winged tiger" for its fierce and rapacious skills as a predator. These birds' wing feathers have serrated edges, which allows them to fly silently. Their eyes are the size of a human adult's, but their vision is one hundred times more acute. Even with these incredible physical attributes, it's their hearing that is really special. Their feathered facial disk acts as a giant ear, capturing sound that, coupled with their amazing sight, allows them to hunt in near-complete darkness.

This owl's primary diet is rabbits, mice, and other rodents, although it freely hunts any animal it can overtake, including middle-sized mammals such as cats and skunks, various birds, reptiles, amphibians, and invertebrates. This bird is sturdy, with a barrel-shaped body, a large head, and broad wings. Its hooting (*Hoo oo oo . . .*) occurs in the middle of the night, with the female's song having a slightly higher pitch on the last sound.

the canyon, where flash floods can originate, this route follows and crosses two arroyos. Arroyos should never be crossed when they contain water, as they can easily sweep a hiker off his or her feet and downstream. Be smart and avoid this hike if a rainstorm/thunderstorm is on the way or there is a storm upstream.

■ THE HIKE

Park at the Embudo Trailhead–Indian School Road parking lot.

Hike east (toward the mountains) on the Embudo Trail (0.5 mile). Pass the dam and head up to where the trail intersects with Trail 365 at the Open Space/ USFS property boundary fence.

Turn left at this junction. Look for a small, unmarked trail that climbs the small hill to the north and east. There are several small trails in this area: choosing the ones heading to the east and slightly north will lead into the valley with the hanging rock. The best one climbs up and over this initial hill, then turns more northward and hugs the base of the hill as it leads up the valley. Other trails descend into the valley, some leading into the channel. If you find yourself in the channel prematurely, turn upstream and continue hiking to the canyon area. It's a little over 0.5 mile to the canyon area from the junction, regardless of which trail is taken.

Once at the canyon, continue hiking upstream for a short distance to the hanging rock. Usually there is ample room to crawl under the rock and continue upstream, but climbing over is also a fun option. This canyon is a bit brushy and becomes steep fairly quickly. Hike upstream as far as desired, then return along the channel to the Embudo Trail and the parking area, about 1 mile.

IF YOU LIKED THIS HIKE, try **HIKE 38: Embudito Canyon Route/Loop** for hiking in a larger canyon or **HIKE 43: Sunset Canyon Route** for a similar valley experience.

FOR THOSE USING GPS DATA
(DATUM: WGS 84)
Intersection of Embudo Trail with small trail that leads into Hanging Rock Canyon:
   –106.47165, 35.09932
Intersection of the small trail and the upstream canyon area: –106.46578, 35.10399

EMBUDO TRAIL LOOP TO UPPER WATERSHED/HEADWALL

Difficulty	4	
Distance	4.3 mi (6.9 km) round-trip	
Hiking Time	2–4 hours	
Elevation	800 ft. gain (244 m)	Peak elevation: 7,000 ft. (2,134 m) at upper valley end; Low elevation: 6,200 ft. (1,890 m) at parking
Trail Condition	Good	Open Space– and USFS-owned and -maintained
Trail Users	Hikers and horses	Bikers along foothills trails
Best Time	Spring and fall	
Parking Lot	Embudo Trailhead	Parking lot is Open Space–owned and -maintained
Fees	None	

SPECIAL INFORMATION: Snow and ice can accumulate on these mountain trails during the winter months.

THE EMBUDO TRAIL and Valley is by far one of the most special areas in the Sandia Mountains, mostly because the Embudo Watershed is so unexpected. The trail follows the valley for many miles, leading first through the foothills, then up a wide arroyo valley that squeezes through a small, tight canyon area with a spring, and then surprisingly opens into an incredible upper valley area with an expansive view of the sky, hillsides, and the mountains, a vista that just can't be beat. This wide-open upper valley area is a rarity in the Sandia Mountains. The valley's sidewalls are set back, creating a beautiful, extensive, high-elevation valley with relatively flat spots and gently rolling hills.

This wonderful valley is a fantastic place to visit and stay for a while. Finding a quiet spot for a picnic is a classic use and well worth the effort. As with all mountain trails, the further a hiker walks, the more likely he or she is to see a large animal. Browsing animals such as deer

ALTERNATE/EXTENDED ROUTES

1. Canyon Side Trail (from End of Main Trail)
Difficulty: 4
Distance: Additional 0.74 mile
Hiking Time: 3–4.5 hours
Elevation: 960 ft. gain; peak elevation: 7,160 ft. at first channel crossing

2. Three Gun Spring Trail Junction (from End of Main Trail)
Difficulty: 5 (includes the steepest section of the Embudo Trail)
Distance: Additional 2.5 miles for a total of almost 7 miles
Hiking Time: 3.5–6 hours
Elevation: 1,720 ft. gain; peak elevation: 7,920 ft. at trail junction

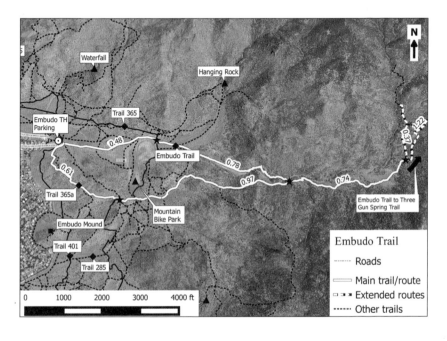

little more, try either climbing up to the Three Gun Spring Trail junction or stay in the upper valley area and take a side adventure over to the canyon and stream before the main trail climbs to the ridge. For fantastic views of the Embudo Watershed, Three Gun Spring Watershed, and Sandia Mountains and distant views of Albuquerque, finish the climb to the Three Gun Springs junction. This area is fully within a mountain forest and can be used to access the South Crest Trail by turning left (north) and then east onto the Embudito Trail.

Another good option for hikers in the Embudo Watershed is a visit to the canyon/stream channel. This option veers left off the Embudo Trail near the end of the main hike and follows a small trail to the channel as it turns to the north. This unmaintained, unnamed trail snakes its way through the upper watershed, then descends back into the Embudo channel. The densely vegetated channel is a great place to explore or simply sit in some deep shade and relax.

As with most hikes involving an arroyo or canyon, these portions of this route should be avoided during inclement weather, especially when there are mountain thunderstorms brewing. If caught on this hike in a rainstorm, take the Horse Bypass route back to the car, as this portion of the hike avoids the Embudo Arroyo/Canyon area.

■ THE HIKE

Park at the Embudo Trailhead–Indian School Road parking lot.

Walk on the Embudo Trail until it passes the dam, meets up with Trail 365, and turns right to descend the small hill into the valley bottom (0.5 mile).

frequent this valley. The variety of terrain along this trail will please every hiker; there is a little bit of everything, from wide-open sandy trails to steep-step bouldering in the short canyon area.

For the return route, the Horse Bypass trail is recommended to make this hike into a loop. This slightly longer return route is a well-kept trail with a larger variety of views of both the mountains and the city. It stays high for a fair distance, and most of the descent occurs just before it reaches Trail 365. It is located on the southern valley hillside and provides wonderful perspectives on the valley trails and the canyons that drain the northern ridge, such as Hanging Rock Valley.

For those adventurers who want a

Springs: Timing Is Everything

Simply speaking, a spring is where groundwater flows up to the surface to form either a pond or a creek. For the springs described in this guide, water travels though the bedrock in the mountains before surfacing in one of the deep canyons. Because these springs come from water flowing through cracks in the rock, each one has its own character and its own specific flow season, which depends significantly on the cracks feeding it.

Here are some general rules of thumb. In the Sandia Mountains, springs tend to flow from midwinter until early summer; some flow for shorter periods and others year-round. From year to year, each spring can change depending on whether the mountains are experiencing a wet or a dry climatic cycle. If you want to visit a flowing spring, early spring (March) is generally the best time for the ones described in this book. However, if it has been a very dry winter or the area is in a long-term drought, many of these springs will have a wet period of just one to two weeks or will not flow at all.

Once in the valley bottom, turn left to walk on the sandy trail that heads up into the mountains. At about 0.5 mile, the valley walls tighten and the trail snakes through the small canyon area. A couple of tallish steps near the springs area take all four limbs to climb. After another 0.25 mile, this trail meets up with the Horse Bypass trail from the south side of the valley.

The wide-open, relatively flat valley extends up the trail for another 0.75 mile and is well worth exploring. Beyond the end of the valley, the trail begins to climb up to the valley/watershed ridgeline, which is quite steep, with long switchbacks. The end of the valley is the designated turnaround point for this hike.

There are two good return options: either return along the Embudo Trail or, for the loop option, turn left (south) onto the Horse Bypass trail, about 0.75 mile from the upper valley edge. USFS signs mark the entrance to the bypass trail.

If on the bypass, follow this high trail back to Trail 365, about 1 mile. Turn left onto Trail 365 and, after less than 0.1 mile, turn right onto Trail 365A to return to the parking area (0.6 mile).

FOR OTHER LARGE-TRAIL MOUNTAIN HIKING options, try **HIKE 6: El Rincon via Piedra Lisa Trail**, **HIKE 22: Pino Trail to the Dead Trees**, or **HIKE 37: Embudito Canyon Overlook Loop**. For a similar experience, try **HIKE 1: Upper La Cueva Overlook via La Luz Trail**.

FOR THOSE USING GPS DATA (DATUM: WGS 84)

Location of Trail 365 as it turns south to cross the reservoir area: -106.471589, 35.099592

Upper Watershed where a small trail veers north to reach the main Embudo channel: -106.450051, 35.097536

Intersection of the Embudo Trail with the Embudo (Horse) Bypass Trail: -106.460146, 35.095742

Intersection of Bypass Trail with Trail 365A: -106.474859, 35.094224

EMBUDO MOUND LOOP

Difficulty	2	Hills increase the exertion.
Distance	2.93 mi (4.7 km) loop	
Hiking Time	1–2 hours	
Elevation	300 ft. gain (91 m)	Peak elevation: 6,500 ft. (1,981 m) near Trail 365/365A junction; Low elevation: 6,200 ft. (1,890 m) at parking
Trail Condition	Excellent	Open Space– and USFS-owned and -maintained
Trail Users	Hikers, bikers, horses	Bikes especially along the large named trails
Best Time	Fall through spring	
Parking Lot	Embudo Trailhead	Parking lot is Open Space–owned and -maintained
Fees	None	

SPECIAL INFORMATION: Add an extra mile to either loop option by parking at the Menaul parking area.

THIS MEDIUM-LENGTH foothills loop hike is similar to the shorter Embudo Dam Loop route, but adds a different landscape: the Embudo Mound south of the parking area. For this route, hikers explore about 1 mile of Trail 365 as it hugs the eastern foothills south of Embudo Dam. This rugged area has a variety of hills that look suspiciously like mounds; the trail passes between them and the steep mountain hillsides. Some of the ruggedness of this trail is due to deep erosive channels that have cut into the soil. Because this is a high-maintenance area, in some locations, boardwalks have been constructed to convey hikers and bikers across the waterways. This more rough landscape comes to an end as Trail 365 drops down to Trail 285, a gently sloping foothills trail that follows the fall line of the outwash plain toward the Embudo Mound.

After a short jog on Trail 401, the route goes "behind" Embudo Mound, where an unnamed public trail is pinched between its rocky sides and a tall residential fence line. This tightly confined but short section of trail is interesting as it gives hikers a close-up view of the talus (rock debris) that has fallen off the mound. This route, and an optional hike to the summit, have an adventurous feel, despite the close proximity of the residences.

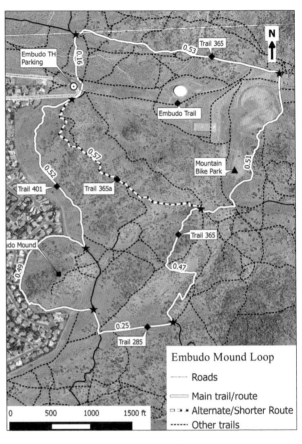

Embudo Mound Loop

- - - - Roads

===== Main trail/route

▫ ▫ ▪ Alternate/Shorter Route

----- Other trails

ALTERNATE/SHORTER ROUTE

Embudo Dam Loop (Trail 365A)
Difficulty: 2
Distance: 1.8-mile loop
Hiking Time: 30–60 minutes
Elevation: Same as main trail
Parking: Embudo Trailhead

Snakes

Snakes are common residents in the deserts of New Mexico, with an estimated sixty different species. The one snake that seems to spark the most concern is the Western diamondback; this member of the pit viper family has an extensive range in the state, including all of the Sandia Mountains and the foothills. Despite their exaggerated reputation for aggression, rattlesnakes do not prey on humans and make a significant effort to leave us alone. Unfortunately, humans don't always have the same philosophy. Although visitors occasionally disturb a rattlesnake, hikers are more likely to encounter one of the many other, nonvenomous varieties. The darker-colored snakes, such as the mountain patchnose, are easily identified as a different species; however, bull snakes are often mistaken for rattlesnakes due to their large size. These easygoing nonvenomous snakes are more common in the foothills, and are the most likely snakes encountered.

Hikers can usually easily identify a Western diamondback with a simple visual inspection—from a distance. As their name suggests, they have a diamond-shaped skin pattern. Other distinctive characteristics are its large, triangular head and alternating black-and-white bands near the end of its tail, reminiscent of, a raccoon's tail. Interestingly, they also have what appear to be a second set of nostrils (known as "facial pits"); these are heat receptors that help them locate warm-blooded prey, especially when hunting at night.

These snakes are best known for their ability to defend themselves with a poisonous bite, but they usually send a warning first, by rattling their tails. A snake's striking distance depends on many conditions: its size and length, its body temperature and that of the air, their location, the substance on which they are lying, and their fear level. Common rules are that snakes can strike at least a third of their body length (many snake professionals say two-thirds), and may attempt to do so several times if extremely agitated. When they strike several times, they can cover a distance more than one body length. Smart hikers who encounter a rattlesnake will immediately back up, respect the snake's space, and leave it alone.

Most of this loop follows larger, well-maintained trails with excellent signs and well-packed soils, making them very easy to follow. These trails are particularly popular with runners and bike riders. As such, they can be busy on weekends, but with so much space, they are rarely crowded to excess.

■ THE HIKE

Park at the Embudo Trailhead–Indian School Road parking lot.

Hike north on Trail 401 for about 0.16 mile.

Turn right (east) onto Trail 365 and follow it as it passes by the Embudo Dam, then turns to pass behind/upstream of the dam (0.5 mile).

After a short distance, Trail 365 climbs a notable hill and meets up with Trail 365A, on the mountain side of the mound (0.5 mile).

Continue past Trail 365A and descend to Trail 285 (0.5 mile).

Turn right (west) onto Trail 285 and follow to Trail 401. Turn right (north) and follow it a short distance until another trail veers off on the left (0.25 mile).

Veer left to hike around the small mound next to the residential/private boundary (0.5 mile).

Turn left onto Trail 401 after completing the partial perimeter trail and return to the parking area (0.5 mile).

IF YOU LIKED THIS HIKE, try HIKE 49: Embudo Dam Loop for a similar landscape, or try one of the other mound hikes: HIKE 54: U-Mound Perimeter Loop, HIKE 56: Two

Mound Loop, HIKE 57: Hilldale Mound Loop, HIKE 58: Four Mound Loop, or HIKE 60: South Mound/I-40 Loop.

FOR THOSE USING GPS DATA
(DATUM: WGS 84)
Intersection of Trail 401 and Trail 365A:
–106.480295, 35.098649
Trail 401 and northern intersection of small trail that circles the base of the Mound:
–106.479743, 35.092664
Trail 401 and southern intersection of small trail that circles the base of the Mound:
–106.479428, 35.090198
Intersection of Trail 285 and Trail 365:
–106.476107, 35.089689
Intersection of Trail 365 and Trail 365A:
–106.474872, 35.09427
Location of Trail 365 as it turns west after crossing the reservoir area:
–106.471589, 35.099592
Intersection of Trail 365 with Trail 401:
–106.480145, 35.101223

EMBUDO—U-MOUND OVERLOOK LOOP

Difficulty	5	
Distance	4.6 mi (7.4 km) loop	
Hiking Time	3–5 hours	
Elevation	900 ft. gain (274 m)	Peak elevation: 7,100 ft. (2,164 m) at overlook; Low elevation: 6,200 ft. (1,890 m) at parking
Trail Condition	Good with poor sections	Open Space– and USFS-owned and -maintained
Trail Users	Hikers	Bikers along foothills trails
Best Time	Fall through spring	
Parking Lot	Embudo Trailhead	Parking lot is Open Space–owned and -maintained
Fees	None	

SPECIAL INFORMATION: Snow and ice often cover the trail in the winter season. Given the remoteness of this trail, it should not be hiked in inclement weather or when trails are icy.

THIS IS ONE OF THE harder hikes in the area but is also one of the few that crosses multiple watersheds. The route is relatively long and exposed, with little shade available, so choose a cool day to explore it. But, as is often the case on these harder hikes, the reward lies in reaching an area of rare beauty that few hikers explore. At the top of the steep hill is an extensive, high-quality mountain bench area filled with dense grasses that dance in the wind. These grasses get quite tall in wet years, and are reminiscent of a ripe wheat field just before harvest. The bench area is tranquil

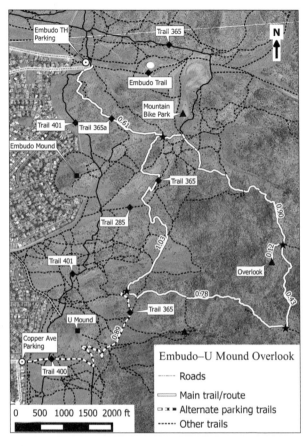

Embudo–U Mound Overlook

------- Roads
======= Main trail/route
❑━■ Alternate parking trails
------- Other trails

0 500 1000 1500 2000 ft

Copper Ave. parking lot

and definitely inspires some reverence. In contrast, the steep trails are intense, giving everyone a real workout.

To access this loop, hikers must walk a short trail to get to another small trail that climbs the mountains. Parking is available at both Embudo Trailhead–Indian School Road and Copper Ave. The access from Indian School Road is a little shorter, while the trail to Copper Ave. is longer but a little easier. Either way, at the end of the loop for this hike, the walk back to the car feels long.

Although this route is one of the longest in the guide, its difficulty ranking is due mostly to the poor quality of the uphill and downhill trails, which are steep and rocky. As such, this hike is not for the beginner. It goes mostly straight up to the bench area and then straight down to the foothills area. The unnamed trails have a nice assortment of everything that makes a trail difficult: very steep hills, loose rocks filling the trails, barely-there trail sections,

bedrock outcrops, slippery slopes covered in pea gravel, and, of course, the requisite boulder steps. Without a doubt, it is a difficult hike, best suited to experienced hikers or moderately experienced hikers with a desire to test their skills, endurance, and vigilance, especially on the steep downhill route, where a tumble could be particularly painful.

■ THE HIKE

Park at the Embudo Trailhead–Indian School Road parking lot.

Start the hike on Trail 365A, heading to the southeast (0.6 mile).

Turn left (north) onto Trail 365 and hike just a short distance, then turn right on a small unmarked trail that leads up the hillside. There are at least two decent trails that climb up this hill. The first is close to the Trail 365/365A junction. A slightly better trail just to the north of the junction starts uphill after Trail 365 travels north and around the small "nose" of this hill. After a short uphill distance, the two trails merge. Continue hiking

The Intense Summer Sun

The summer sun in New Mexico can be summed up in just one word: intense. At its height in June, New Mexico's hottest month, nothing seems to protect a hiker's body from its effects. Maybe it's the extra-long days or the relentless sunny weather, or maybe it's the lack of humidity in the air. Whatever the cause, when you are in the full sun in the heart of summer, you feel it. Regardless of sunscreen or how much water you drink, your body reacts to the force of the summer sun, and this must be taken seriously.

In the old days, many New Mexicans would take a siesta after lunch, moving into a deeply shaded napping spot. Although that lifestyle has faded away, the most important

lesson is to take it easy when the sun is at peak intensity. For the purposes of this guide, that translates into hiking early or late, but not in the afternoon.

If you need to hike throughout this part of the day, do everything you can to provide shade to your body. Beyond sunscreen, this includes dark, polarized UV-protection sunglasses, a full-brimmed hat, and lightweight clothing that protects your arms and legs. Although sunglasses and hats are items that seem to be celebrated by hard-core hikers, wearing long sleeves and long trousers still needs a little attention. Nothing protects your skin like clothing.

up the hillside to the bench area (0.9 mile). This is a steep and rocky trail with sections that are of poor quality, but it has wonderful views toward the Embudo Dam/Tank.

Once on the bench, this small trail intersects another small, unnamed trail trending in the east–west direction; the segment leading to the west goes to the boulder-filled overlook area (0.12 mile), while the trail to the east heads up into the greater mountains.

After a short stop at the overlook, return to the main bench trail and continue to head south along the bench area. The trail will descend and rise out of a shallow drainage, then join up with a larger trail in a large grassy field (0.4 mile from the overlook).

Turn right (west) and follow the main trail downhill, returning to Trail 365 in the foothills area. Be prepared: the downhill trail is steep and a bit rough, with sections that are in poor shape (0.8 mile).

Turn right onto Trail 365 and follow back to Trail 365A (1 mile).

Turn left onto Trail 365A and return to parking area (0.61 mile).

IF YOU WOULD LIKE TO TRY an easier small-trail mountain hike, try either **HIKE 44: Candelaria Bench Loop** or **HIKE 59: Tijeras Canyon–Four Hills Overlook Loop**. For harder small-trail mountain hikes, try **HIKE 39: Embudito North Ridge Trail Loop** or **HIKE 40: Embudito South Ridge Trail to Boulder Cave**.

FOR THOSE USING GPS DATA (DATUM: WGS 84)

Intersection of Trail 365 and Trail 365A: −106.474872, 35.09427

Intersection of bench trail and the small trail leading to the overlook: −106.466573, 35.087004

Intersection of bench trail and the small unnamed trail that leads to Trail 365: −106.46642, 35.081437

Intersection of small trail leading from Trail 365 to the bench trail: −106.477415, 35.083915

U-MOUND PERIMETER LOOP

Difficulty	1	
Distance	1.2 mi (1.9 km) loop	
Hiking Time	1–2 hours	
Elevation	240 ft. gain (73 m)	Peak elevation: 6,160 ft. (1,877 m) at U-Mound/Trail 365; Low elevation: 5,920 ft. (1,804 m) at parking
Trail Condition	Excellent	Open Space– and USFS-owned and -maintained
Trail Users	Hikers, bikers, horses	
Best Time	Fall through spring	
Parking Lot	Copper Ave.	
Fees	None	

U-MOUND IS THE MOST obvious natural feature anywhere in the foothills area. Hikers, climbers, and riders from all around come to see it up close. With the look of a miniature Mt. Fuji, the mound is tall with a narrow peak, wide base, and relatively even side slopes. The whole area around U-Mound is a popular recreation spot where either short or very long hikes can easily be completed with or without much planning. Several large Open Space trails not only surround U-Mound, but extend out from it, creating a dense network and numerous hiking opportunities all around the mound. The official Open Space trails are well-maintained, graded with switchbacks, and marked with signs, which makes this area an easy place to navigate. The unofficial trails that crisscross this greater foothills area also tend to be in good condition, which makes for pleasurable exploring throughout this area.

The U-Mound perimeter loop is short and focused on hugging the edge of the mound. Of course, it can be extended

easily by hiking along one of the other trails in the area. From the perimeter loop, a good trail ascends the mound, leading off of Trail 365 at the back (east side). For people who simply wish to see the view from the top, it is fantastic and worth the climb. This hike is especially popular with groups and families. (For smaller crowds, try it on a weekday.) Given that it is short, hikers are never too far from their vehicles and can spend a short time exploring or a long one, depending on their desires.

■ **THE HIKE**

Park at the Copper Ave. parking lot.

Hike east on Trail 400 (0.25 mile).

Turn left (north) onto Trail 365 and follow it to the back of the mound (0.3 mile).

If you want to ascend the mound, turn left onto the designated trail, about 0.12 mile, to end of trail near the top.

If you want to continue on the perimeter route, keep walking straight (north)

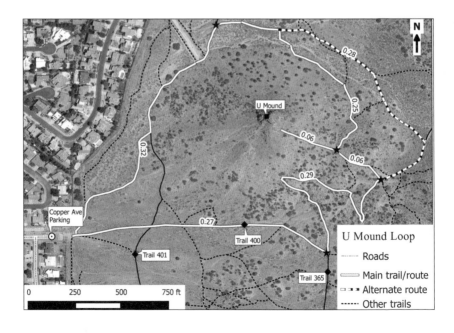

U Mound Loop

‑‑‑‑‑ Roads
▭▪▪ Main trail/route
▭▪▪ Alternate route
‑‑‑‑‑ Other trails

on Trail 365, which descends into the arroyo channel (0.1 mile). Turn left and walk along the arroyo trail, heading west (0.2 mile). This unnamed route crosses in and out of the arroyo, but as it nears Trail 401, a well-defined trail emerges.

Turn left onto Trail 401 and follow it back to the parking area (0.3 mile).

SUMMIT OPTION

Difficulty: 3, due to steep and rocky trail to the top

Distance: 1.3-mile loop

Hiking Time: 30–60 minutes

Elevation: U-Mound peak is 6,300 ft.; trail to top climbs 140 ft. in 0.1 mile

Parking: Copper Ave. parking area

IF YOU LIKED THIS HIKE, try **HIKE 56: Two Mound Loop** to see more of this landscape/ area or try one of the other mound hikes: **HIKE 53: Embudo–U-Mound Overlook Loop, HIKE 57: Hilldale Mound Loop, HIKE 58: Four Mound Loop,** or **HIKE 60: South Mound/I-40 Loop.**

FOR THOSE USING GPS DATA
(DATUM: WGS 84)

Intersection of Trail 400 with Trail 365:
–106.479753, 35.07891

Intersection of Trail 365 and the U-Mound Summit Trail: –106.4788, 35.080186

Intersection of Summit Trail and an alternate return trail: –106.481762, 35.082858

Intersection of small arroyo trail with Trail 401:
–106.47959, 35.080702

Beep, Beep!

The Greater Roadrunner is one of the most identifiable birds in Albuquerque and throughout the Southwest. These courageous and curious birds are a special treat to see, one that you are likely to tell your friends about. Because roadrunners are not particularly afraid of hikers or dogs, they go about their business with or without your presence, sometimes crossing your path just feet in front of you. Many southwestern people feel a kinship toward this iconic bird, as it is highly adaptable to city life, making sightings common not only in the foothills but throughout Albuquerque.

Roadrunners are large ground birds with streaks and flecks of brown intermixed with tans and white colors, a solid white/tan breast and underparts, a large, thick bill, a long tail, and a shaggy head crest. With an odd-looking set of toes—two pointing forward and two facing back—the roadrunner leaves an X footprint in the sand. But its most identifiable feature is its long legs, on which it runs about, hunting for things to eat. Its diet consists of insects, lizards, cactus fruits, scorpions, tarantulas, and snakes (even rattlesnakes). Although roadrunners do fly, it is their brave, free spirit

that attracts so much attention as they sprint from bush to bush focused on catching their favorite food, lizards.

Interestingly, these birds use a variety of calls to communicate with their mates and offspring. Two common sounds are a sort of coo used primarily during mating and a short barking sound similar to the deeper yip of a coyote. But unlike the cartoon, New Mexico's roadrunners don't go "beep! beep!"

OLD MAN CANYON LOOP

Difficulty	5	For climb up waterfal	
Distance	2 mi (3.2 km) loop	0.9 mi to base of falls	
Hiking Time	1–2 hours		
Elevation	600 ft. gain (183 m)	Peak elevation: 6,520 ft. (1,987 m) at top of hill above falls; Low elevation: 5,920 ft. (1,804 m) at parking	
Trail Condition	Good with poor sections	Open Space– and USFS-owned; Unmaintained	
Trail Users	Hikers	Horses and bikes along the base of the mountains	
Best Time	Fall through spring		
Parking Lot	Copper Ave.		
Fees	None		

SPECIAL INFORMATION: The canyon has a sandy bottom in between tall bedrock steps. The waterfall is moderately difficult to climb, but hikers who are not comfortable with heights or the look of the climb should turn around at the base and return along the same route.

THIS IS A GREAT dry-waterfall hike that is easy to reach and explore. From Trail 365 and U-Mound, trail users can see a glimpse of the upper falls, which is a glowing white color. The white comes mainly from the color of the granite, but, like the falls in the Piedra Lisa Watershed, some of the rocks are also covered with a chalklike white coating. The reason for this waterfall's name is evident to hikers who climb to the top of the upper falls: a rock structure there looks like the profile of an old man. The "old man" sits stoically at the upper falls, keeping watch on the surrounding area. Only those hikers adventurous enough to reach the top of the waterfall can boast of seeing this handsome rock.

The trail leading up the small valley from Trail 365 is small and a bit brushy, but following the arroyo will certainly get a hiker to the canyon area. Once within it, the valley walls are relatively tight to the top of the waterfall, then fall away

upstream from it. Ascending to the upper falls area is not for the faint of heart and should only be attempted by hikers who are confident in their "scrambling/ climbing" abilities. (Although the climb may look easy from the bottom, it has a fair bit of exposure, such that a slip or fall would likely result in a dangerous tumble. A better falls hike for beginners is **HIKE 45: Piedra Lisa Falls and Bench Loop**, where hikers access the top of these same falls via a marked trail.)

From the top of the falls, the loop takes off to the north and descends along a

SHORTER OPTION (ROUND-TRIP TO BASE OF FALLS)

Difficulty: 2 (due to some steep bedrock in arroyo channel)
Distance: 1.8 miles round-trip
Hiking Time: 1 hour
Elevation: 480 ft. gain (est. 6,400 ft. at waterfall)
Parking: Copper Ave. parking area

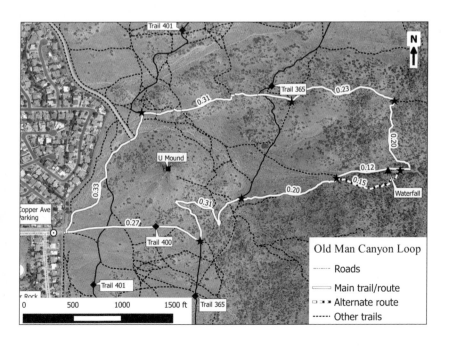

fair-condition unnamed trail, which inter-sects directly with Trail 365. Overall, this is a favorite hike that doesn't seem to be overly used, but traveled enough to keep the trail in decent shape.

The falls area and the trail that ascends the valley should be avoided during inclement weather of any kind, with slick rock and flash floods the primary con-cerns. The bedrock in this canyon, espe-cially at the falls, has been worn smooth over time and can be slippery even when it is not wet. The bench area and the descent down the mountainside would not be fun during or just after a rain-storm, but they are the better trail choice in comparison to the falls area.

■ THE HIKE

Park at the Copper Ave. parking lot.

Hike west on Trail 400 until it inter-sects with Trail 365, about 0.25 mile.

Turn left (north) onto Trail 365 and hike a short distance as it descends into the small valley just to the north of U-Mound. After about 0.3 mile, look for a small, unnamed trail that heads up into the small valley on the right (east) side.

Turn right (east) and hike up the unnamed trail into the valley. The trail up this small valley is sometimes obscured by thick vegetation. After a short distance, the valley tightens and boulder-bedrock steps begin as it quickly climbs. From this point, the path is easier to follow. At about 0.2 mile from Trail 365, the valley bottom narrows and the trail enters the canyon area.

Another 0.1 mile reaches the base of the upper falls. For the loop option, care-fully climb the dry falls. If not climbing the upper falls, turn around at this point and return along the same route.

From the top of the falls, a relatively well-worn trail heads up and out of the channel on the north side. Although there are several of these small trails heading north, they all seem to converge up this hillside. Continue up the hill to the ridge-line. Just beyond it, this small trail joins with another, slightly better and larger trail that follows the ridgeline from the upper mountains, about 0.2 mile from the falls.

Turn left and follow this trail to descend the lower mountains to a high trail just uphill from Trail 365, 0.23 mile. Once on this trail or Trail 365, turning left (south) will return hikers to Trail 400 and

Hydrate before Hiking

It's hard to explain the effects of full-on high-desert conditions to people who have not experienced them. Everyone has experienced some sort of heat and has a reference point to start from. But the factors that inexperienced desert hikers seem to miss are the extremely dry air, the high altitude, and the raw intensity of the desert sun. These can easily take those unprepared hikers by surprise and lead to problems. In the Grand Canyon, where visitors number in the millions during the hot summer months, the desert heat is the number one cause for hiker rescue requests. In fact, rangers report that hikers are rescued from the elements every day during the height of summer, even though there is a massive educational campaign in the park to help visitors understand this risk.

The most important preparation for hiking in hot, dry desert conditions is to be hydrated before hiking. The second most important detail is to stay hydrated throughout the hike. An average-sized person is capable of losing 1.5 to two quarts of fluids (three to four pounds) per hour when hiking in high heat conditions. In extreme conditions this can rise to two to eight quarts per hour. A complicating factor for staying hydrated or recovering from dehydration is that a person can only absorb fluids consumed at a rate of 0.5 to one quart per hour. This means that a person hiking in extreme, dry heat will always be dehydrating. So be wise: always start your hike hydrated and be prepared to drink enough water during the hike to stay as hydrated as possible.

---

the parking area. For different scenery and the full loop, continue straight down the hill on the unnamed trail.

Continue to hike due west on the unnamed trail about 0.3 mile, until it intersects with Trail 401. This route takes hikers to the north of U-Mound and also completes a loop around it.

Turn left onto Trail 401 and follow back to the parking area, about 0.33 mile.

IF YOU LIKE THIS falls/small-trail mountain loop, try HIKE 45: Piedra Lisa Falls and Bench Loop for an easier falls climb but longer mountain hike or HIKE 5: Hidden Falls Canyon Route for a harder/similar falls climb but easier return loop hike.

FOR THOSE USING GPS DATA
(DATUM: WGS 84)
Intersection of Trail 400 with Trail 365:
–106.479753, 35.07891
Intersection of Trail 365 with first trail that leads into Old Man Canyon: –106.478375, 35.08032
Start of Old Man Canyon:
–106.475165, 35.080969
Old Man Canyon Falls: –106.473026, 35.081214
Intersection of low-bench trail with a moderate-sized trail that leads to Trail 365:
–106.473228, 35.083477
Intersection of Trail 365 with moderate-sized trail leading uphill into the southern bench area: –106.47669, 35.08345
Small trail that connects Trail 401 with Trail 365:
–106.481742, 35.083108

TWO MOUND LOOP

Difficulty	2	Ascending a mound increases the difficulty
Distance	3.34 mi (5.4 km) loop	
Hiking Time	1–2 hours	
Elevation	240 ft. gain (74 m)	Peak elevation: 6,160 ft. (1,878 m) near Embudo Mound; Low elevation: 5,920 ft. (1,804 m) at parking
Trail Condition	Excellent	Open Space– and USFS-owned and -maintained
Trail Users	Hikers, bikers, horses	
Best Time	Fall through spring	
Parking Lot	Copper Ave.	
Fees	None	

TWO MOUND LOOP is named for the two large mounds at the northern end of this hike, but really it could be called "Hundred Mound Loop," as there are little mounds scattered all around this area. Once you know what to look for, the various mounds are easy to spot, even when they are surrounded by streets or have a home on top. The smallest ones are simply piles of large boulders, which, of course, are great for bouldering. In fact, on weekends, it is not uncommon to see small groups of climbers bouldering until their arms are too tired or their fingers are too sore. The larger mounds tend to be very large piles of semicoherent rock, with boulders and trails scattered along their hillsides, making them prime attractions for those hikers who like to reach summits.

This route snakes its way north through small mounds to where an obvious perimeter trail circles the oblong-shaped Embudo Mound. Trail 401 cuts between this mound and a taller one to the east. Embudo Mound is probably the easiest of the large mounds to ascend, from a bench along Trail 401 in the saddle area on the east side of the mound. From the top of either of these mounds, or from any of the smaller ones along the way, views of U-Mound, the mountains, the foothills, and the city are great. Pick your backdrop and capture a nice photo.

This whole loop is along large well-maintained trails with excellent signs and well-packed soils. If you want to explore some of the small mounds, they

ALTERNATE PARKING

Embudo Trailhead parking lot (6,200 ft. elevation)

are typically easy to reach; well-worn trails lead to just about every one of them.

■ THE HIKE

Park at the Copper Ave. parking lot.

Hike north on a small side trail that leads to Trail 401 and the concrete conveyance channel, about 0.28 mile.

Turn left (west) onto Trail 285 and follow it alongside the v-shaped conveyance canal toward the west (0.6 mile). At the northern end of the canal, an unnamed trail turns off to the left while Trail 285 veers right to cross with Trail 401.

Turn left (west) to circle Embudo Mound

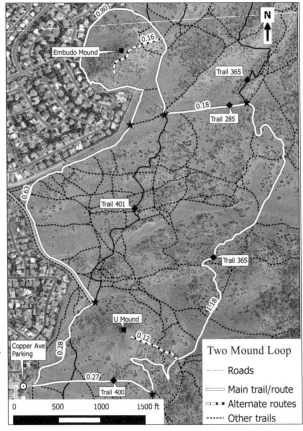

Two Mound Loop
······ Roads
═══ Main trail/route
▭·▪▪ Alternate routes
······ Other trails

Embudo Hills Park

This beautiful city park, just north of the parking area at Copper Ave., is located near Lomas Boulevard and Monte Largo Road. Street parking is available around most of the park and provides a good option for when Copper Ave. is too busy or for foothill trails north of U-Mound. Grass, playground equipment, fitness stations, and a paved path circle the grassy area and extend along Lomas Boulevard to Turner Street. At Turner, a small bridge crosses the channel and a set of user-formed trails follow the concrete-lined channel uphill, leading into the publicly owned Open Space and Trail 401 in the foothills. This alternate access is a good option for **HIKE 54: U-Mound Perimeter Route**, **HIKE 55: Old Man Canyon Loop**, **HIKE 56: Two Mound Loop**, or really any hike in this general area. If you choose to use this alternate parking area, please respect the rules of street parking and especially the local residents by staying off their land.

(0.8 mile). This trail sneaks between the mound on the right and the residential unit to the left until it turns northeast toward Trail 401 and breaks out of the tight area.

Turn right (south) onto Trail 401 and follow it up the small hill to the bench area. Hikers inclined to summit Embudo Mound will find a nice ascending trail to the right at about the bench area. Otherwise, continue on Trail 401 down the hill to Trail 285.

Turn left onto Trail 285 and follow this wide and somewhat sandy trail as it climbs up to Trail 365 (0.18 mile).

Turn right onto Trail 365 and follow to Trail 400, about 1.2 miles.

Turn right onto Trail 400 and follow back to parking area, 0.27 mile.

IF YOU LIKED THIS HIKE, try **HIKE 52: Embudo Mound Loop** for a similar landscape and area or try one of the other mound hikes: **HIKE 54: U-Mound Perimeter Loop**, **HIKE 57: Hilldale Mound Loop**, **HIKE 58: Four Mound Loop**, or **HIKE 60: South Mound/I-40 Loop**.

FOR THOSE USING GPS DATA (DATUM: WGS 84)

Intersection of Trail 400 with Trail 365:
  –106.479753, 35.07891
Intersection of Trail 285 and Trail 365:
  –106.476107, 35.089689
Intersection of Trail 285 And Trail 401:
  –106.479223, 35.08924
Intersection of Trail 401 and Trail 285:
  –106.481948, 35.082307

HILLDALE MOUND LOOP

Difficulty	1	
Distance	1.6 mi (2.6 km) loop	
Hiking Time	1–2 hours	
Elevation	200 ft. gain (61 m)	Peak elevation: 6,120 ft. (1,865 m) at Hilldale Mound/Trail 365; Low elevation: 5,920 ft. (1,804 m) at parking
Trail Condition	Excellent	Open Space– and USFS-owned and -maintained
Trail Users	Hikers, bikers, horses	
Best Time	Year-round	
Parking Lot	Copper Ave.	
Fees	None	

HILLDALE MOUND

is just to the south of U-Mound but, surprisingly, is a little off the beaten path. This rounded mound has a very wide base and is lower and simply less spectacular compared to U-Mound. Despite its slightly reduced popularity, an easy-to-follow trail rings the mound about midway up the side slopes, creating an interesting higher-elevation perspective. The trails leading to and from, as well as around this feature are mostly flat, making this one of the easier hikes in the guidebook. As with other hikes in the foothills, one of the options follows a trail that is tightly confined by a hill on one side and a fence on the other. When this section of trail opens up, Hilldale Mound is a little bit of a surprise, as it pops out right in front of you.

To access the Hilldale Mound perimeter route, hikers can walk either along the well-marked Open Space trails (Trail 365 or Trail 401) or follow the property line trail that leads directly south from the parking area. Regardless of which access trail is chosen, the other trail options make great alternatives for the return trip. All of the hiking options cross the rolling foothills area, which is covered in the classic desert vegetation this area is known for: grasses, cacti, and yuccas, with the occasional tree and set of bushes.

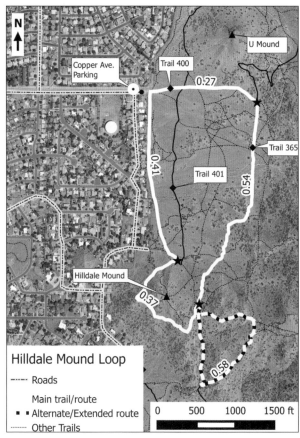

Hilldale Mound Loop

----- Roads
Main trail/route
▪ ▪ Alternate/Extended route
.... Other Trails

0   500   1000   1500 ft

■ THE HIKE

Park at the Copper Ave. parking lot.

Hike south along the property boundary on the unmarked fence line trail. As it nears the mound, follow the better trail that veers left away from the property line, which almost meets up with the end of Trail 401 (0.4 mile).

Turn right (west) onto the Hilldale Trail to begin hiking around the mound. This trail climbs a little at the start before contouring along the mound. This trail meets with Trail 365 near the southeastern edge (0.4 mile). At this point, hikers have four options:

Rio Grande Migratory Corridor

The latest count by the Sandia Ranger District found that 244 types of bird, nearly a third of all the species occurring in North America, resided at least occasionally in the Sandia Mountains. This great diversity is due to two specific features: first, mountains so high that they include four distinct life zones, and second, their location next to one of the most important North American bird migration corridors, the Rio Grande Migratory Corridor. In fact, about two-thirds of the Sandia bird species (171 of the 244) are migratory birds. The primary reason birds migrate is to utilize the variety of climates in North America, so that they can nest in warm weather and over-winter in less-frigid climates.

Two migratory birds commonly seen in the foothills are Oregon juncos and humming-birds. Juncos nest throughout the northern regions of North America and then migrate to New Mexico and other southern states for the winter months. Although a few of these dark-hooded, pink- or white-beaked sparrows call New Mexico home year-round, most arrive in late fall and leave in spring, fashioning a large winter junco population. These wintering residents can be found throughout the foothills, searching the grassy fields for seeds and visiting local bird feeders.

Hummingbirds use New Mexico as one of many summer habitats. In fact, the "hummers" that oversummer in the state might be considered short-hop commuters, as hummingbirds are found throughout North America during the summer months, with all returning to South America for the winter.

Given the large bird-migratory population, these mountains and their foothills have different birds for each of the seasons. Knowing just a little bit about the different migrants can lend hikers many excuses to explore the region throughout the year.

If you want to ascend the mound, this is probably the best location to start climbing; however, there are no marked trails leading to the peak.

If you want to extend the hike with the optional loop, turn right onto Trail 365 and head south.

If you want to continue on the perimeter route and return to the parking area via Trail 401, continue to veer to the left.

Or, to complete the main hike, continue north on Trail 365 as it descends the mound and intersects Trail 400 (0.5 mile). Turn left onto Trail 400 and follow it back to the parking area (0.27 mile).

IF YOU LIKED THIS HIKE, try **HIKE 49: Embudo Dam Loop** for a similar landscape and difficulty or try one of the other mound hikes: **HIKE 52: Embudo Mound Loop**, **HIKE 54:**

U-Mound Perimeter Loop, **HIKE 56: Two Mound Loop**, **HIKE 58: Four Mound Loop**, or **HIKE 60: South Mound/I-40 Loop**.

FOR THOSE USING GPS DATA
(DATUM: WGS 84)
Intersection of Trail 401 and Hilldale Trail:
     −106.48310, 35.07351
Intersection of Hilldale Trail with Trail 365:
     −106.48215, 35.07204
Intersection of Trail 400 with Trail 365:
     −106.479753, 35.07891

EXTENDED ROUTE OPTION

Difficulty: 3 due to steep and rocky trail
Distance: 2.2 miles with the additional 0.6 mile loop
Hiking Time: 1–2 hours
Elevation: 240 ft. gain; peak elevation: 6,160 ft.
Parking: Copper Ave. parking area

FOUR MOUND LOOP

Difficulty	3	
Distance	4 mi (6.4 km) loop	
Hiking Time	1.5–3 hours	
Elevation	400 ft. gain (122 m)	Peak elevation: 6,120 ft. (1,865 m) at Hilldale Mound/Trail 365; Low elevation: 5,720 ft. (1,743) near I-40
Trail Condition	Good	Open Space– and USFS-owned and -maintained
Trail Users	Hikers, bikers, horses	
Best Time	Fall through spring	
Parking Lot	Copper Ave.	
Fees	None	

THIS ROUTE EXPLORES the four large mounds between the Copper Ave. parking area and Interstate 40, while experiencing the distinctly different terrain to the south of Hilldale Mound. Although still present, the amount of classic foothills landscape diminishes greatly in this area, as the base of the lower Sandia Mountains seems to extend out. Additionally, this far southern portion of Open Space does not have the typical views of the city; they are blocked by Hilldale and Powerline Mounds. Even though trail users are not far from civilization on this hike, it feels like the back woods (but not exactly wilderness, as many of the trails are old road beds). With few hikers south of Hilldale Mound, this is certainly an overlooked area and has a high potential for seeing wildlife.

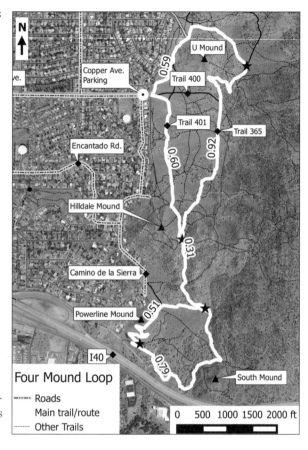

Four Mound Loop
---- Roads
　　 Main trail/route
·······Other Trails

0　500　1000　1500　2000 ft

The four mounds visited along this trek are U-Mound, Hilldale Mound, Powerline Mound, and South Mound. Although close to each other, each of these mounds has a different character and shape. U-Mound is the best known: it is pinnacle-shaped and sits visibly apart from the lower Sandia Mountains near Copper Ave. Hilldale Mound, just to the south of U-Mound, has a very wide base and a more rounded top. Powerline Mound, on the western edge of the Open Space, has a wide base with two small but vertical rocky tops. South Mound is the little sister of the other three and is located next to I-40; it is smaller than the others and, although it sits distinctly apart from the Sandia Mountains, it can be overlooked due to its small size. This mound has a conical shape, although it tilts toward the west and is missing the pinnacle top.

Trail 365 is the main trail that visits each of the mounds as it travels across the lower-mountain area. It climbs up and over a large saddle that separates the northern mounds from those near I-40.

Coyotes

Coyotes are a common mammal of the foothills and, like the roadrunner, an icon of the southwest. Both of these animals are smart and successful hunters. The coyote is often described as cunning, strong, and tough, with an incredible flexibility to adapt to just about any situation, including living in the city. This is a survivor species and it thrives throughout the foothills.

One of the most adaptable animals in the world, the coyote can change its breeding habits, diet, and social dynamics to survive in a wide variety of habitats. Coyotes typically mate for life, with each litter producing between two and eight pups. Mating season ranges from January through April, with gestation lasting about two months. Their dens are usually hidden from view, with the coyote digging its own den or fixing up an old badger hole or natural hole in a rocky ledge.

Coyotes are opportunistic hunters and foragers. Their principal diet is mice, rabbits, ground squirrels, other small rodents, insects, reptiles, frogs, and the fruits and berries of wild plants. As with the common housedog, the coyote is an omnivore, and will eat just about anything, including small pets and human garbage.

Despite what some people say, coyotes do not attack humans. (However, rabid mammals of any species are always a concern.) An important benefit of these clever creatures is their desire to hunt rodents. With rodent-carried diseases that affect humans prevalent in New Mexico, such as the plague, coyotes naturally help keep their spread—and the local small-mammal populations—in check. As with most of the animals in the foothills, these larger mammals avoid humans and usually run away at first sight.

The trail is in good shape, but requires a little more exertion on these steeper hills.

■ THE HIKE

Park at the Copper Ave. parking lot.

Start hiking north from the parking area to reach Trail 401 near the conveyance channel. After passing U-Mound, find the well-worn arroyo trail that leads to the east, and continues to track along the mound's base. Follow it to reach Trail 365 and the back of U-Mound (0.6 mile).

Hike south (right turn) on Trail 365 to Hilldale Mound (0.92 mile) and pass the saddle to reach the southern portion of the foothills area. Here, Trail 365 makes a sharp turn to the right (0.31 mile).

Turn right to stay on Trail 365 and follow it up and over Powerline Mound. At

the bottom of the mound, the trail ends (0.51 mile).

After Trail 365 officially ends, another main trail veers to the right. Follow this as it skirts I-40, then turns northeast to lead to South Mound (0.8 mile).

From South Mound, turn left (north) on a side trail and start to ascend. This trail intersects with Trail 365 about halfway up the hill.

Continue north (right turn) on Trail 365 up the hill to Hilldale Mound (0.3 mile).

Veer left at Hilldale Mound, taking the unmarked trail that leads to the left and to the base of the mound at the location where Trail 401 begins (0.3 mile).

Follow Trail 401 to return to Copper Ave. parking (0.6 mile).

IF YOU LIKED THIS HIKE, try one of the other mound hikes: HIKE 52: Embudo Mound Loop, HIKE 54: U-Mound Perimeter Loop, HIKE 56: Two Mound Loop, or HIKE 60: South Mound/I-40 Loop.

FOR THOSE USING GPS DATA
(DATUM: WGS 84)

Intersection of small trail connecting Trail 401 and Trail 365 on north side of U-Mound: –106.478016, 35.0808481

Intersection of Trail 365 and Hilldale Trail next to Hilldale Mound: –106.482158, 35.0716543

Intersection of Trail 365 and loop trail leading to South Mound: –106.480552, 35.06803

End of Trail 365: –106.484843, 35.0661013

TIJERAS CANYON—FOUR HILLS OVERLOOK LOOP

Difficulty	5	
Distance	3.1 mi (5 km) loop	
Hiking Time	2–4 hours	
Elevation	960 ft. gain (293 m)	Peak elevation: 6,880 ft. (2,097 m) at I-40 overlook area; Low elevation: 5,920 ft. (1,804 m) at parking
Trail Condition	Fair with poor sections	Open Space– and USFS-owned and -maintained
Trail Users	Hikers	Bikers and horses on the lower trails
Best Time	Fall through spring	
Parking Lot	Copper Ave.	
Fees	None	

SPECIAL INFORMATION: Snow and ice often cover the trail in the winter season. Given the remoteness of this trail, it should not be hiked in inclement weather or when trails are icy.

THIS HIKE HAS A unique feature: it passes by a set of high-elevation mounds. These mounds appear small, but only due to the large mountains that form the backdrop. As with the other mounds, each of these has a unique shape, with one being more like a pinnacle and another more blunt. Regardless of shape, each of them has little trails leading to the summit or at least close to it.

The beginning of this route overlooks the U-Mound area, with fantastic views of the mound as well as the surrounding landscape and city. After more climbing past the mountain mounds, this route reaches a high bench area. The main trail turns south for a beautiful walk across the bench before reaching the last ridgeline at I-40. The bench area is filled with dense grasses, yuccas, cacti, shrubs, and trees, but has more of a desert feel than similar areas to the north. Here,

the desert species seem to dominate over the grasses, with lots of prickly pear and yucca spread across the rolling hills. Regardless, this area is a great place to spend some time on a little break or a long lunch stop.

At this overlook area, hikers have excellent views of Tijeras Canyon, the Four Hills area, the southernmost parcel of Open Space lands (Manzano Open Space), the Sunport (Albuquerque's airport), and, of course, the Manzano Mountains in the distance. The descent is along the last tall ridgeline before reaching I-40, so the hiker has views of this major interstate all the way down from the mountains.

This is one of the harder hikes in this guidebook. The route ascends quickly into the mountains to access a variety of small trails that can easily lead hikers astray. This is a great hike for people with intermediate or better mountain and

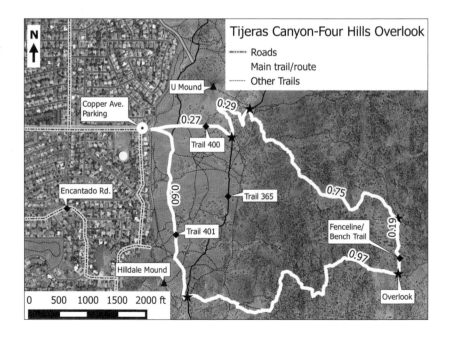

Tijeras Canyon-Four Hills Overlook

N

----- Roads
——— Main trail/route
········ Other Trails

U Mound

Copper Ave. Parking

0.29

0.27

Trail 400

Encantado Rd.

0.60

Trail 365

0.75

Trail 401

Fenceline/ Bench Trail

0.19

0.97

Hilldale Mound

Overlook

0   500   1000 1500 2000 ft

route-finding skills, or for those who hope to improve these types of skills.

■ THE HIKE

Park at the Copper Ave. parking lot.

Start hiking on Trail 400 to Trail 365 (0.25 mile).

Turn left onto Trail 365 and continue to climb up to the U-Mound summit trail (0.3 mile).

At this junction, turn right (east) and climb up the hill/ridgeline on a small, unnamed trail. A couple of trails in this area ascend the hill; be aware that even the best one is steep, with several rocky sections. There are several small trails along the way that veer off to overlooks; the correct path is the largest of these unnamed trails, which continues to veer to the right (south) as it ascends to the bench area and an old fence line, about 0.75 mile from Trail 365.

Once on the bench, follow this south-trending trail to the Tijeras–Four Hills overlook area/ridgeline (0.2 mile).

Turn right at the overlook and start to descend. Staying to the left on the main trail, follow this ridgeline down to Trail 365, about 1 mile. As this trail gets to the bottom of the lower mountains, it crosses the power line access route; this may look like a good trail option back to the U-Mound area, but its hills have difficult, steep sections covered in slippery pea gravel. It is recommended to avoid the power line route and return along the lower Trail 365.

Turn right onto Trail 365 and return to the parking area (0.6 mile).

Manzano/Four Hills Open Space Area

This City of Albuquerque Open Space area is readily visible from the Tijeras Canyon–Four Hills Overlook area, as it is due south of I-40, sandwiched between a residential neighborhood and the northeast boundary of Kirtland Air Force Base. Similar to the Sandia Foothills, and feeling like an extension of the Southern Trails area, this landscape is within the Upper Sonoran life zone, with a vast array of mounds all around. The trails that climb up and over these rocky hills are wide and sandy. Some lead to a variety of overlooks; others follow the edge of the residential area. If you liked the Southern Foothills area, try this one: it has a similar landscape and trail network, but is less crowded.

To find these public lands, turn south onto Four Hills Road from Central Avenue. This intersection is located immediately south of Tramway Boulevard. Drive south along Four Hills Road and, when this main artery splits, veer left onto Stagecoach Road. Continue around a corner or two to the end of the road, which essentially dead-ends at the Open Space boundary. Signage at the gate clearly marks the public lands and provides hiking hours and hiking/safety information.

Two words of warning. First, parking is along the streets. Please be courteous of the local landowners and obey all parking laws. Second, be smart and stay off the Air Force lands; they are clearly marked with a fence, which should never be crossed.

IF YOU WOULD LIKE to take an easier small-trail mountain hike, try HIKE 44: **Candelaria Bench Loop**. For harder small-trail mountain hikes, try HIKE 53: **Embudo–U-Mound Overlook Loop**, HIKE 39: **Embudito North Ridge Trail Loop**, or HIKE 40: **Embudito South Ridge Trail to Boulder Cave**.

FOR THOSE USING GPS DATA
(DATUM: WGS 84)
Intersection of Trail 400 with Trail 365:
  –106.479753, 35.07891

Intersection of Trail 365 with small trail leading into the southern bench area:
  –106.478775, 35.080197
Bench trail: –106.470193, 35.075355
Bench trail and overlook area:
  –106.470135, 35.072846
Intersection of Trail 365 with small trail that connects with the bench trail:
  –106.482152, 35.07165

SOUTH MOUND/I-40 LOOP

Difficulty	2	
Distance	1.7 mi (2.7 km) loop	
Hiking Time	30–60 minutes	
Elevation	240 ft. gain (74 m)	Peak elevation: 5,960 ft. (1,817 m) along Powerline Mound; Low elevation: 5,720 ft. (1,743) near I-40
Trail Condition	Good	Open Space–owned and -maintained
Trail Users	Hikers, bikers, horses	
Best Time	Fall through spring	
Parking	Camino de la Sierra by I-40	
Fees	None	

SPECIAL INFORMATION: Parking near this hike is on-street. Please be considerate of residential properties and park appropriately.

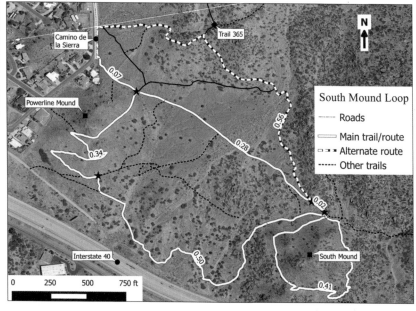

AT THE SOUTHERN FRINGE of the Sandia Mountains and its foothills is a small, isolated, somewhat mysterious area that feels a little bit forgotten. Part of its mystery may be that it is quite hard to see from any vantage point from within the city; likewise, while in this area, the "normal" views of Albuquerque are absent. Mounds surround this little piece of land on three sides, while the steep lower Sandia Mountains bound it on the fourth. The land surface tilts toward the Tijeras Canyon and Four Hills area, meaning that all of its water drains toward I-40. The area looks as if it has been scooped out like a melon: its little drainages have eroded the center, forming almost a bowl shape. Because you can't simply drive up to it and look in, the only way to find out what is in this little space is to walk or ride in. Judging by the well-worn trails throughout this area, many people have done just that.

Powerline Mound and its little sister,

South Mound, line the southern and western edges of this interesting area. Old abandoned access roads, now used as trails, cut across the bowl, with an active maintenance road/trail running up Powerline Mound. A pleasing loop takes trail users out to the South Mound area, where a side trail circles around the base and provides an overlook of I-40 and the beautiful *Aluminum Yucca* sculpture. This small area contains two loop options, with the longer one taking trails that lead around South Mound and then up and over Powerline Mound. For another, longer hike option with easier parking, start your hike from the Copper Ave. parking area and add another two miles onto the loop; see **hike 58: Four Mound Loop** for trail information.

■ **THE HIKE**

Park along the street at Camino de la Sierra, near I-40.

Aluminum Yucca Sculpture

The *Aluminum Yucca* sculpture can be a surprising find for recreationists hiking or biking around the South Mound. The New Mexico Cultural Corridors Program commissioned Gordon Huether to create this sculpture in 2002 as part of Albuquerque's One Percent for Art program, with grant support from the US Department of Transportation. The art is meant to be seen and experienced by travelers on Interstate 40 and Route 66, but coming across it in this unlikely spot can be startling to hikers. This beautiful sculpture serves as a gateway to the City of Albuquerque for I-40 travelers, and reminds all of the unique riches in our landscape. The twenty-two-foot-tall installation is made from salvaged aluminum fuel tanks from military aircraft, polished to a mirrorlike shine. The artist sliced these hollow forms vertically to resemble the scooped shape of the native datil yucca leaf. During the day, the shiny metal naturally reflects the New Mexico sun, while at night, the sculpture is illuminated by a slow-moving, solar-powered color wheel.

This sculpture is particularly endearing to locals, as the blossom of the yucca has been the state flower since 1927. The yucca flower was selected by the schoolchildren of New Mexico and recommended to the government by the New Mexico Federation of Women's Clubs. Interestingly, the legislation does not specify a particular species of yucca. With between forty and fifty species of perennials, shrubs, and trees available, there are plenty of choices for everyone's favorite yucca flower.

Start hiking straight (southeast) from the street to reach Trail 365. Continue straight on the main trail that contours over to South Mound (0.4 mile).

Just before this main trail reaches South Mound, it turns west. Keep going straight (southeast) on the smaller South Mound perimeter trail, which curves due south as it starts to circle the mound, returning to the same junction (0.4 mile).

After completing the circle around South Mound, return to the main trail, turning toward the west to continue on the larger loop. The main trail drops into a little channel that hugs South Mound for a short distance, then follows the southern property boundary, which overlooks I-40 (0.5 mile).

From here, climb up Powerline Mound via the trail with the large switchbacks. This trail climbs near the top, then drops down near the street (0.3 mile).

Turn left at the bottom of the hill and return to the parking area (0.1 mile).

IF YOU LIKED THIS HIKE, try extending it with HIKE 58: Four Mound Loop, which covers more of the same area. For other mound hikes, try HIKE 52: Embudo Mound Loop, HIKE 54: U-Mound Perimeter Loop, HIKE 56: Two Mound Loop, or HIKE 57: Hilldale Mound Loop.

FOR THOSE USING GPS DATA
(DATUM: WGS 84)
Intersection of Trail 365 with trail leading to
   South Mound: –106.483648, 35.067945
South Mound circumference trail:
   –106.479451, 35.065361
Intersection of several trails near the end of Trail
   365: –106.484519, 35.066117

ALTERNATE/EXTENDED ROUTE

Difficulty: 3
Distance: 1.9-mile loop
Hiking Time: 45 minutes–1.25 hours
Elevation: 240 ft. gain; peak elevation: 5,960 ft.
   along Powerline Mound
Parking: street parking along Camino de la
   Sierra near I-40

Directions to Parking Areas

1. LOWER USFS FEE STATION: Turn onto FR 333 from Tramway Road Park in the first parking area just within the fee area. Lot elevation: 6,080 ft. (1,853 m). Unpaved parking lot with space for approximately five cars. No designated handicap parking. No water, toilets, or garbage collection. This lot is within the USFS fee area and has a fee station: $3 per car or $10 per high-occupancy vehicle (fifteen or more passengers).
GPS: –106.504047, 35.202631

2. JUAN TABO CABIN (PULL-OUT): Turn onto FR 333 from Tramway Road. Drive a short distance uphill and into the USFS lands. Park in the first or second pull-out on the right (south) side of FR 333, about half a mile from the first fee area. (A "pull-out" is simply a wide place in the road. These narrow mountain road features are used for roadside parking or turning around; on single-lane roads, they provide the extra space needed for two cars to pass each other.) The second pull-out is closest to the ruins. Lot elevation: 6,240 ft. (1,902 m). Unpaved parking area with space for approximately three cars. No designated handicap parking. No

water, toilets, or garbage collection. This lot is within the USFS fee area: $3 per car or $10 per high-occupancy vehicle (fifteen or more passengers). Closest place to pay is the Lower Fee Station located near Tramway Road.
GPS: –106.498533, 35.205911

3. LA CUEVA: Turn onto FR 333. The access road is the first road off of FR 333, near the first fee station. It is marked with a USFS sign. If the road is open, drive about 1.25 miles to the parking areas. If the road is closed (gated), hiking on it is permitted. Lot elevation: 6,520 ft. (1,987 m). Three paved parking lots with space for thirty or more cars. No designated handicap parking. Toilets and garbage collection are available. No water available. This lot is within the USFS fee area and has a fee station: $3 per car or $10 per high-occupancy vehicle (fifteen or more passengers). This parking and picnic area is closed from October 15 to May 15.
GPS: –106.487911, 35.203489

4. OLD 333 ROAD: Turn onto FR 333 from Tramway Road. The unmarked parking lot is located about 1.5 miles up from the Lower Forest Service Self-Service

Fee Area near Tramway Road, just before the entrance to the Juan Tabo Picnic Area loop road. Lot elevation: 6,720 ft. (2,048 m). This unpaved parking area is on the left (north) side of the road and has space for three or four cars in the primary area. Several other pull-outs nearby provide additional parking options. There is no designated handicap parking. No water, toilets, or garbage collection. This lot is within the USFS fee area: $3 per car or $10 per high-occupancy vehicle (fifteen or more passengers). The nearest fee station is at the Juan Tabo Picnic Area.

GPS: –106.487408, 35.216703

5. JUAN TABO PICNIC AREA: Turn onto FR 333 from Tramway Road and drive approximately two miles to where the paved road turns right to climb up to the La Luz Trail. Near the turn is the primary Juan Tabo Picnic Area parking area with fee station. (This area is open year-round.) Just beyond this first picnic area parking area is the Juan Tabo loop road, FR 333E, which turns right off the paved road leading to the La Luz parking area. The loop road is one-way and closed between October 15 and May 15. Lot elevation: 6,920 ft. (2,109 m). Multiple paved and unpaved parking areas exist within the loop and near the fee station, with space for more than thirty cars. No designated handicap parking. Toilets and garbage collection are available. No water available. This lot is within the USFS fee area and has a fee station: $3 per car or $10 per high-occupancy vehicle (fifteen or more passengers).

GPS: –106.486000, 35.219139

6. FR 333/333D INTERSECTION: Turn onto FR 333 from Tramway Road and follow the paved road to the FR 333/ FR 333D intersection. A large parking area is located on the left (north) side of the intersection. Lot elevation: 6,800 ft. (2,072 m). This unpaved parking area has space for five or six cars. There is no designated handicap parking. No water, toilets, or garbage collection. This lot is within the USFS fee area: $3 per car or $10 per high-occupancy vehicle (fifteen or more passengers). The nearest fee station is at the Juan Tabo Picnic Area.

GPS: –106.486914, 35.219658

7. LA LUZ TRAILHEAD: Turn onto FR 333 from Tramway Road and drive to the end of the paved road/FR 333 (follow signs). Lot elevation: 7,040 ft. (2,146 m). A primary paved parking area at the end of the pavement has space for approximately twenty cars, including one space designated for handicap parking. Overflow parking occurs at several pull-out areas along the road near the lot; however, there are also designated areas (marked with signs) where parking is not allowed. The Piedra Lisa Trailhead parking area also serves as additional parking, requiring a short hike along the La Luz–Piedra Lisa Trail, which connects the two parking areas. Toilets and garbage collection are available. No water available. This lot is within the USFS fee area and has a fee station: $3 per car or $10 per high-occupancy vehicle (fifteen or more passengers).

GPS: –106.480947, 35.219667

8. PIEDRA LISA TRAILHEAD (near Albuquerque): Turn onto FR 333 from Tramway Road and follow the paved road to the FR 333/333D intersection. Veer left onto FR 333D (a dirt road) and follow until you reach the parking area, which is marked. Lot elevation: 6,960 ft. (2,121 m). This unpaved parking area is on the left (north) side of the road and space for approximately fifteen cars. No designated handicap parking. No water, toilets, or garbage collection available. This lot is within the USFS fee area: $3 per car or $10 per high-occupancy vehicle (fifteen or more passengers). The nearest fee station is at the Juan Tabo Picnic Area. GPS: –106.483564, 35.222753

9. PIEDRA LISA TRAILHEAD (near Placitas): From I-25 north, take the NM 550/ NM 165 exit in Bernalillo and turn right onto NM 165. Drive approximately three miles and turn right onto FR 445. The trailhead is about two miles along this road, just before the Del Agua Canyon trail. Lot elevation: 6,040 ft. (1,840 m). This unpaved parking area has space for five or six cars. No designated handicap parking. No water, toilets, or garbage collection. No parking fees. GPS: –106.477006, 35.282425

10. SPRING CREEK: Turn onto Tramway Road from Tramway Boulevard, as if going to the Sandia Peak Tram. Turn left onto Juniper Hill Road, second road on the left. Turn left onto Ridge Dr., then left onto Juniper Hill Loop. The trail parking area is a large pull-out on the right, in the bottom of a wide arroyo crossing (Spring Creek Arroyo). There are no other arroyo valleys in the area. Lot elevation: 6,240 ft. (1,902 m). This unmarked, unpaved USFS parking area is fully surrounded by residential properties, and has space for five or six cars. No designated handicap parking. No water, toilets, or garbage collection. No parking fees. GPS: –106.490672, 35.197183

11. SANDIA PEAK TRAM: Turn onto Tramway Road from Tramway Boulevard and follow the signs to the Sandia Peak Tram and its associated parking lots. Lot

elevation: 6,520 ft. (1,987 m). Along with the tram, a restaurant and small store are located near the trails and provide water, toilets, and garbage collection. The paved tram parking area holds more than one hundred cars and includes designated handicap parking spots. This is a fee area: the $2 per car fee is collected at a booth on the way to the parking area. GPS: –106.479233, 35.191697

12. ELENA GALLEGOS PICNIC AREA: Turn east (toward the mountains) from Tramway Boulevard onto Simms Park Road just north of Academy Boulevard. Follow the signs to the picnic area and parking lots, which are located at the end of the paved road. Multiple paved parking lots with space for more than fifty cars, including several designated handicap parking spaces. Toilets, water, and garbage collection are available. This area is within the City of Albuquerque Open Space Division fee area. Fees are collected at a booth on the way to the parking area: $1 per car Mon.–Fri., $2 per car Sat.–Sun. On days with no attendant, use the self-serve pay station at the booth.

Cottonwood Springs parking lot elevation: 6,400 ft. (1,950 m). GPS: –106.47338, 35.16567

Outer Loop parking area elevation: 6,440 ft. (1,963 m) GPS: –106.47012, 35.16265

13. MICHIAL EMERY TRAILHEAD: Turn east from Tramway Boulevard onto Spain Road just north of Montgomery Boulevard. Follow Spain Road toward the mountains to the end of the road and turn right onto High Desert Street. The parking lot is located on the left before the arroyo crossing. It is owned, operated, and maintained privately by the High Desert Residential Owners Association. Lot elevation: 6,160 ft. (1,877 m). This paved lot has space for approximately thirty-three cars and includes two designated handicap spaces. Water, a portable toilet, and garbage collection are available at this lot. No parking fees.

GPS: −106.48244, 35.14621

14. EMBUDITO CANYON: Turn from Tramway Boulevard onto Montgomery Boulevard and follow it up the hill into the Glenwood Hills neighborhood. Turn left onto Glenwood Hills Drive. Turn right onto Trailhead Road Drive and follow it to the end of the road and the Embudito Trailhead parking lot. This paved lot is owned and maintained by the City of Albuquerque Open Space Division. It has space for approximately thirty cars, including two designated handicap parking spaces. No water or toilets available. Garbage collection is available. No parking fees. Lot elevation: 6,240 ft. (1,902 m).

GPS: −106.48196, 35.13598

15. JOHN B. ROBERT DAM: Turn downhill from Tramway Boulevard onto Montgomery Boulevard. Turn north (right) onto Juan Tabo Boulevard and drive for about half a mile. The dam is on the right. Parking area is in front of dam. The unpaved lot is owned and maintained by the Albuquerque Metropolitan Arroyo Flood Control Authority. This lot has space for approximately twenty cars. No designated handicap spaces. No water, toilets, or garbage collection available. No parking fees. Lot elevation: 5,960 ft. (1,817 m).

GPS: −106.51575, 35.13829

16. SUNSET CANYON ACCESS POINT: From Tramway Boulevard, turn east on Montgomery Boulevard and drive up into the residential area. Pass through two stop signs to Sunset Canyon Drive, turn left, and continue up the hill. Sunset Canyon Drive ends when it reaches the base of the mountains. Park along the street near this access point. A better access point for the USFS land is actually at the "end" of Cedarbrook Ave., one street to the north. Because this is street parking, parking is limited to the space available. No water or toilets are available. City of Albuquerque Open Space Division often makes garbage collection available at these obvious Open Space access locations. Pay special attention to any posted restrictions such as no parking between certain hours. Lot elevation: 6,360 ft. (1,939 m).

GPS: −106.48094, 35.13081

17. COMANCHE ROAD (or Candelaria Road) Access Point: Turn east from Tramway Boulevard onto Comanche Road. Drive to the end of this road, which is a T-intersection with Camino de la Sierra. Park along the street near the access point. Because this is street parking, it is limited to spaces available. No water or toilets are available. City of Albuquerque Open Space Division often makes garbage collection sites available at these obvious Open Space access locations. Pay special attention to any posted restrictions such as no parking between certain hours. Lot elevation: 5,960 ft. (1,817 m).

GPS: −106.48964, 35.12334

18. PIEDRA LISA CANYON: Turn east from Tramway Boulevard onto Candelaria Road. Drive to the end of this road, which

is a T-intersection with Camino de la Sierra. Turn right onto Camino de la Sierra and follow a short distance to the Piedra Lisa parking lot, on the left (east) side of the street. This lot is owned and maintained by the City of Albuquerque Open Space Division. It has space for more than twenty cars, including one designated handicap space. Although paved, there are no painted lines in the parking area. No water or toilets available. Garbage collection available. No parking fees. Lot elevation: 6,000 ft. (1,829 m).
GPS: –106.48849, 35.11226

19. EMBUDO CANYON TRAILHEAD (Menaul Boulevard Parking Lot): Turn east from Tramway Boulevard onto Menaul Boulevard. The road ends at this parking lot, which is owned and maintained by the City of Albuquerque Open Space Division. This paved lot has spaces for more than twenty cars, including two designated handicap spaces. No water or toilets available. Garbage collection available. No parking fees. Several shaded picnic tables are located close to the parking area. Additional parking is available along Menaul Boulevard; pay special attention to posted restrictions such as no parking between certain hours. Lot elevation: 5,960 ft. (1,817 m).
GPS: –106.48839, 35.10500

20. EMBUDO CANYON TRAILHEAD (Indian School Road Parking Lot): Turn east from Tramway Boulevard onto Indian School Road. Drive to the end of this road, which ends at this parking lot. This paved lot has space for approximately thirty cars and has five designated handicap spaces. A paved pull-out just outside the gate area has space for an additional five cars; pay special attention to any posted restrictions such as no parking between certain hours. No water or toilets available. Garbage collection is available. No parking fees. Lot elevation: 6,200 ft. (1,890 m).
GPS: –106.48014, 35.09891

21. COPPER AVE.: Turn east from Tramway Boulevard onto Copper Ave., which ends at this parking lot. This paved lot has space for approximately eight cars, including one designated handicap space. Additional parking is available along Copper Ave.; pay special attention to any posted restrictions such as no parking between certain hours. No water or toilets available. Garbage collection is available. No parking fees. Lot elevation: 5,920 ft. (1,804 m).
GPS: –106.48474, 35.07916

22. CAMINO DE LA SIERRA ACCESS POINT near I-40: Turn east from Tramway Boulevard onto Copper Avenue. Drive nearly to the end of this road and turn right onto Supper Rock Drive. Following the edge of the open space, turn left onto La Jolla Place and then right onto Camino de la Sierra. Park along this street at the access point near Powerline Mound. Pay special attention to all posted restrictions, such as no parking between certain hours. Because this is street parking, spaces are limited to those available. No water or toilets available. City of Albuquerque Open Space Division often makes garbage collection sites available at these obvious Open Space access locations. Lot elevation: 5,840 ft. (1,780 m).
GPS: –106.48452, 35.06867

Timeline of Post–Pueblo Revolt Land Ownership and Management of the Sandia Foothills

1690s: Spanish settlers returned to the Albuquerque/Santa Fe area following the Pueblo Revolt of 1680.

1694: A land grant of the north and east Villa de Alburquerque area was issued to Captain Diego Montoya. (It had to be reissued in 1712 after the original grant papers were lost.) These approximately seventy thousand acres later became known as the Elena Gallegos Land Grant. The property spanned the lands between the Pueblo of Sandia in the north, Villa de Alburquerque in the south, Rio Grande in the west, and the crest of the mountains in the east.

1706: The Villa de Alburquerque was officially founded.

1712–1716: Captain Montoya died and passed title of the land grant to widow Elena Gallegos. Elena was a prominent Hispano society figure, a rancher with her own registered brand and associations with the Spanish colonial government. It's not clear why the captain chose her as his heir, as he had five children of his own. Most likely, he simply sold or gave the land to Elena Gallegos,

reportedly a distant relative. However, some historians suggest that the two were in love. In fact, they reportedly shared a large residence in Bernalillo, New Mexico. (This building is currently known as La Hacienda de la Luna. Prior to that, it was called La Hacienda Grande Bed and Breakfast, but its original name was the Montoya-Gallegos House.)

1731: Elena Gallegos died and passed the land grant to her son and only heir, Antonio Gurulé. He married in the mid-1700s and fathered nine children.

1761: Gurulé died and willed each of his heirs a portion of the land grant. Subsequent heirs continued to subdivide the property, a large portion of which—although this is not clearly documented—was set aside to be used for common activities such as grazing and timber harvest. This "community" land was located in the foothills and the mountains, and was left wild and essentially unimproved.

1812: The General Land Office (GLO) was formed as part of the US Department of the Treasury. This agency's purpose was twofold: first, to aid in the transformation of wilderness and public lands (especially in the west) to agricultural lands, and second, to create an income source for the government through the sale of public land. It aggressively reviewed all "public lands" and worked diligently to redistribute them to new owners. The GLO reviews of land grants were particularly contentious.

1861–1865: The US Civil War. Several small skirmishes occurred in the New Mexico territory, which was claimed by both sides. In 1862, local residents/soldiers joined with the Union and defeat the Confederates.

1881: The US Department of Agriculture's Division of Forestry was temporarily established. The formation of this agency evolved out of the general concern and acknowledgment that public lands nationwide were being overused in the mistaken assumption that natural resources were limitless. Congress was particularly concerned about the ongoing timber harvest trends in the eastern forests. A study had found that nearly all of the mature trees had been fully harvested and projected that it would take many decades for new ones to replace them. This led to the controversial recommendation to reserve and protect existing forests and wild land for future use. Also at this time, overhunting was causing extinctions of local game populations, as occurred with elk in New Mexico. Luckily, a combination of private and state and federal agency funding allowed a successful reintroduction program to begin in 1911.

1891: The Forest Reserve Act was ratified by the US Congress. This "Creative Act" gave the president the authority to "set

apart and reserve" public lands. On March 30, 1891, President Benjamin Harrison established the first reserve: the Yellowstone Park Timberland Reserve (now part of the Shoshone and Bridger-Teton National Forests in Wyoming).

1891: The US Court of Private Land Claims was established to deliberate Treaty of Guadalupe Hidalgo land claims in the territories of New Mexico, Arizona, and Utah and the states of Nevada, Colorado, and Wyoming. The Elena Gallegos Land Grant was one of these.

1893: Thomas Gutierrez, on behalf of himself and more than three hundred heads of families in the Elena Gallegos Land Grant, began the process with the US Court of Private Land Claims to confirm their grant boundaries. This was a long and difficult process, but eventually, the court confirmed that the original territory was granted to an individual (Diego Montoya) and that its eastern boundary was the crest of the Sandia Mountains (*Gurulé v. United States*, No. 51). This ruling was vitally important to the heirs, as the federal government was systematically assessing all of the land grants in the West to determine which were "community" properties and officially determining grant boundaries. In many instances, these boundaries were redefined (usually as smaller parcels than previously), and many "community" properties were later determined to be "public" and taken from grant heirs.

1897: Congress approved guidelines for designating reserved public lands and arranging for their care and management. The Organic Act of 1897 came about in part due to an exceptional public outcry against President Grover Cleveland's naming of thirteen new Western forest reserves. A month later, Congress amended a sundry civil appropriations bill to set criteria for establishing new reserves and provide for management of the lands. New reserves were to include, at minimum, lands for forest protection, watershed protection, and/or timber production.

1905: The US Forest Service (USFS) was established to consolidate and manage federally owned forested public land.

1906: The Manzano National Reserve was established. This included both the Manzano Mountains and the Sandia Mountains. In 1907, the reserve was converted to a National Forest.

1908: The USFS Albuquerque District Office and five others were formed as a move to decentralize and improve local decision-making.

1915: Albert G. Simms moved to Albuquerque to practice law and other professions, including politics and banking. In 1929, he began a term in Congress representing the State of New Mexico.

1917: Jaral Ranger Cabin was built and used by the USFS. In the late 1970s, the building was destroyed by vandals and currently remains as a ruin. A functioning spring sits next to a set of concrete steps with inlaid rock that lead into a pile of cabin debris. Unlike the later Civilian Conservation Corps buildings at the Juan Tabo–La Cueva picnic areas, concrete was used here as the primary component of the walls, with rock acting more as a filler material than structural support. Brick and metal were used for the fireplace and other easily obtained commercial products such as milled lumber and sheet metal for the walls and roof. *Jaral* is Spanish for "willow thicket," a name that likely referred to the area around the unimproved spring.

1931: The Cibola National Forest was created. This now contains a number of mountain chains and other landscapes, including the Manzano Mountains (formerly part of the Manzano National Forest), the Sandia Mountains (now part of the Sandia Ranger District), Mt. Taylor, the Magdalena Mountains, and the eastern grasslands.

1932: Albert G. Simms returned to New Mexico with second wife Ruth Hanna McCormick Simms. Ruth, a former Congressional representative from Illinois, was a prominent and active woman of her generation. In addition to being a high-standing member of many social and political activist groups, she was also a businesswoman who owned two newspapers, a radio station, and several farms. Together, the couple purchased a large part of the Elena Gallegos Land Grant to establish the Los Poblanos Farm and ranch. This encompassed about eight hundred acres of the Elena Gallegos Land Grant and extended from the present-day ranch near the Rio Grande to the crest of the Sandia Mountains. Albert and Ruth Simms were also instrumental in founding the Manzano Day School, Sandia Preparatory School, Albuquerque Academy, and Albuquerque Little Theater.

1936: The Civilian Conservation Corps (CCC) finished several construction projects in the Juan Tabo–La Cueva Picnic Areas. In an effort to draw visitors into the national forests, the CCC was instructed to build user structures within national forests throughout the country, including the Sandia Mountains. The Juan Tabo–La Cueva structures—shelters, toilets, and picnic tables—are still present and usable. The ruins of the Juan Tabo Cabin are located near the National Forest boundary just off FR 333; this temporary base or "side camp" for the CCC was used during construction of the picnic area buildings. The structures were composed primarily of native-granite boulders and massive timbers and were used as examples of ideal and appropriate methods of "rustic architecture" for CCC projects in other forests. In 1938, the National Park Service documented them in *Park & Recreation Structures,* a manual that described rustic architecture as "a canny combination of pioneer building skills and techniques, principles of the Arts and Crafts movement, and the premise of harmony with the landscape."

1963: The Arroyo Flood Control Act of 1963 was passed by the State of New Mexico Legislature, creating the Albuquerque Metropolitan Arroyo Flood Control Authority (AMAFCA). John B. Robert was hired as the agency's first engineer-manager. Once formed and funded, the AMAFCA didn't waste time: it began planning, design, and construction of flood-control projects almost immediately, focusing on the populated areas of the city. Over the next few years, it recommended several land-use and new development zoning regulations as the city expanded; these kept development out of flood-prone areas, provided on-site infiltration (locations where storm water could effectively soak into the ground), and created engineering waterways and arroyos to reduce loss of life and property damage due to storm water runoff.

1964: On Albert G. Simms' death, the Los Poblanos Farm and ranch were deeded to his nephew, Albert Simms. The elder Simms bequeathed twelve thousand acres of undeveloped land to be held in trust for the Albuquerque Academy.

1969: The City of Albuquerque's City Goals Committee agreed upon open space goals "to preserve the unique natural features of the metropolitan area by achieving a pattern of development and open space respecting the river, land, mesa, mountains, volcanoes, and arroyos." Up to this time, the city had acquired many parcels of land that were being used by the public as open space; however, it had no formal structure to manage them. After the official sanction of open space, several volunteer citizens groups formed to monitor these lands.

1974: As Albuquerque expanded toward the Sandia Mountain foothills, AMAFCA developed components of a City Drainage Master Plan. This included substantial flood-control projects for the Bear Arroyo near Spain Road and the northern arroyos east of Tramway Boulevard.

1975: The Open Space Task Force was formed, led by Philip Tollefsrud. In addition, the City/County Comprehensive Plan was published, which called for active acquisition of important lands for open space, such as the west mesa volcanoes and land along the Sandia Mountains. During the 1970s, about a thousand acres in the Sandia foothills was purchased.

1976: Planning began for the Juan Tabo Dam, later renamed the John B. Robert Dam.

1978: President Jimmy Carter signed the Endangered American Wilderness Act, which redesignated 30,981 acres of the Sandia Ranger District's land as the Sandia Mountain Wilderness.

1982: In a land purchase and exchange between the Albuquerque Academy, the City of Albuquerque, and the USFS, approximately eight thousand acres of the Elena Gallegos Land Grant became public land. This was a more complex transaction than this sentence implies. The city paid the Academy with funds raised through a local three-year quarter-cent sales tax. It retained 640 acres of the property to create the Elena Gallegos Picnic Area and Albert G. Simms Park, exchanged the remainder with the USFS for bits and pieces of "surplus land," then sold the latter and placed the proceeds in a permanent trust fund for open space management. Meanwhile, the lands acquired by the USFS became part of the Cibola National Forest, with most of those more than seven thousand acres used to expand the Sandia Mountain Wilderness Area.

1984: The City of Albuquerque Open Space Division was created to manage and maintain the city's open space. The Open Space Division currently has three sections: Operations and Maintenance, Resource Management, and Visitor Services. It had a Law Enforcement section for a brief period, which was later moved to the Albuquerque Police Department.

1994: The Open Space Division organized a Trail Watch Volunteer Program to "serve as extra eyes and ears for the Division."

Digital Data: How Do I Use It with My Smartphone?

Smartphones and Geospatial Data Use

The primary way to use geospatial data on a smartphone is through an application, or app. Once a geospatial app is on your phone, it will display Keyhole Markup Language (KML) with no difficulty and will map your location as you walk along the route. KML is a lightweight XML-based file format designed specifically for use with Google Earth in 2008. (XML—Extensible Markup Language—is the most commonly used format for these types of data.) Today, the KML file format can be used and viewed in a variety of applications, including Geographic Information Systems (GIS). Because it stores a minimum of data, the files are very small, a major benefit when storing sixty routes on a smartphone or iCloud account.

Every year, more and more geospatial apps are developed for smartphones. Because many are free, everyone can use these data without a special device. Below is a partial list of some of the more popular free apps available at the time this guidebook was written. Hikers willing to purchase an app will find many, many more, often offering other options such as the ability to modify or create one's own routes, save points, add different maps, and the like.

How Do I Open the App/Route Data on My Smartphone?

1. Download a geospatial application such as Google Earth and install it on your phone.
2. Download a KML file and save it in an online server such as iCloud, store it on your phone (in the app or Notes), or send it to your e-mail account and store it there.
3. To open the file: Go to the file (whether it is stored on your server, in Notes, or your e-mail) and double-click or hold the file icon to open it, which also opens the app. The phone will present a series of available apps that can open the file (e.g., Google Earth). Or open it directly from the application (e.g., Google Earth's "File" menu) and the app will look in your server account for potential files to open.
4. Once the file is open in the app, the trail/route should be automatically displayed on a map, aerial photograph (Google Earth), or another background depending on the app.

NOTE: Before using these data on a hike, practice downloading and opening the KML files. Also practice with the app, including learning how to use it to locate yourself. Each app does this slightly differently: some continuously locate the user with a blinking dot, others only when the user taps a button on the screen. The power-hungry Google Earth app will locate you when you tap the little arrow in the lower left-hand corner of the screen.

Initial List of Free Smartphone Apps

Most of these apps can be found on the Internet or at sites such as iTunes and Google Play. These apps are forever evolving, merging, and simply disappearing. Digital data users are encouraged to try out a few of the apps beforehand to determine which one fits your needs the best.

APPLE/IOS: Google Earth, MapPlus, mophie outdoor, Vectorial Map Lite, Easy Trails GPS Lite, Head GPS, Bird View, Walk-Trk

ANDROID: Google Earth, GPS Map, MyTrails, Hiking and Outdoor Navigation, Maps.ME–GPS Navigation and Map, All-In-One Offline Maps, Backitude GPS Location Tracker, Hiking Route Planner Lite, AlpineQuest GPS Hiking (Lite)

INDEX